A World
in a Grain of Sand

– Poulton –
a Cotswold village revealed

Tom Boyd

Half of the revenue from the sale of this book is donated to
the Poulton Parish Church

Englang
Publishing

Supported by
The National Lottery®
through the Heritage Lottery Fund

heritage
lottery fund

First published in 1994 by
Englang Publishing
Poulton House
Cirencester, Gloucestershire GL7 5HW
England
Revised edition 2012

All rights reserved. No part of this publication may be reproduced, stored in a retrieval system, or transmitted, in any form or by any means, electronic, mechanical, photocopying, recording or otherwise, without the prior permission of the copyright owner.

Copyright © 2012 by Tom Boyd.

The right of Tom Boyd to be identified as Author of this Book has been asserted by him in accordance with the Copyright, Design and Patents Act 1988.

Cover: Aerial photograph of the village of Poulton, 1992
          (courtesy of Airpic)

Frontispiece: Owen Ash farms the fields of Poulton, c. 1930
          (courtesy of John Ash)

To see a world in a Grain of Sand.
And a Heaven in a Wild Flower
Hold Infinity in the palm of your hand
And Eternity in a hour.

                                    William Blake

'Britain is a world by itself, and we shall nothing pay for wearing our own noses.'

William Shakespeare

This book is dedicated to all those who were born or have made their home in the Parish of Poulton since its earliest beginnings. And to my wife Sally, whose help was invaluable.

Composite views of Poulton on a 1930s postcard

Contents

Preface
p. 1

I
Prehistoric Poulton
The Ranbury Ring p. 5

II
Romano-British Poulton
First to the fourth Centuries p. 11

III
Saxon Poulton
Fifth to the Eleventh Centuries p. 17

IV
Mediaeval Poulton
Twelfth to the Fifteenth Centuries p. 29

V
Tudor Poulton
The Sixteenth Century p. 59

VI
Jacobean Poulton
The Seventeenth Century p. 69

VII
Georgian Poulton
The Eighteenth Century p. 87

VIII
Victorian Poulton
The Nineteenth Century p. 109

IX
Poulton in the Twentieth Century
p. 141

X
Poulton in the Twenty-First Century
p. 215

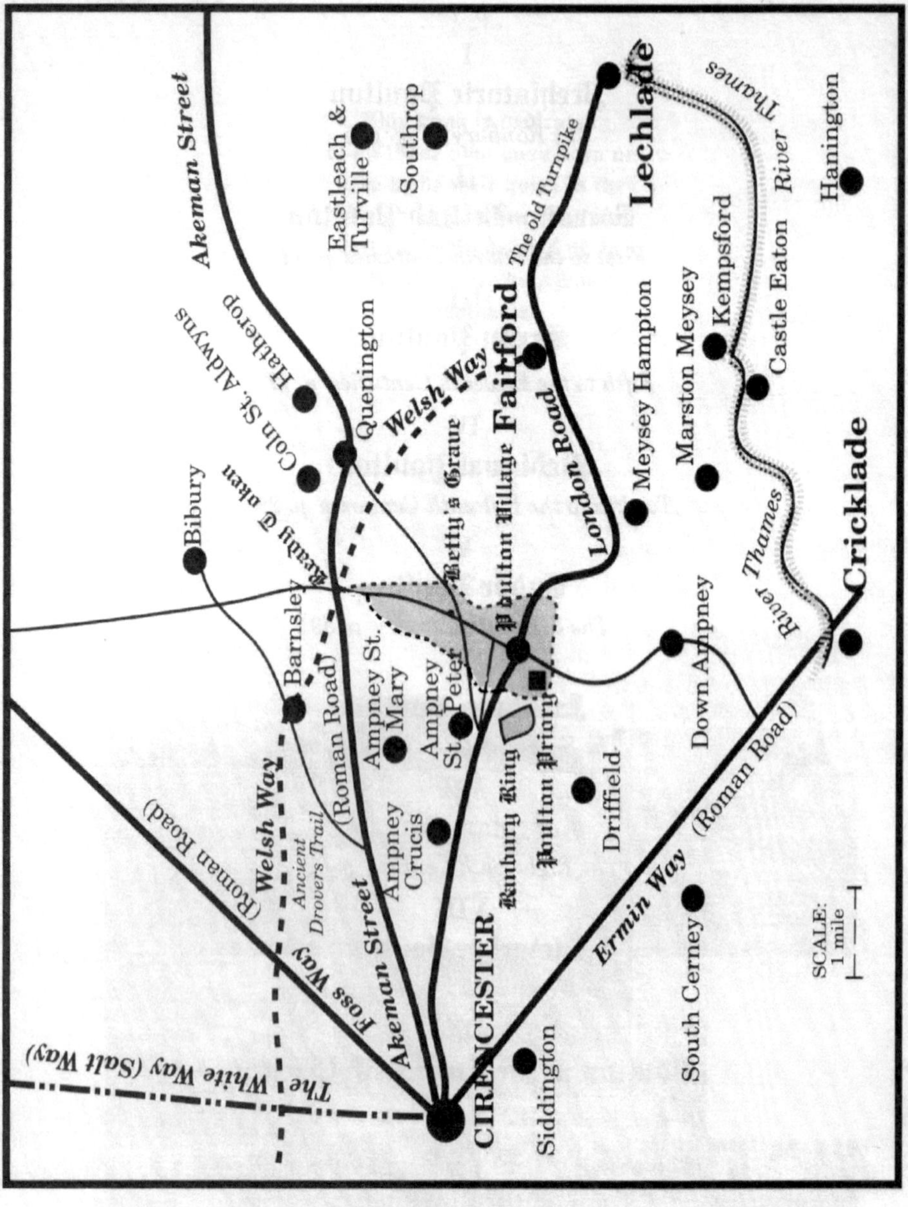
The White Way (Salt Way)
Foss Way
(Roman Road)
Welsh Way
Ancient Drovers Trail
Akeman Street
Akeman St.
Akeman Street
CIRENCESTER
Siddington
Ermin Way
(Roman Road)
South Cerney
SCALE: 1 mile
Ampney Crucis
Driffield
Ranbury Ring
Poulton Priory
Ampney St. Peter
Ampney St. Mary
(Roman Road)
Barnsley
Bibury
Ready Token
Coln St. Aldwyns
Hatherop
Quenington
Welsh Way
Betty's Grave
Poulton Village
Down Ampney
Cricklade
River Thames
Meysey Hampton
Marston Meysey
London Road
Fairford
The old Turnpike
Kempsford
Castle Eaton
Eastleach & Turville
Southrop
Lechlade
River Thames
Hanington

Preface

When it was suggested that I write the history of Poulton in 1993, I imagined it would take only a matter of weeks to produce a slim volume from the minimal material I was at first presented with. After all, Poulton is a small village of no particular distinction or outstanding claim to historical importance, so not all that much to get down – or so I thought. Once I began, I realised how wrong I had been. Perhaps I should have known that any settlement of human beings that has survived for over two thousand years would have more than a few good tales to tell.

As more and more residents and ex-residents came forward with aging documents, family photograph albums, scrapbooks, and true yarns of sometimes bizarre characters and events in the life of the village, it became clear that Poulton is no less than a microcosm of all society; its history is the history of the Cotswolds, the history of England, and even the history of Europe. Although Poulton's population has never reached the 500 mark, all life, as the cliché goes, was here at one time or another. This is possibly equally true of any village, anywhere, but what is special and particularly interesting about Poulton is that it is so typical on the one hand, and yet so singular and idiosyncratic on the other.

Certainly it is similar to many hamlets in the Cotswold area, both physically and functionally; like its neighbours, it has spent the centuries ploughing its fields, raising sheep for the 'Cisiter' wool market that brought such prosperity to this region, and quarrying its silver-grey oolite limestone that has provided so many villages in the Cotswolds with such a distinctive architectural unity. It has all the expected amenities and landmarks of an English village: an Anglican parish church, a village hall, a cricket ground, a children's playground, a provisions shop and post office, an old pub, a manor house and the ubiquitous village war memorial. But that's about it. Poulton can offer no famous battleground, no castle in romantic ruins, no stately home, and now not even a mediaeval church to detain a tourist on his way from one rather better known and more picturesque Cotswold village to another.

Nonetheless Poulton, or *Pulton*, as the Saxons named it, is *sui generis* in a number of ways, not least its long history as a border village, forever on the furthest edge of tribal boundaries and political divisions: a football between the warring *Dobunni* and *Catuvellauni* tribes; a Saxon enclave engulfed by Angles; a frontier outpost between the Kingdoms of Wessex and Mercia; and, after the creation of the counties, a Wiltshire island surrounded by a sea of Gloucestershire – or, more literally, the See of Gloucester. For nearly a thousand years, the Parish of Poulton was ringed on maps to show that it was, in this way at least, something special.

But what makes Poulton ultimately so fascinating is not its long and unique place in Cotswold socio-political history, but the actual flesh and blood mortals who spent all or a portion of their lives in its handful of houses; a mixed bag of heroic, villainous, ordinary, extraordinary, comic, and occasionally tragic souls who have all bequeathed, by their mortal presence here, a richness of village lore belonging exclusively to Poulton.

T.B.
Poulton, June 1994
Revised, July 2012

ACKNOWLEDGEMENTS

I wish to thank all those residents and ex-residents of Poulton, who have given such invaluable help towards compiling this book by lending their family photographs, documents, scrapbooks, maps, mementos, etc. and by giving me information or the opportunity to hear their stories and reminiscences about the village and the people who have lived here. I am also obliged to those who have no connection with the village, but offered their expertise in one field or another.

Mr Reg Adams, Mrs Sally Adams, Mr John Ash, Mr and Mrs Les Ball, Mr John Barnard, Mrs Freda Baylis, Ms Beth Bishop, Air Vice-Marshall Ian Campbell, Mrs Zélide Cowan, Professor James Davis, Mrs Margaret Edwards, Mr Charles Esmond-Cole, Mr St John Foy, Mr Wilfrid Freeth, Mr John Griffiths, Mr and Mrs Mike Hargreaves, Dr Rowland Hill, Dr Edgar Hope-Simpson, Mrs Catherine Jackson, Mr Julian Jackson, Mrs Des Jobbins, Mr Stephen Langton, Mr & Mrs Geoffrey Lavin, Mr Mark Lomas, Mrs Cathy Lynn, Mrs Clarissa Mitchell, the Revd. Robert Nesham, Miss Joan Nunn, Mr John Nunn, Mrs Polly Palmer, Mr & Mrs Dick Peters, Mrs Erica Mary Sanford, Mr Mike Smith, Mrs Hilda Strange, Mrs Janet Crouch née Hill, Mrs Margaret Thorne, and the Women's Institute.

And for this 2012 revised edition, I would like to thank Geoff Chapman for his dogged determination to get the funding for the printing cost, and thanks to the *Heritage Lottery Fund, the Langtree Trust, the Gloucestershire Diocese* and the *All Churches Trust* for providing the grants to the Poulton Parish Council that subsidised the project.

The Parish of Poulton Today

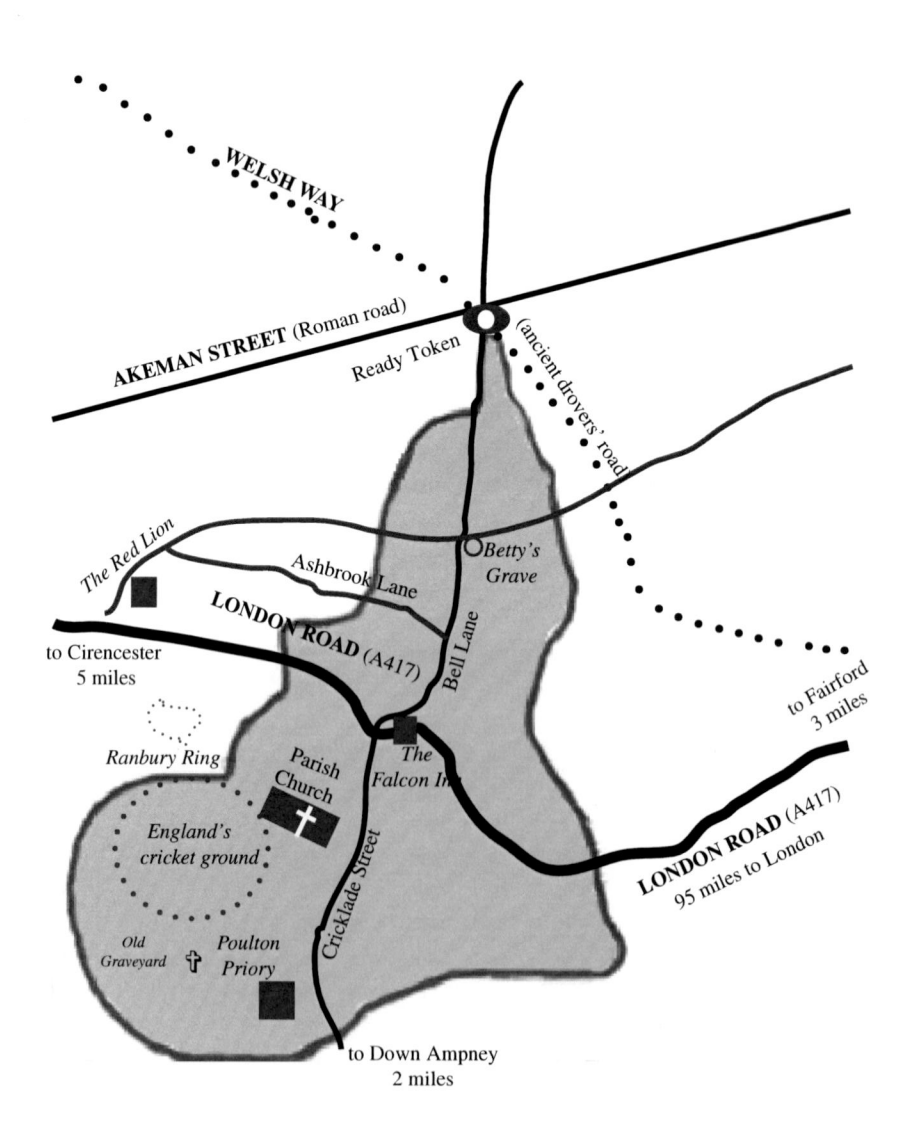

I
Prehistoric Poulton
The Ranbury Ring

The area around Poulton has doubtless been inhabited for as long as man is known to have lived in the Cotswolds, over a quarter of a million years. The countryside in the Southeast Gloucestershire/North Wiltshire region surrounding Poulton is sprinkled with ancient burial mounds, henges, barrows, ditches, dykes; a mass of prehistoric sites of one kind or another that enable archaeologists to follow, or at least guess at the course of human activity round and about here since the last years of the Ice Age. For each prehistoric monument discovered and documented, there must be hundreds of sites still buried beneath the ground, and it isn't at all far fetched to assume that there may be remnants from the Stone Age or the Bronze Age* lying undisturbed beneath the herbaceous borders of many a Poulton garden. The first concrete evidence we have of a settlement here, however, dates from the Iron Age, that roughly spanned a thousand years before the birth of Jesus of Nazareth until the Roman invasion of Britain, in the first century AD.

The Ranbury Ring, lying in the fields just to the west of the present Poulton Parish Church, and now part of Ranbury Farm, owned by the Poulton Priory estate, was an Iron Age hillfort settlement of the type found all round this area: at Eastleach, Ashton Keynes, Perrott's Brook, Bibury, North Cerney, and the much-excavated Iron Age settlement at Lechlade. The Ranbury Ring would probably have been built during the

---

Since this book was first published, a cache of 59 Bronze Age items from 1300-1100 BC, was discovered in a field in Poulton in 2004. Details of this important find, known as the 'Poulton Hoard', or 'Poulton Gold' will be included in the final chapter.

middle to latter part of the Iron Age, that archaeologists call *'the age of the hillforts'*, and it probably survived some hundreds of years as a 'British' village until military occupation of the South Cotswolds by the Romans between AD 43 and AD 45.

Although the Ranbury Ring itself has never been excavated, the design and construction is so typical of Iron Age fortifications nearby that we can assume that what is known from other local excavations would equally apply to the settlement at Poulton.

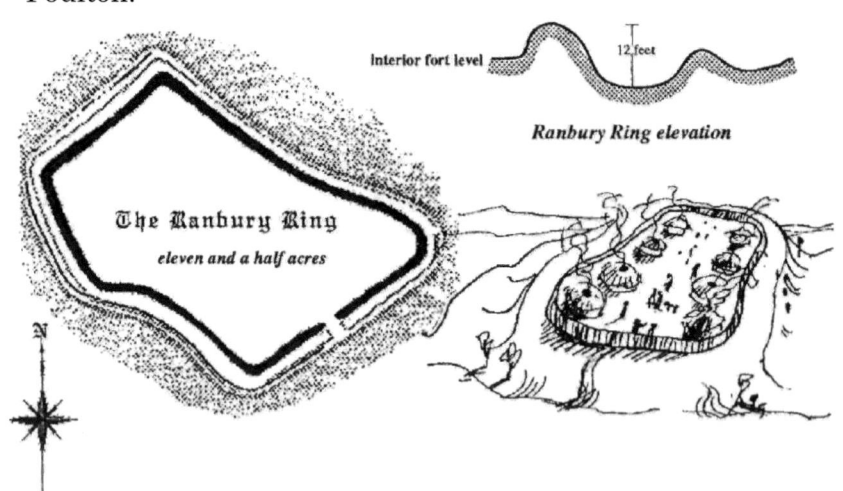

[Figure: Diagram of The Ranbury Ring, eleven and a half acres, with interior fort level marked 12 feet, and a Ranbury Ring elevation sketch]

The Ranbury Ring hillfort, some 310 feet above sea level, was bivallate; that is, it had two defensive ditches and banks surrounding the perimeter, for protection from warring enemies. (As Julius Caesar noted, the Britons of this period were extremely warlike and seemed to accept fierce battles as a day-to-day part of their lives.) The outer ditch is 12 feet wide, and the inner ditch 30 feet wide, with a 35 foot wide bank that rises some 12 feet above the ditch and 7 feet above the interior, where the settlement was built. Much of the original ditches-and-banks structure is still clearly evident today, over two thousand years on. The ditches enclose a settlement area of eleven and a half acres, which is now one cultivated field growing rape and flax. At the top of the inner bank there would have been a defensive stone wall built from limestone taken from the same local quarries that have provided the material for the houses of Poulton for centuries. The Iron Age walls were similar in construction to the dry-stone walls in Poulton today, though the Ranbury Ring 'fence' would probably have been reinforced with timber or possibly iron clamps to give more protection from attackers.

An artist's impression of life in the settlement at Ranbury in Poulton, c. 500 BC to the first century AD

The settlement must have been somewhat similar to villages that still exist in Africa today. Within the stockade perimeter wall they built their crude, undecorated circular huts, about fifty feet in diameter, made of wood supported by poles, and covered by a conical, layered thatched roof with a hole in the centre to allow smoke to escape. The central fire was, of course, for heating as well as for cooking. (The Cotswold winters, it is said, were much colder then than now.) There might have been perhaps as many as twenty of these houses within the Ranbury

The Ranbury Ring as it is today, showing what remains of the Iron Age defensive ditch. The author's wife and dogs are at the lowest point, and the figure seen twelve feet above is standing on the level where the hillfort settlement would have been built.

Ring, and a watchman with a fierce guard-dog would have been stationed in a hut at the compound entrance gate. The entrance can still be seen as a gap on the South East side of the Ring.

When privacy was required, the interior of the houses could be partitioned off with wickerwork screens or leather dividers to form various cubicles, though the polygamous families actually slept together on skins spread out on the floor.

Woad, used by the Ancient Britons to dye their bodies blue

For a physical description of these Iron Age Britons, we have to rely on the writings of Julius Caesar. He reported, after his visits to Britain in 55 and 56 BC, that they had long hair and wore moustaches, but shaved off all other bodily hair and painted their naked bodies with woad to make their skin blue. Considering the climate of the island of Britain, it seems inconceivable that the Britons, hearty though they may have been, were prancing about in the buff, so quite how Caesar came by this bit of intimate intelligence gives pause.

Although it seems that the Celts (as the late Iron Age Britons were called) made no attempt whatever to decorate their houses, inside or out, they apparently had a passion for personal adornment, covering themselves in all kinds of jewellery: bronze and gold necklaces, brooches, belts, buckles and rings, some of which, along with Celtic swords, daggers, shields, helmets and other paraphernalia of war, have been found in the Cotswold excavations and now grace museums at Cirencester, Gloucester and the Ashmolean at Oxford.

During the day, when these long-haired, moustachioed, blue-bodied Poultonites weren't actually out waging war with settlements at Coln St Aldwyns or Sidbury, they ploughed the fields surrounding the *Ring*, and grazed their sheep and cows (which, like the Masai in Kenya, they would bring into the compound for protection when under threat) and hunted birds and boars. Even before the Iron Age, sheep-rearing was important in this area, and the Poulton Celts would certainly have known how to weave wool to make their clothing: heavy hooded winter cloaks that were striped, checked and multi-coloured which the Romans, who had never seen such garments elsewhere, named *'Birris Britannicus'*, and tunics and even trousers for the men. Trousers seemed most peculiar to the toga-wearing Romans, but on observing how practical they were for riding (the Celts were great horsemen), the Roman army soon adopted them for their own cavalry regiments.

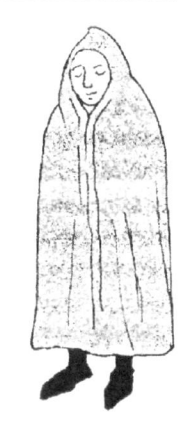

The Birris Britannicus that kept out the cold Cotswold winds.

As well as weaving, the Britons at Ranbury would also have been skilled at such domestic crafts as metalwork, making pottery, leather shoes and sandals, glass beads, shale bracelets etc. and would use these to trade with other settlements within the area, or even much further afield. Iron Age trade was considerable and extensive. Pottery found in Abbeydale, just outside Gloucester, had come originally from Cornwall, and there were well-established Iron Age trading links between Cotswold Celts and the Continent, all the way down to the Mediterranean; an Etruscan jug from the fourth century BC turned up in Tewkesbury, and a fifth century BC vase found in Gloucester is claimed by the experts to be of Southern Italian origin.

The Poulton Celts would probably have used whatever they produced within the Ranbury Ring enclosure to exchange for salt, a precious necessity for curing their meat, and for iron ore needed to make their swords and shields. They would have obtained the salt from the saline springs in Droitwich, transported to Ranbury in ceramic containers down the prehistoric route that is still known as the Salt Way or the White Way, and they would have had to go as far as The Forest of Dean or Bristol to barter for iron ore.

Evening entertainment in the settlement would have consisted of story-telling round the fire, singing eulogies accompanied by the lyre, and playing board games, one of which was the immediate precursor of chess.

Until the arrival of the Romans, vegetables were raised for medicinal rather than culinary use, and the diet of the Ranbury Ringers would have consisted almost entirely of small amounts of bread which they made by milling their two types of wheat into flour with quern-stones (several of which have been found on similar sites in this area), and vast amounts of meat – pork being the favourite – that was either roasted on a spit or boiled in an iron cauldron suspended by chains from a cross-beam over the fire. This was all washed down with considerable quantities of beer brewed from barley, mead from honey, and various other potent tipples, passed around in a communal loving cup, which would send them off into a deep sleep.

These Pagan Celts were worshippers of nature; the sun, moon, water, and certain medicinal plants, and the 'Cathedral' for the Poulton area would have been at Avebury, which had been a sacred Druidical centre since the early Bronze Age.

Like the Egyptians, they firmly believed in an after-life world and prepared themselves for the journey by being buried with ample food, surrounded by their treasures and favourite trinkets. Thus far, no Celtic burial grounds have been discovered at Poulton, but that is not to say there aren't any here. They have been found all round this area and a complete Iron Age settlement in Winson, near Cirencester, remained undiscovered until as recently as 1985.

Celtic Druids

II
Romano-British Poulton
First to the Fourth Centuries

Britons living in the Poulton area would have seen Roman soldiers tramping over their fields by the middle of the first century AD. Although there was fierce resistance from the Catuvellauni tribe of South-East England to the Roman invaders in AD 43, it appears that the Dobunni tribe in the Cotswolds, whose capital was at Bagendon (a couple of miles north of modern Cirencester), virtually welcomed them with open arms. This was due, it is said, to a bit of a sell-out deal by Boduoccus, King of the Dobunni, who surrendered his entire kingdom to the Roman commander, Aulus Plautius, the minute the imperial forces set sandalled foot upon the beaches of Kent. In fact the quisling King Boduoccus had pledged allegiance to the Emperor Claudius before the first battle for Britain had even been fought. Aulus Plautius sent half a legion (3,000 foot soldiers) more or less straightaway up to the Cotswolds, and it must have been a bit like the German troops marching into Austria. History doesn't record if the Cotsallers actually turned out to wave SPQR flags, but there is no record of skirmishes or even any *Romans-Go-Home* sentiment in this area.

The Roman Command positioned a strong military encampment in the southern end of where Cirencester now is, and set about constructing the Fosse Way as a military link with their garrison in Lincoln in about AD 47, followed by building

Roman soldiers arrived in the Cotswolds in the mid-first century AD

Akeman Street, which runs along the northern boundary of the Parish of Poulton at Ready Token on its way to Verulamium (St Albans) and then on to Colchester. These Roman roads, brilliantly engineered, solidly constructed and straight as the crow flies, were better than any roads that were built in mediæval Britain, and are, of course, still extensively in use today.

The Britons in the Cotswolds were already civilised to a great extent when the Romans set up camp here, and were familiar with Roman culture and life-style, as they say these days, due to years of trading with Roman Gaul. This must have led to easy fraternising with the foreign troops, and before long a civilian town grew around the protection of the original encampment, and this became Corinium Dobunnorum, later to be known as Cirencester. Small settlements and grand villas sprang up in the surrounding countryside. Twenty villas have so far been discovered within ten miles of Cirencester, including an impressive one in Barnsley Park, less than two miles from Ready Token, and there was certainly a small Romano-British settlement in Poulton village itself, sited just behind St Michael and All Angels Church on what is now Englands, the present cricket grounds. Concentrations of pottery, tile fragments and limestone slabs (many reddened) of the second to fourth century have been found there and suggest at least three or four Romano-British structures, probably farmhouses, in an area covering three acres. The pottery found there is now in the Gloucester City Museum.

Finds at Poulton were first made in 1877 when pottery shards were discovered during examination of the church's foundation. Also an oval piece of lead covering Romano-British human bones, denoting a burial ground, were found in the vicarage garden, along with six Roman coins. A Roman coin of Constans was found in another Poulton garden, and is now in the Corinium Museum in Cirencester, and in 1958, the Vicar of Poulton, the Revd Tidmarsh, found an old piece of Roman plate and a flagon at the bottom of the Poulton Church vestry. Masses of Roman coins have been found in Ready Token where Akeman Street crosses the even older drovers road, the Welsh

Way, and there is, in the garden of Ready Token House, a well some 130 feet deep through solid stone, sunk during the Roman occupation. At least three old barns in Poulton, at the Manor, at Jenners, and another at Home Farm, contain stone columns, thought to be Roman, which were incorporated into the structure of the buildings.

Roman pottery has been found at Englands, in Poulton.

Historians have speculated that the Ranbury Ring was turned into a Roman military encampment, which, considering the defensive advantages of its location and the Iron Age fortification structure already in place, is logical and in keeping with the Roman practice of further developing existing fortifications for their own military purposes. An urn containing a hoard of Roman coins was found in a garden not far from the Ranbury Ring.

By the second century AD, Corinium covered 240 acres and was the second largest city in Britain, a mere 90 acres smaller than Londinium itself, and by the fourth century it had become the bustling capital of Britannia Prima, one of the four Roman provinces of Britain. Here was a major commercial and cultural centre just a few miles from Poulton – a big cosmopolitan metropolis that would clearly have been a terrific draw for rural settlers.

The sheep-raisers and farmers from Poulton must have periodically gone into Corinium to sell their produce in the market hall adjacent to the forum. After flogging their fleece, corn, or vegetables, the Poulton farmers, pockets bulging with imperial gold coins, would doubtless head down the covered colonnade to the centrally-heated shopping centre that stretched between the market hall and the cavalry fort, on the present site of the St Michael's Park tennis courts, to stock up with such luxuries as shell-fish from the coast and olive oil, which was imported from Spain in large jars called amphorae. They might well have made a day of it, meeting up with chums from other nearby Roman settlements like Ampney

Crucis and Fairford for a chin-wag in the forum, having a splash in the public baths, or possibly taking the opportunity to visit the doctor. There were two known eye specialists in Corinium and prescriptions for various salves, tinctures and ointments made from alum, frankincense and poppies for easing pain and inflammation have been found carved on stone in Cirencester. To round it all off, the Poulton day-trippers might have taken in the latest Roman comedy at the Corinium municipal theatre or gone to cheer and boo the gladiators, wrestlers, boxers or bear-baiters at the amphitheatre on Querns Hill, one of the largest in Roman Britain which could hold over 8,000 spectators.

Artist's reconstruction of the 2nd C. Amphitheatre in Cirencester, where Poulton day-trippers could watch major sporting events. (Corinium Museum)

The Roman occupation was curiously similar to the British Raj in India. A very few highly placed Romans were able to rule and control a great number of 'natives' without much resistance or difficulty. The top echelon, the administrative officials and army officers, were posted here for a limited tour of duty from other outposts of the Empire, and arrived in Britain often accompanied by their entire families and household possessions. The lower orders of the native Britons worked as their household servants, or, as often the case, slaves. Higher ranking local Britons were given fairly unimportant administrative jobs by the Roman colonial governors, as minor civil servants, rather like the old babus of Calcutta. A great many other Britons served in the Imperial army under the command of foreign officers. It will be remembered that the British Celts were highly accomplished horsemen and it was natural that a large number were offered places in the Roman Cavalry, which kept two different regiments at Cirencester. By the end of the second century, the Roman forces in Britain numbered 50,000, which is larger than any mediæval army ever formed by an English king.

The local Britons were proud to say *'civis Romanus sum'* and learned to speak Latin as well as their native Celtic language. In time some native Britons became rich under the Roman occupation and owned their own stately villas in the area (there were more Roman villas in the Cotswolds than anywhere else in Britain), sometimes even sending their sons away to Rome to study law, just as the maharajas used to send their sons to Oxford. As upper-caste Indians often became more English than the English, so the upper-class Britons aped the more 'civilised' Romans in speech, dress, and religion, and developed exotic and expensive tastes for things like oysters and imported French wine. The Romano-British of Poulton though were probably simple farmers with limited access to the delicacies that their grand neighbours at the Barnsley villa enjoyed, but they added to their traditional crops some new food plants that the foreign invaders had brought from the Mediterranean; it is said that the wild garlic which keeps popping up as a weed in so many Poulton gardens today is the direct legacy of the Romans.

Some Britons became Christian as early as the second century, and yet more after news of Alban's martyrdom in Verulamium in the early part of the third century. Although still a time of official persecution, we know clandestine Christianity was practised in Corinium from finding the now famous graffiti word-square or cryptogram in 1868, scratched on a wall in Victoria Road, Cirencester, which reads the same forwards, backwards, downwards and up:

```
R O T A S
O P E R A
T E N E T
A R E P O
S A T O R
```

The translation: *'the sower Arepo holds the wheel carefully'* must have seemed quite innocuous to the casual pagan passer-by or official Christian persecutor, but the early followers of

Jesus knew how to re-arrange the letters as an ingenious anagram of the beginning of *the Lord's Prayer* in the form of a cross. The outstanding two sets of the letters A and O , or in Greek A Ω, the first *(alpha)* and the last *(omega)* letters of the Greek alphabet signifies 'the beginning and the end' from the *Book of Revelation* – a religious inspiration to the secret believers.

```
A           P           O
            A
            T
            E
            R
P A T E R N O S T E R
            O
            S
            T
            E
A           R           O
```

In AD 312 the Emperor Constantine the Great (whose father had died in York and whose mother, Helena, legendary daughter of King Cole of Colchester, was a British Christian who was later canonised), decreed Christianity the official religion throughout the Empire, and within two years there were native British bishops. It is believed by historians that a bishop from Cirencester was one of four of who attended an international ecclesiastical conference at Arles, in the South of Gaul, in AD 314. It is therefore fair to assume that by this time the residents of the settlements in and around Poulton were practising Christians.

Emperor Constantine

By the fourth century, many of the officers of the Roman Imperial Army in Corinium were actually native British, and by the end of the century, the officers who were non-British, seeing the writing on the wall, began to clear out. Most Continental Roman civilians went back home with all their belongings during the reign of Constantine II in 407, though like some British businessmen and civil servants after Indian independence, there were those who stayed on. By 410 AD the army was nearly depleted and too weak to defend Corinium from attacks by the Saxons, so the local Britons took over nearly everything that had been Roman, declared their independence from Rome, and the Empire was finished forever.

III

Saxon Poulton

Fifth to the Eleventh Centuries

The Saxons probably arrived at Poulton, or Pulton (a settlement around pools), as they named it, sometime in the fifth century. We know that large groups of wealthy Saxons sailed up the Thames to Lechlade and were settled there in the latter part of the fifth century, and others went on to Fairford, which they called *Fagrinforda* meaning 'a fair (easy) ford' across the River Coln, a bare three miles east of Poulton. There is a large Anglo-Saxon necropolis near Horcott Hill, on the Poulton side of Fairford, which was excavated in 1850. The artifacts found there are in the Ashmolean Museum in Oxford. From the Fairford base they made their assaults on the ancient British hillmen to the west, which would certainly have included Poulton.

The Saxons sailed up the Thames to Lechlade in the fifth century.

Meanwhile the Angles were sweeping in from the north east and founded the Kingdom of Mercia down to Corinium, called by them Cirenceaster *(ceaster* from the Latin castra meaning 'camp'). By then this once great Roman city had become a ghost of its former self, was for the most part derelict and had been all but abandoned by the Romano-British, probably due to economic misfortune or a plague, or both.

Piggy in the Middle

The next centuries saw a struggle for the enlargement of Mercia against the pushing ever-westward of the West

Poulton's position c. AD 600

Saxons, who in time formed the Kingdom of Wessex. Poulton seems always to have been on the border of these two super-states whose battles shifted their boundaries backwards and forwards, with little Poulton being surrounded some years by one kingdom, some years by the other. So far as we can tell, however, it always remained a Saxon village, even when encircled by Mercian Angles of the *Hwicce* tribe. Down Ampney for example, only two miles away to the south, was apparently an Anglian stronghold, and one article about Poulton history in the *Wilts & Gloucestershire Standard* claims that there was a battle between the Angles, presumably from Down Ampney, and the Saxons of Poulton that took place on Englands (the present cricket ground), the site of the Romano-British settlement. This is unproved, but we do know from the *Anglo Saxon Chronicle* that great battles between the Hwiccians of Mercia and the Saxon 'men of Wilton' took place all around the Poulton area for centuries.

The Venerable Bede, the first English historian, tells us that the Cirencester area was conquered by the West Saxons in the sixth century at the battle of Dyrham (Deorham) in 577. Thirty years later, St Augustine came to the Poulton area and, according to Bede, met with the British bishops and teachers at what is referred to as *Augustine's Oak* on the border of the Hwicca Mercians and the West Saxons. The exact

St Augustine met with the British bishops near Poulton.

spot where they met has not been conclusively identified, but it is thought this may have been a couple of miles south of Poulton. There is an ancient Saxon cross in Down Ampney which, it is said, was put up to mark the occasion. After two hundred years of Germanic paganism, this area, by the seventh century, was Christian again, and the Saxons built small churches in most villages around Poulton: at Down Ampney, Peteramney (Ampney St Peter) Holiroodeamney (Ampney Crucis), South Cerney, Kynemeresforde (Kempsford), Driffield, and Meysey Hampton. There are no remains of a Saxon church at Poulton, but it would seem more than probable that there was one sited at the Priory which was torn down or built over, as was often the case, when the Normans arrived and constructed a new church there.

According to the *Anglo-Saxon Chronicle*, Penda, the King of Mercia, attacked the West Saxon kings and recaptured all this territory in 'the battle of Cirencester' in 628 (the year, incidentally, that Mohammed founded Islam), and thereby greatly enlarged the Anglian Kingdom of Mercia. From Mercian coins of the reign of Penda, we get the word 'penny', derived from the king's name.

Silver Penny of the Kingdom of Mercia

Two centuries later the Angles and the Saxons were still at each other's throats and another major battle between the Hwiccians and the Wiltshiremen took place a few miles southeast of Poulton at what is still locally referred to as the 'Battlefield', a meadow on the banks of the Thames between Ettone (Castle Eaton) and Kynemeresforde or Chenemeresforde (Kempsford). In 799 A.D., a Mercian army led by Æthelmund crossed the Thames at Kempsford into Wessex territory. Egbert, King of Wessex, met them head on and a great battle raged in which both leaders were slain, but the men of Wilton won the day and drove the invaders back, possibly through Poulton.

A Saxon Lantern

The First Recorded Mention of Poulton

By the 9th century, however, the kingdoms of Mercia and Wessex were at peace, united in common interest both through marriage and through defence against mutual enemies. In 853, Burgred, King of Mercia, married Æthelswith, the daughter of the Saxon King of Wessex, and appealed to his father-in-law Æthelwulf to join forces with Mercia to fight against the marauding Welsh and the onslaught of the invading Vikings. To raise capital for his army, Burgred sold a parcel of his land to the Bishop of Worcester. The Charter of Sales, which is in Latin, was signed in 855 by Burgred, and witnessed by his Queen. It cited the grant of lands which included the villages of **EADBOLDINGTUN** (Ablington), **BERINDESLEA** (Barnsley), **ESEG** (Eysey or Eisey, a manor on the outskirts of Cricklade), and **PULTUNE** (Poulton). For this, it is recorded that he received two *bradiolae*, or armlets of gold.

Burgred's brother-in-law (King Æthelwulf's youngest son, Ælfred), was crowned King of Wessex in 871. As every English schoolchild knows (or used to know) this was Alfred the Great, styled King of the English, who united the Mercian Angles and Wessex Saxons in a joint struggle against the Danes, and preserved Christianity from the pagan invaders.

In accordance with old Germanic tribal tradition, districts were divided into 'hundreds', originally each containing one hundred warriors. Poulton is thought to have been in the Cricklade 'hundreds', certainly by Alfred's time, and possibly well before. Sometime in the tenth century, the kingdom of *Englaland* was divided into counties, or shires, administered by a royal official known as the *shire reeve,* or sheriff. Poulton once again found itself on a border, this time of Gloucestershire and Wiltshire. Although the boundary of the shire of Gloucester was drawn beyond Poulton, to the south east as far as Cricklade and Lechlade on the River Thames, the village of Poulton and its adjacent fields, some miles well within this boundary, was singled out to be given to the shire of Wilts, for reasons history does not disclose. This political peculiarity of the Poulton *enclave* remained for the next nine centuries.

Saxon Life in Poulton

The political to-ing and fro-ing of Poulton throughout the Anglo-Saxon era probably affected the people who lived in the village not a whit. Quite likely they were mostly peasants; agrarian Saxons who simply got on with their day-to-day farming duties, which meant spending half the working week ploughing their own strip of land and the other half working on the lands of the lord of the manor, who in return guaranteed them security. Not all that different, in a way, from today's P.A.Y.E. taxes in exchange for various social benefits from the state. Some villagers may well have been slaves, but even a slave was given a strip of his own land, and the lord was obliged to provide the free peasantry with furnished timber houses stocked with household utensils, tools and farm animals: at least one pig, a team of oxen, a few sheep and the odd horse or cow. When the tenant died, the manorial lord reclaimed everything and passed it on to a young able-bodied peasant of productive and re-productive age, and so it went on. It is also the case that a slave could save up and buy his freedom from the lord.

Poulton would have had a village smith – an important figure in the community, as the peasants relied on him to repair their ploughs and harrows, and shoe their oxen and horses. The miller too had a special status. Without him there could be no 'staff of life', and even the smallest villages would consume dozens of loaves of bread a week. The diet of the Poulton Saxon was, according to modern thinking, extremely healthy and nutritious with lots of fibre from wholemeal bread, beans and leeks, and plenty of nuts, apples, sloes, and all kinds of berries. Hunting rights did not extend to the peasantry, but it's fairly likely that poaching was commonplace and what was a fairly monotonous vegetarian diet was no doubt jollied up by a festive hare or occasional pigeon for the pot, and when the family pig was slaughtered, it would provide enough pork, ham and bacon to feed all the family throughout the winter months.

Though there are no signs of real deprivation in Anglo-Saxon life, the necessary physical strength for a day's work in the fields was extremely demanding. From Ælfric's Colloquy, a tenth century account of an Anglo-Saxon peasant's life, we get a picture of what it must have been like for many a Poulton farm labourer at the time:

> *I work hard. I go out at daybreak, driving the oxen to the field, and then I yoke them to the plough. Be the winter ever so stark, I dare not linger at home for awe of my lord; but having yoked my oxen, and fastened ploughshare and coulter, every day I must plough a full acre or more. I have a boy, driving the oxen with an iron goad, who is hoarse with cold and shouting. Mighty hard work it is, for I am not free.*

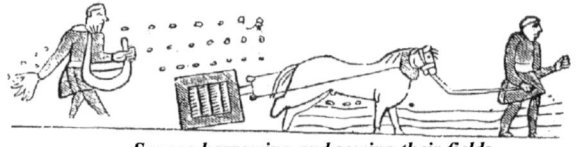

Saxons harrowing and sowing their fields

A hard life, yes, but it was an extremely ordered society in which everyone played their part and knew what part to play. The church and the lord of the manor were expected to and did provide a mass of holidays and feasts throughout the year to raise the village spirits: harvest festivals, spring celebrations and the by then established annual highlights of the church calendar – Christmas, Easter etc., which cleverly corresponded to existing pagan festivals. Every year the lord gave a great communal feast for all the villagers, a tradition that in a sense went on in Poulton for centuries; as you will later read, some of the village grandees, like the Joiceys and the Mitchells of Poulton Priory and the Hon. Mrs Duncan Campbell of Poulton House were opening their gates and staging similar annual social events for the entire population of Poulton a thousand years later.

It was forbidden to ask anyone to work on Sundays, and the village Saxons, after attending mass, would spend the day at leisure, playing board games such as chess – just as the Ranbury Ring Celts had entertained themselves a thousand years earlier.

English-speaking Poulton

If pleasures and pastimes seem to have passed through the centuries unchanged, the rocks and rills of Poulton have witnessed dramatic shifts of local language from Iron Age Celtic, to Latin, to the Saxon dialect that became Old English (a term that covers what was spoken here from the fifth century to around the latter part of the eleventh century). The English spoken today, in spite of all the linguistic interference that came in with the Norman conquest and the Renaissance, still favours its primary Anglo-Saxon roots. Churchill attributed the power of his oratory to his preference for Anglo-Saxon vocabulary over those English words of latinate derivation, and certainly what we call our nearest and dearest in Poulton today is not very different from the Old English words our Saxon ancestors used here over a thousand years ago: *wif, modor, fæder, sweostor, brothor,* and *cild*. From Saxon gods *Tiw, Woden, Thunor* and *Frigg*, we get Tuesday, Wednesday, Thursday, and Friday and Easter takes its named from the Saxon goddess of Spring, *Eostre.* The world-famous Anglo-Saxon 'f' word and 's' word have changed even less – and you can certainly hear a rich stream of those in Poulton these days!

In Saxon times the woman (*wifmann*) made all the family's clothes at home, mostly of wool, and nearly every house had a loom. The younger women of the household were expected to devote most of their time to spinning, thus the term *spinster* to describe an unmarried woman came into the language and remained there until the modern feminists gave it the thumbs-down along with that other uniquely Old English creation *lady* (a word which curiously travelled

Original Spinster

up-market into gentility from its down-to-earth Saxon origins, *hlæfdige,* meaning someone who kneads bread, i.e. the common housewife).

The eventual intermingling with the Vikings brought about a marriage of Norse with the dialects of the Angles and the Saxons that matched arm (Saxon) with leg (Norse), door (the Saxon *duru*) with window (the Norse *vindu*) and not least in this linguistic and often literal marriage between Danes and Anglo-Saxons, the Old English *wife* was teamed up with the Scandanavian *husband*. We had to wait for the input of French to get *partners*.

So dominant was the influence of Old English in the Cotswolds that whereas in many other areas of Britain, Celtic and Latin place-names survive to this day, nearly all British or Latin-influenced place-names in the Poulton area were replaced by names of entirely Anglo-Saxon origin – almost as if the Celtic and Latin influences had never existed here. We spoke in the last chapter of Akeman Street, the important Roman road that forms the northern border of the Parish of Poulton. What the Romans called it we know not, but *Akeman Street* is a pure Anglo-Saxon invention, as is the name of the ancient hillfort at Ranbury. *Bury* meant a fortified place and the Anglo-Saxon word *ram* meant garlic. Considering the prevalence of wild garlic in Poulton today, it seems likely that it was originally Rambury, the fort where the Saxons found garlic growing freely.

The Coming of Common Law

Under old Germanic law, Saxon women were treated as perpetual minors, forced to obey the command of their fathers or husbands, but with the advent of Christianity their status and power grew and by the late Anglo-Saxon times, women could own and inherit property on a sizeable scale and leave it to their children, and men could no longer divorce wives at will. What we call 'common law', the legal system now entrenched all over the English-speaking world, was developing, with its roots firmly planted in English soil; a curiously Anglo Saxon concept quite unlike the legal machinery which the Romans left as a legacy all over the Continent. The *lex et consuetudo Angliæ*, was based not on codes, but on the universal custom of the realm as determined by judges following precedent. Although we are today swamped by one parliamentary statute after another, the most important areas of jurisdiction are still left subject to historical precedence as authority, from matters constitutional to manslaughter and murder.

By the eighth century the basis of English common law was in place with the establishment of its first, foremost and loftiest edict: *there shall be only one law that applies to every person, rich or poor*, which has been deemed inviolate and cited in various forms throughout history from Magna Carta, when it was asserted that even the king is subject to the law, to Watergate, which applied the Anglo Saxon precedent that *'no one is above the law'* to an American president. Although the concept gets flaunted regularly for political expediency, with recent statutes on the books and still more being constantly passed at Westminster, Brussels and Strasbourg that define application or immunity in terms of age, sex, means, ethnic and cultural background and religious claims, *One law for all* has been, in theory, the cornerstone of the English constitution for over a thousand years.

Vikings in Poulton?

The Danes were thought to be strolling the streets of Cirencester in the ninth century, and in 1015, King Cnut's army crossed the Thames at Cricklade and, according to the *Anglo-Saxon Chronicle,* 'marched through Gloucestershire to Warwickshire and ravaged and burnt and killed all they came across.' Down Ampney and Poulton would have been dangerously in the path of their devastation, and may have been victim to Viking rape, plunder and pillage. Well, let's hope they took the Driffield/Preston route instead, and spared poor Poulton that bit of unpleasant history.

The Normans Take Over

During the reign of King Edward (the Confessor, 1042 – 1066), the Manor of Poulton was held by a Saxon called Siward, who, according to the *Domesday Book*, paid tax on 5 hides, which is 600 acres. The land was listed as 8 carucatæ, a *carucata* being what one plough could till annually. Of this land, 420 acres were 'in lordship', with 8 serfs and land for 4 ploughs there. It also states that there were 8 villagers and 7 cottages with 4 carucatæ of land, and also 15 acres of meadow and a pasture 3 furlongs long and 1 furlong wide. The Manor was then valued at £12.

Although the Norman conquerors promised to uphold the existing English common law, they nonetheless set about introducing continental-type feudalism, and William the Conqueror had no qualms about confiscating English land, including the 'Manor of Pulton', and parcelling out the manors and lordships to his Norman friends and relations. He also replaced Saxon ecclesiastics with Norman clergy from rectors to bishops. Everybody, right down the hierarchy, was the King's man first and foremost, and all tenants and sub-tenants in Wessex had to go to Salisbury and take an oath of allegiance to William.

According to one source, Siward was replaced as Lord of the Manor of Pulton by one Earl Edwin, but his lordship could only have lasted for five years and we know nothing about him. We do, however, know quite a bit about his successor, Roger de Montgomery. Roger had led the centre of the Norman army at the battle of Hastings, and grateful William immediately gave him the earldoms of Shrewsbury and Arundel, along with other lands at Chichester. The fact that Roger's wife, Josceline, was a cousin of the Conqueror didn't exactly hamper the Earl's career prospects either. He was made Governor of Normandy, and he founded several religious houses there as well as founding the Abbey of St Peter and St Paul at Shrewsbury.

In 1071 Earl Roger de Montgomery was made Lord of the MANOR OF PULTON, as well as acquiring the Wilts. manors of Ettone (now Castle Eaton) and Mildestone (now Milston).

To facilitate taxation, William I instituted a survey of the realm, which culminated in the production of the Domesday Book, completed in 1086. Under TERRA ROGERII COMITIS (Land of Earl Roger) in the Wiltshire section of the *Domesday Book* is the record of POLTONE as his holding, stating the current value had risen to £16. For Latin scholars and history buffs, I include the entry in its original form:

Idem Comes tenet POLTONE. Siwardus tenuit tempore Regis Edwardi, et geldabat pro 5 hidis. Terra est 8 carucatæ. De hac terra sunt in dominio 3 hidæ et dimidium, et ibi 4 carucatæ, et 8 servi; et 8 villani, et 7 coscez, cum 4 carucatis. Ibi 15 acræ prati. Pastura 3 quarentenis longa, et una quarentena lata. Valuit 12 libras; modo 16 libras.

The invasion and conquest by the Normans brought the Anglo-Saxon period to an end, and Poulton became tri-lingual with the return of Latin, spoken in clerical circles, French, spoken in lordly circles, and Old English, now looked down upon, but still on the lips of the largely illiterate Saxon peasants who, in spite of foreigners as top dogs at the manor and the parish church, doubtless stayed put, got on with their lives, and regenerated the village.

King William I parcelling out English land to his Norman relations (here, to his nephew, the Earl of Brittany). He handed over the Manor of Poulton to a cousin, Roger de Montgomery.

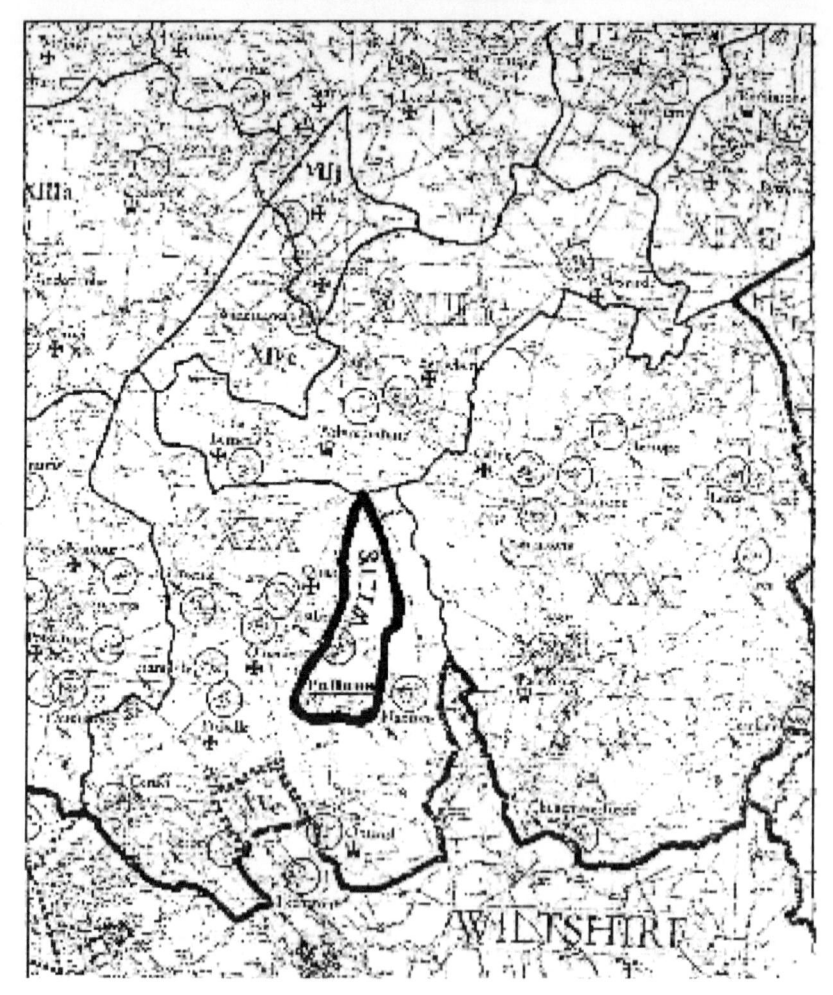

Map of Gloucestershire showing Poulton as an island belonging to Wiltshire
(from reproduction based on the Domesday Book)

Poltone and its Surrounding Villages in 1086

Becheberie (Bibury)
Bernesleis (Bamsley)
Cemei (S.& N. Cemey)
Chenemeresforde (Kempsford)
Culne (Coln St. Aldwyns)
Drifelle (Driffield)

Etherope (Hatherop)
Fareforde (Fairford)
Hantone (Meysey Hampton)
Harehille (Harnhill)
Lecce (Eastleach)
Lechetone (Latton)

Omenie (Ampney Crucis,
St. Mary & St.Peter
Ominel (Down Ampney)
Prestitune (Preston)
Quenintone Quenington)
Sudintone (Siddington)

IV
Mediaeval Poulton
Twelfth to the Fifteenth Centuries

Earl Roger de Montgomery died in 1094. According to some authorities he was slain by the Welsh between Cardiff and Brecknock. We have no record of the Lords of the Manor of Poulton from then until 1256, when Henry III granted the Manor of Pulton, initially for only five years, to Nicholas de Sancto Mauro (colloquially, St Maur), of Castle Cary in Somerset, but residing in a 'mansum', a great house in Ettone (now Castle Eaton) about four miles from Poulton. It is probable, however, that during the 162 years between Roger de Montgomery and Nicholas St Maur, Poulton was owned by the Meysey family, as they had succeeded Roger as lords of the manor of Ettone, which was still linked with Poulton when Nicholas acquired both manors. The Meyseys were major Norman landowners in this area and gave their name not only to Ettone, which became *Eton Meysey* (before it was Castle Eaton), but also to the nearby villages we know today as Marston Meysey and Meysey Hampton. Whether there was a marriage descendancy link between the family of Roger de Montgomery and the Meyseys and the St Maur family is hard to say, but that is a possibility. Arranged marriages to amass acreage was the wont of aristocratic families in the Middle Ages and the St Maurs had already increased their fortunes by marrying into the land-rich de la Zouche family.

Seal of Henry III

From the time of the original grant, eight years in fact elapsed before the King confirmed Nicholas de St Maur as hereditary *Lord of Poulton Manor* and gave permission to him and his heirs to hold a weekly market in the parish on Tuesdays, and the right to stage a yearly fair at Michaelmas, from 28 to 30 September – 'the vigil, the feast and the morrow', as it was quaintly put. This may have been Poulton's initial connection with St Michael, or possibly this feast-day was chosen because the existing church in Poulton was already dedicated to the Archangel.

In 1297, the Diocese of Salisbury appointed the Norman, Thomas de Lecchelade, to be rector of 'Pulton', with his living provided by Nicholas de Sancto Mauro, and this rector was succeeded in 1301 by another Norman, Ricus le Venour. (After his four year stint in Poulton, Thomas de Lecchelade went on to be rector of Eton Meysey to further serve his St Maur patron.)

In the fourteenth century, political intrigue in the area was so rampant and dangerous that St Maur felt threatened, surrounded as he was by powerful enemies in nearby manors, such as the de Cardurcis family in neighbouring Kynemeresforde or Chenemeresforde (Kempsford), just across the Thames from his manor house, and their relations, the treacherous Despencer family in Hannington, a few miles to the south. Nicholas de St Maur was the first person in Wiltshire to request permission to fortify his residence, and in 1311 he was granted Royal Licence to 'crenellate' the house. He then added battlements and turned the place into a veritable castle. Thereafter the village of Eton Meysey once again changed its name to Castle Eaton and is known as such to this day. There is now no trace of the original castle, but it is thought to have stood near the Norman church of St Mary the Virgin, which Nicholas de St Maur endowed.

Nicholas de St Maur was 'summoned to Parliament in the eighth year of Edward II', which would have been 1315. He died two years later, leaving the manors of Castle Eaton and Poulton to his son, Sir Thomas, a knight, or 'chivaler', as they were called in those days.

By 1334, Sir Thomas had anglicised the Norman name St Maur to *Seymour*, and thus began a surname which was to have prominence throughout English history. Seymour has remained, from that time to the present, the family name of the Dukes of Somerset, whose seat, with typical English perversity, is not in Somerset, but in Wiltshire, and the Marquesses of Hertford, who likewise live nowhere near Hertford but at Ragley Hall in Warwickshire.

The Seymour dynasty reached the peak of prominence when a descendant, Jane, in 1536, became Henry VIII's third Queen. She died giving birth to Henry's only son, Edward VI. The Seymour family went on to produce some notorious sixteenth-and seventeenth-century power-crazed scoundrels, one of whom, also named Thomas Seymour, married Henry VIII's surviving Queen, Catherine Parr, to advance his position. It is thought that he poisoned her at his Cotswold home, Sudeley Castle, 'to make room for a still nobler consort'. His plan was to arrange a marriage between himself and Elizabeth Tudor when she was still a child princess, living in his house. Had the plot not failed, we would need a new sobriquet for the Virgin Queen. This blackguard Seymour also tried to do in his more powerful brother, the Lord Protector Somerset, but he was charged with treason and beheaded in the Tower of London, not a moment too soon.

But back to the earlier Thomas Seymour, potentate of Poulton, who was a rather holier figure. In 1337 the good knight endowed a chantry, a mediaeval practice of paying for a Mass or prayers to be said daily for the soul of a specified person, the specified person usually being the endower himself. In Sir Thomas's case a licence was granted for him to give one hundred acres of land and eight acres of meadow belonging to the Manor of Poulton to a chaplain to celebrate divine service daily 'in the Parish Church of Pulton for the good estate of the King and the said Thomas in life and for their souls after death'.

Another licence was granted in 1344 to Sir Thomas Seymour, or *de Sancto Mauro* as he was still officially called, allowing him to relinquish the responsibility for 'the Church of St Michael, Pulton', which was to be appropriated by five chaplains of the Diocese of Salisbury. In return, Sir Thomas agreed to build a chantry chapel in the rectory of St Michael's Church, Poulton, and there the chaplains would continue to celebrate divine service daily for the souls of the King Edward and Sir Thomas.

Meanwhile, across the river and within view of Sir Thomas's manor house at Castle Eaton, was the castle of John of Gaunt, a son of King Edward III, and his wife Lady Blanche, daughter of the first Duke of Lancaster, whose lifestyle was definitely more temporal than spiritual. Their Kempsford castle was the scene of endless house parties for the cream of Norman society and John and Blanche played hosts not only to his royal brothers, the Dukes of Clarence, York and Gloucester, but to Lady Blanche's protégé, that promising young writer from London, Geoffrey Chaucer. So well did Chaucer fit in with the Kempsford smart set of his patroness that he, later on in life, married into the family and became John of Gaunt's brother-in-law. Sir Thomas Seymour did not live long enough to see his neighbour John become one of the most despised men in the Kingdom, and one of the prime causes of the Peasants Revolt of 1381.

John of Gaunt – his castle was at Kempsford, near Poulton

The Black Death at Poulton

The arrival of history's most horrific plague must have been something like an all-out nuclear strike on this island today. In scarcely more than one year, two and a half million people, that is, half the total population of the Kingdom, had died quick but agonising deaths. The origin of the Great Pestilence, as it is sometimes called, is debatable; some historians say it began in Constantinople, others that it swept west along the trade routes from Eastern Asia. Knights returning to Europe from the Crusades are given some credit for bringing it into France, notably at Avignon, whence it spread south to Italy and Spain, and northwards to Calais and thence across the Channel entering England, it is reckoned, at Melcombe Regis (now part of Weymouth) in Dorset in July, 1348. It devastated the West Country first, halving the population of Bristol and Gloucestershire several months before reaching London the following winter. One source says, 'no spot, however isolated escaped its rage; England became a mere pest-house' and one can be sure that this would have included Poulton and its surrounding villages.

This form of plague is said to have caused a massive infection of the blood, causing inflammatory boils or buboes to break out all over the body, eventually bursting and spewing 'black filth', hideous black blotches to appear on the skin, and haemorrhaging and vomiting of blood so poisoned that this too appeared black. Some people died almost upon contact, others within twelve hours, but most were in their coffin, if they were lucky enough to be provided with one, within three or four days of contracting the disease. The fact is that so many fell victim that there was virtually no one about ablebodied enough to bury the corpses, much less make them coffins. Small wonder it was almost immediately known as The Black Death.

Apart from the obvious panic, suffering and mayhem caused by the plague, its effect was twofold: dwellings became so infected that surviving villagers often burnt down their entire clusters of wood and wattle houses and resettled their communities on higher sanitary ground some distance away and started life anew. This can most vividly be seen at Ampney St Mary, down the road from Poulton, where the tiny Norman church, known as *The Ivy Church*, was once the village centrepiece, but now sits isolated in an empty field. The present village of Ampney St Mary, re-built on a hill, is not even within sight of its church. It must have been around 1349 or so that the village of Poulton, too, physically shifted from the environs of the Priory to its present location, a half mile or so north of the original settlement. Some of the replacement houses were built of stone and there are still bits of barns and stone walls incorporated into houses that now stand, which could date from the late fourteenth century, when Poulton relocated after the plague had passed.

The second result of the plague dramatically affected both the social structure and the economy of the village. So many peasant farmers and field workers died that there was, thereafter, a great shortage of labour and a surplus of agricultural land and livestock in almost exact opposite proportions to what there had been before. It's an ill wind that blows no good, and this illest of winds blew away the feudal power of the manorial system. The lords could no longer require farm workers to till their fields as an obligatory service; the surviving labourers had the whip-hand and refused to work without considerable compensation. In spite of statutes passed to try and stop the peasants exploiting their situation, they downed their ploughs and scythes and continued striking until the lords had no alternative but to pay, and pay handsomely. Overnight, wages in coin doubled or trebled. This meant that the survivors became relatively affluent; serfs were quickly able to buy their freedom, and freemen had cash aplenty to buy up land of their own as well as flocks of sheep and other livestock, thus forming a new prospering class of landowners independent of the Manor. The generations of yeoman farmers in the Hill family, late of Home Farm, Poulton, for example, can be seen as a direct continuation of this fourteenth-century post-pestilence reform. Once the yeoman farmers and skilled craftsmen began replacing the villeins, and a Prior replaced the authority of the Lord of the Manor, Poulton, starting life afresh on new ground, was never to be the same again.

The Founding of the Priory of St Mary at Poulton

Various reports are contradictory regarding the date and founding of Poulton Priory. *The Victoria History of Wiltshire* (Vol.III, *'The Religious Houses of Wiltshire'*) states that 'in 1350, under an agreement between [Sir Thomas] Seymour and the King [Edward III], the manor and advowson of Poulton (except a *messuage* [a dwelling house, outbuildings and surrounding land] and 10 acres of land) were granted to the Prior and Canons of Sempringham to found a priory of St Mary, and licence was given to appropriate Poulton church.' On the other hand, Dr. Rose Graham, in her book *St Gilbert of Sempringham and the Gilbertines* writes: 'In 1348 Thomas Seymour obtained a licence from Edward III to grant his manor of Poulton in Wilts, to the canons of Sempringham for a house of their order.'

A Royal inquest held at Cricklade concerning the foundation, to which Dr. Graham may have been referring, is dated 'the second of August, in the twenty-first year of the Reign of King Edward the Third after the Conquest', which, considering Edward III ascended the throne on 1 February, 1327, sounds very like it was 1347.

The Wilts and Gloucestershire Standard, in an extensive article about Poulton written in 1955, states that Sir Thomas Seymour *died* in 1347 and *'in his will* [my italics] he expressed the wish that the Manor of Poulton and advowson of the church should be passed on to the Master of the Gilbertine Order at Sempringham, Lincolnshire.' The author, who signed himself J.B.G., claims to have seen the original inquest document, written in Latin, in the possession of the Vicar of Castle Eaton. If this is true, it seems strange that he didn't notice that Seymour appears to have been present at the

Gold coin of Henry III

inquest, and that the King refers to 'his beloved and trusty Thomas de St Maur kt.' in the present tense, which would, in the words of Mark Twain, make reports of his death greatly exaggerated. Over is the transcript of the inquest:

INQUEST *taken before Thomas de St Maur, Escheater of our Lord The King in the County of Wilts at Cricklade, on the second day of August in the twenty first year of the reign of King Edward the Third after The Conquest, in execution of a Writ of our Lord The King drawn up for this same Inquest, on the oath of William Colnham and others.*

T*he which declare upon this oath that it is not to the loss nor prejudice of our Lord The King or of any other, that our Lord The King should grant to his beloved and trusty Thomas de St Maur, kt, to give and assign The Manor of PULTON with the appurtenances Thereof, and the advowson of the Church of the same Manor to his well-beloved in Christ, The Master of the Order of SEMPRINGHAM for a house to be newly established according to the Order of the same Master for a certain number of Canons of the same Order, within the bounds of the same Manor, to celebrate the divine offices in the same for the good estate of The King himself The while he yet liveth, and for his soul when he shall have departed this life, and for the souls of his forbears and his heirs; and for the souls of the aforesaid Thomas and his heirs; and for the souls of all the faithful deceased; to be had and be held by the same Master and Canons and their Successors in free, pure and perpetual alms and (that our Lord The King should grant) to The same Master and Canons to appropriate the aforesaid Church themselves, and to hold it thus appropriated for their own uses, themselves and their successors aforesaid.*

A*nd they declare that the aforesaid Manor with the appurtenances Thereof, with the Advowson of The Church of the same, are held of our Lord The King in chief by the service of half a knight's fee; and they do say that aforesaid Manor with the appurtenances thereof is worth ten pounds a year in its whole revenues, according to the true value of the same, and the Advowson of the Church is worth Cs. And that there are lands and tenements remaining to the same Thomas besides the Manor and Advowson aforesaid;*

to wit The Manor of ETON Meysy with The Advowson of the Church of the same Manor and little CHELESWORTH; and that the Manor of Eton, with the Advowson of the Church of the same, are held of The Earl of Gloucester by the service of half a knight's fee and the said Manor of Chelesworth is held of the Earl of Salisbury by the service VI a year. And that the Manor of Eton with the Advowson of The Church of the same are worth XX pounds a year, in their whole revenues according to the true value of the same. And the aforesaid Manor of Chelesworth is worth Cs a year in its whole revenues according to the true value of the same.

In witness whereof the aforesaid jurors have affixed their seals to this Inquest. Given the day, place and year aforesaid.

At any rate, for reasons never explained, the entire Manor of Poulton and the Parish Church were indeed given by Sir Thomas Seymour to the monks of the Gilbertine Order of Sempringham to form a new southern cell (there was another Gilbertine house in Marlborough which had been there since c.1200, though most were up in Lincolnshire and Nottinghamshire). Sir Thomas Seymour continued to be Lord of the Manor of Castle Eaton until 1361 when, presumably, he died, but the parish church there was in the patronage of the Seymours and their la Zouche cousins for the following 189 years.

The Gilbertines were the only monastic order ever founded by an Englishman, St Gilbert of Sempringham. Gilbert was highly educated and from a well-to-do family (his father Jocelin was a Norman knight) but his social conscience was such that he devoted himself first to 'serving the poor and ignorant' who worked or lived on his father's large estate. In 1131, he founded a school, a hospital and a small community

St Gilbert of Sempringham

of nuns, and later added laymen and canons. Some sixteen years later he received the Pope's authority and his home-grown monastic order was officially recognized by the Vatican.

Gilbert lived to be more than 100 years old. When he died in 1189, his order marched on and by 1200 there were sixteen foundations or cells, and another eight were added during the thirteenth century, most of which were hostels for the poor and the sick. Gilbert was canonised by Pope Innocent III in 1202.

A Victorian depiction of St Gilbert from the St Gilbert of Sempringham church, Brothertoft, Lincs

After Sir Thomas's bequest received the King's blessing, the Gilbertine canons came down to Poulton in 1350 and set up the Priory of St Mary which, like their sister priory at Marlborough, was for canons only. This cell also probably served as a hostel for travellers and for the sick and the poor, though the eminent historian G.M. Trevelyan tells us that the English monks of this period were 'worldly and well-to-do, living lives of sauntering comfort in the monastery... having themselves abandoned the manual labour practised by their predecessors, they maintained armies of servants to carry on the daily routine.' How much of Trevelyan's description below of life in a mid-fourteenth century priory applies to the small monastic house in Poulton is anyone's guess, but there is no real reason to assume that the Gilbertine monks were different from any other order.

A Gilbertine Canon.

'The monks performed in person their obligations of prayers and masses for the living and the dead, their patrons and their founders. They gave daily alms in money and broken meats to the poor, and showed lavish hospitality to travellers, many of whom were wealthy and exacting guests. The rich fed at the table of the Abbot or Prior, while humbler wayfarers were accommodated in the guest house of the Monastery.'

In any case it is reasonable to assume that the Priory offered a fair amount of employment to the Poulton villagers, either as servants, farm labourers, or shepherds. The primary source of profit came from the Priory flocks and doubtless the Prior sold the fleeces at the great wool market in Cirencester, or Cisitur as it was then called, to subsidize the extensive building programme at the Priory. Quite what they built is pure speculation as only a few walls and some arches have survived, but there was surely a sizeable stone house for the canons which must have been on the site of the present Priory Farm House, the east wall of which is an original wall of the Priory. The version of St Michael's Church that existed when the Gilbertines arrived was probably of Norman design, which is likely to have been built over an earlier Saxon church. The Gilbertines then set about re-building it once again in the latest fourteenth-century Gothic style, which would certainly have required a considerable local workforce. This mediaeval church, which stood unaltered until the end of the nineteenth century, has been described as a perfect specimen of decorated architecture and probably looked very similar to its contemporary at Ampney St Peter, which is still intact and in use. The Poulton church, however, fell into great disrepair over the centuries and was finally pulled down in 1873, its stonework used to build the present Victorian church.

The mediaeval Church of St Michael and All Angels at Poulton Priory, as it was before demolition.

In 1354, King Edward III granted special privileges to the Poulton monks which included freedom from tolls, tariffs and levies of all kinds, including the 'scot', that mediaeval tax that gives us the expression to be, like these canons, let off *scot free*. Their house was, from then on, under Royal protection. For readers with the patience and perseverance to wade through archaic language, I set out the charter in full, for the sake of historical documentation and authenticity. For those who can't face *panage, murage, pedage, lastage, stallege* and *hidage*, not to mention *frankalmoign* and *Flementhrif*, which wouldn't even be allowed on *Call My Bluff*, I suggest skipping on to the Poulton-Cotswold Sheep Theory on p. 44.

Charter of King Edward the Third of divers liberties and privileges granted to the aforesaid Priory.

EDWARD

by the grace of God King of England and France and Lord of Ireland, to the Archbishops (etc) greeting.

Be it known to you that whereas to the honour of God and Holy Mother Church we have caused a house of Canons regular of the Order of St. Gilbert of SEMPRINGHAM to be founded at PULTON in the County of Wilts, and to be endowed with certain lands, tenements, rents and possessions for the maintenance of the same Canons; in order that the Prior and Canons of the said house might be able in future to attend in greater peace to celebrating the divine offices ordained and hereafter to be ordained therein for us, our heirs and our forbears; We, desiring to establish the said Prior and Canons in the liberties and quittances which by inspection of the Rolls of our Chancery, we find to have been granted to the House of SEMPRINGHAM and the other houses in our Kingdom of England of the said

Order by our aforesaid forbears, as they are hereinunder set forth; have granted for us and our heirs and by this our Charter have confirmed to the aforesaid Prior and Canons and their successors.

To have and to hold for ever all their lands, tenements, rents and possessions whatsoever and wheresoever, well and in peace freely and quietly, wholly, fully and in honour; in wood and in the open; in meadows and in pastures, in waters, in fish-ponds, in stews, in streams and strand; in marshes and forests, in mills and in ponds, in tofts and crofts; and thickets, in ways and paths. And to be quit, both themselves and their men in City, Borough, markets and fairs, in crossing bridges, and the ports of the sea and in all places throughout our whole Kingdom of England and throughout all our lands and waters, of Toll, pontage, passage, panage, murage, pedage, lastage, stallege, hidage, carriage and of wards and works on castles, bridges, parks and walls and ditches and of imposts, tributes, and levies, fird fines and knight-fines and of forest fines, and of escape and of regard and waste everywhere; in the marsh and throughout the whole of our forest of BRADENE and of all gelds, and Danegeld and Woodgeld, Fengeld and Horngeld, Footgeld and Penny geld and Tithingpenny and Hundreds-penny and of Miskenning and the Chevage and Headpenny and Buckstall and Tristris and of all fines and amercements, forfeitures and aids and wapentakes counties, Ridings, Hundreds and shires and tenmentale; and of murder and robbery and concealing (fines) and outflat and homsoon, Grithbreach, Bloodwite, Fleetwite, and forestall and Hangwite, and Leirwite. And furthermore to be free of Scot and wardpenny and Burghalpenny and of all carey and sumage and shipmoney and the building of the King's houses and all manner of works; and of all aids of the Sherriffs and their Minions and scutage and assizes and boons, summonses, and talliages frankpledges and of Bed and Board; and of all pleas and plaints occasions, and customs, and of the seizing their chattels in requistions and of every terrain service and secular tax of their wood for the aforesaid works, nor in no manner for any other thing so ever to be seized.

*A*nd let the aforesaid Prior and Canons and their successors have their Court, and justice, with soke and sake, and toll and team and infang Thief and outfang Thief and Flemenfrith and Ordeal and Oresl, in time and out and with all other free customs and immunities and liberties; and with all their pleas and plaints and quittances. And we have granted, for us and our heirs, and by this our Charter have confirmed that when the Master of the said Prior and Canons shall die, the care and custody of the aforesaid Order, both houses and granges and Churches and properties shall remain alway in the custody and regiment of the Prior and Canons. And we forbid any Sherriff or Minion or other person great or small, within their frankalmoign to take, bind, beat, slay or shed the blood of any man; or to dare to do repine or any violence; nor anyone to presume to seize their chattels from the lands of their frankalmoign in requistion on account of our forfeiture; nor anyone to impound their serfs and their runaways or their cattle, nor to molest them or their men, nor in no manner to hinder men coming to their mills, for any custom or service tax or for any cause in the use of their goods which their men can swear to be their own but let them be quit of all customs taxes, and occasions such as are or can be and generally of all things of all manner which pertain or can pertain to us or our heirs and successors, excepted only jurisdiction of death and members (life and limb).

We have granted furthermore for us and our heirs and by this our Charter have confirmed to the aforesaid Prior and Canons of PULTON in perpetual alms, the amercements and forfeitures of all their men, in all pleas, wheresoever they be indicated; whether in our Court, whether in another as far as to us it doth pertain; and if so be their men shall be condemned to death or loss of limb or to perpetual banishment, to the aforesaid Prior and Canons to have all their Chattels with none to gainsay them; There being retained to us, by our Bailiffs, the execution of justice in life and limb, whereof we grant to them all manner of plaint and suit. And furthermore we forbid anyone to molest or grieve the house of PULTON in these liberties, or to take their sheep or beats in requistion, or stint them in common pasture, on forfeiture to us often pounds and on forfeiture to the Sherriff of twenty shillings, witness the confirmation of the Lord John of famous memory, late King of England, our Forbears, which the house of SEMPRINGHAM holdeth from that time.

Furthermore we have taken into our custody a special protection and defence the said house of PULTON with all its members and the appurtenances thereof, in such wise that the said Prior and Canons might hold them well and in peace, freely, quietly and wholly, with all the liberties and free customs aforesaid. And if any one shall lay claim against the house of PULTON to any of their possessions or wish to vex them in anything or place them in Plea, we forbid the said Prior and Canons to answer for anything, nor enter into a Plea, nor anyone to make them plead except before us or our heirs or our chief justice or (The C.J.) of our heirs, or before the Justices in Eyre. Wherefore we will etc.

Given by our hand at Westminster, the fifth day of February, the twenty-eighth year our Reign in England, the fifteenth of our Reign in France

The Poulton-Cotswold Sheep Theory

Were the famous 'Cotswold sheep' actually bred first at Poulton? This is the assumption that was put forward in 1955 by Mr H.S. Hutchinson, the then Vicar of Poulton who, according to the *Wilts & Gloucestershire Standard* 'has conducted a good deal of research into the history of the area'. The Gilbertines, Mr Hutchinson asserts, were prolific wool growers and would have brought a flock of their native Lincolnshire Longhairs down south with them to Poulton Priory, and the monks subsequently cross-bred these with the local native Romano/British sheep, creating the famous *Cotswold* sheep, a breed that altered the ratio of fleece to flesh in favour of bigger wool profits.

A classic Cotswold sheep, now found only on a rare-breeds farm

The immense prosperity of this area during the Middle Ages, and the funds to build all those magnificent perpendicular wool churches in the Cotswolds such as St Mary's in Cirencester, and St Mary the Virgin in Fairford, came from these obliging shaggy creatures. British wool was recognized as the best in Europe, and Cotswold wool was the finest in Britain. There was a direct export run from Cirencester to Calais, then an English town and to remain so for the next two hundred years. From Calais the Cotswold wool was sent on to the hungry looms of Flanders, Ypres, Ghent, and down to Italy to supply the material necessary for the production of luxury woollens which they could get nowhere else. Not only were the monks in the Priory producing wool, but even the poorest peasant in Poulton would have had a Cotswold sheep or two, if not a small flock, to profit by the almost insatiable European demand for English fleece. Everyone from top to bottom was enjoying this bonanza of prosperity. To quote Trevelyan again: 'The woolsack, the symbolic seat of England's Chancellor, was the true wealth of the King and of his subjects, rich and poor, cleric and lay, supplying them with coin over and above the food they wrung from the soil and themselves consumed'.

In the fourteenth century, the production of woven cloth moved from cities and towns to rural districts, particularly to the Cotswolds, due in part to the immediate availability of the fine and plentiful fleece of the Cotswold sheep, but also because of the skills and crafts available in villages like Poulton. Apart from the shepherding and shearing, the industry called for many cottage crafts that kept local villagers fully employed: carding, fulling, spinning, weaving, dyeing and cloth finishing. There were also individual 'websters' weaving away on looms in separate premises, similar to the fourteenth-century weavers' cottages in nearby Bibury. Local entrepreneurs with money to invest soon began organising and overseeing the manufacture of standardised cloth, from collecting the raw material to commissioning the weavers and processors, to exporting the finished broadcloth to the best markets. Trevelyan says: 'Capitalism as the organizer of industry is first clearly visible in the [fourteenth century] cloth trade.' These capitalist clothiers must surely have been operating in Poulton as well as in surrounding villages. Some of the richest and most powerful of the mediaeval wool merchants were based in Fairford, just three miles away. From 1340 to 1400, the production of broadcloth trebled and the export of same was increased ninefold. England, thanks to the Cotswold villages, which surely included Poulton, commanded the world's cloth market for centuries.

Peasants keeping sheep in the Middle Ages. Sheep raising for the Cirencester wool market and cottage crafts needed for the cloth trade would have brought full employment and prosperity to Poulton.

There are no Cotswold sheep left in Poulton, and scarcely any of these distinctive animals anywhere in the Cotswolds as they are now museum pieces, and can only be seen at a few Cotswold farms specialising in rare breeds. When the love of roast lamb and mutton chops surpassed the demand for blankets and pullovers, a breed of sheep with more flesh than fleece got the jobs and the poor old Cotswold variety were made redundant and dwindled away. Gone but not forgotten; the silhouette of the shaggy beast is a common sight in a public park in Philadelphia, Pennsylvania, where grassy knolls are adorned with a number of bronze statues of Cotswold sheep.

The Parlance of Poulton

The Norman Lords of Poulton Manor would most certainly have been French-speaking, as would the early incumbents of the Parish such as Thomas de Lecchlade and Ricus le Venour. However, by the time Poulton Priory was established c. 1350, Norman French and the 'englysshe' tongue were no longer separate languages, the former of the aristocracy and educated clergy, the latter of the common people. This was the age of the great poets Chaucer and William Langland, of Wycliffe and Wat Tyler, when the English people emerged as a racial and cultural unit. Trevelyan says, of the mid-fourteenth century: 'The upper class is no longer French, nor the peasant class Anglo-Saxon: all are English,' and even though the Parish of Poulton was in the charge of various canons of distinctly Norman origin, such as Robert de Uttaby (1361), Robert de Fakenham (1365), William de Calthorpe (1378), William Mountar (dates uncertain) and William Launde (1392), they would have spoken what we call Middle English with their parishioners when they weren't speaking Latin in their official capacity and within the Priory itself.

Middle English was a sort of *Franglais*, and the melting of the two languages is largely what has given modern English a vocabulary many times the size of other European languages; a dual vocabulary, if you like, that offers us a choice of kingly and royal, freedom and liberty, brotherly and fraternal, hamlet and village, hearty and cordial, foe and enemy etc., not to mention the well-known peculiarity of assigning one set of names (of Germanic origin) to animals and another (of French origin) to their meat: deer/venison, swine/pork and bacon, calf/veal, cow/beef, sheep/mutton, which is unique to the English language and is thought to reflect the fact that it was the Anglo-Saxon peasants who reared the beasts for the table and the Norman upper classes who sat down to feast upon the flesh.

As said before, words for the immediate family members are Old English, but our vocabulary for other relations – uncles, aunts, nieces and cousins – came from French, and though the title of *earl* long pre-dates the Conquest, an earl's wife had to wait for the Normans to arrive to receive the title, countess.

It is the old Saxon genitive that allows us to speak of Poulton's vicar and call Poulton's church St Michael's, whereas it was the introduction of French sentence structure that allows the flexibility to say, alternatively, the Vicar of Poulton and the Church of St Michael and All Angels, and the influence of Norman grammar is still evident in the unEnglish adjective-reversals witnessed in phrases like the Princess Royal, courts martial, knight errant, treasure trove. the lords spiritual and the Church Miltant. Professor C.T. Onions writes: 'The Englishman has dealt with foreign languages at his own sweet will, and French especially,' and indeed, having inherited the word gentil from the Normans, the English played variations on the theme – gentle, genteel, gentile and jaunty – giving us four words for the price of one. As the Norman letters *gu* were interchangeable with the letter *w*, we get both guarantee and warranty, guard and ward, guardian and warden, and guile and wile, from the same source.

So many of the phrases common today not just in Britain but in English-speaking countries all over the world were derived during this Middle-English period. A mid-fourteenth century poem about a poacher shooting a deer ends with the lines:

> *And [it] happened that I hitt hym behynde the lefte sholdire. Dede as a dorenayle doun was fallen.*

This, even in the original spelling, requires only the slightest imagination to be quite comprehensible to modern readers, and the expression *'dead as a door nail'* is as colloquial today as it must have been in Poulton 650 years ago. Certainly every Poulton villein of the time would have known the expression *'by hook or by crook'*. The local authority, whether lord or prior, gave official permission for villagers to collect branches for fuel 'by hook or by crook', i.e. to pull them down from standing trees with such an implement. Or the Norman landowners' outcry calling for the mass pursuit of an escaping poacher – *'hue cri'* – our hue and cry. Other common doublings in English reflect the bilingual situation after the Conquest when an Old English word became coupled with a French synonym in order for everyone in the Kingdom to understand the concept – *'goods and chattels'* (*goods* from Anglo Saxon; *chatel* meaning 'property' in Norman French, from which we also derive the word cattle); likewise *law and order, ways and means, might and main, fair and square,* and *rack and ruin* – redundant doublings that have long outlived their original function, but remain lodged in the language for all time.

Although English is technically a Germanic language, about thirty per cent of the current vocabulary we use today has come from the French of the Norman period, and Britain must surely be the only country in the world which passes its national laws in a foreign language: *'La Reine le veult,'* says the Sovereign's representative in the House of Lords to place a parliamentary bill onto the modern English statute books, meaning 'The Queen wishes it' but delivered from the throne in purest Norman French from the Middle Ages.

The Poll Tax Revolt

In 1377 the population of Poulton, for purposes of the poll tax, is given as 67. Chances are these sixty-seven residents were none too pleased to have to pay up, and they weren't the only ones, by a long shot. By 1381 the poll tax was such a thorn in the flesh of many of the small landowners and villeins all over England, that they began turning rather nasty. Their wrath was aimed not at the boy-king, Richard II, whom they supported with a profound loyalty, but at the hated John of Gaunt and even more so at priors, abbots and other establishment clerics. The Prior of Bury St Edmunds was murdered by his own serfs, and in London Wat Tyler's men beheaded the Archbishop of Canterbury on Tower Hill. The Peasant's Rising, which began in Essex and Kent, soon spread to become a national rebellion in twenty-six counties. Whether the Poulton poll-tax payers actually marched on the Priory and demanded the final end of villeinage and land at fourpence an acre, as Englishmen elsewhere were demanding, is not recorded, but it's likely that they joined the revolt to some degree, and may well have made known their discontent with the Poulton Prior. The rebellion was only quietened when the fifteen-year-old King met the rebels at Mile End in London and convinced them that their requests would be granted. In fact they weren't, but that's government for you.

Poulton in the Fifteenth Century

England was by now a fully fledged and well-defined nation state, full of self-confidence and self-awareness, and the English were cock-a-hoop over a stream of French battlefield victories in the preceding years, from Crecy to Poitiers. Now it was triumph at Agincourt, and in 1415 every village in the realm echoed the triumphal strains of the carol in praise of Henry V:

> Our King went forth to Normandy
> With grace and might of chivalry
> There God wrought for him marvellously,
> Wherefore England may call and cry,
>   Deo Gratias!

...and many a prayer of jubilation and thanksgiving must have been offered up at matins at the Poulton Parish Church by the canon John Cumberworth, who had taken over the incumbency from Richard Lincoln in 1409. Much of France was under the English Crown and St George had been adopted as the country's Patron Saint. Doubtless the white standard bearing his crimson cross would have been fluttering from the top of St Michael's Church, a symbol of nationhood around which the villagers of Poulton could rally with pride.

England, though, was a thorough annoyance to the various kingdoms and dukedoms on the Continent, which considered the English to be bolshy, xenophobic, eccentric, even heretical – Europe's odd man out – even back then. But the English couldn't have given a toss what contempt the French, Italians, Spanish or Germans may have held them in. Their attitude was perfectly expressed a century later when the Bard proclaimed: *'Britain is a world by itself, and we shall nothing pay for wearing our own noses.'*

But even the most critical foreigner grudgingly respected England's military prowess (the most accurate longbow archers in Christendom) and admired her pre-eminence in music. Yes, music. In the fifteenth century England was acknowledged as the mecca of the musical arts, and English composers, singers and instrumentalists, particularly brass players, were offered high-paid jobs in the royal courts and ducal chapels all over the continent. At a time when European composers were still limited to stark early-mediaeval intervals of fourths and fifths in their primitive polyphony, the English avant-garde composers like John Dunstable and Leonel Power had moved on to discover the 'sprightly consonance' of thirds and sixths and were employing the triad chord, as much the harmony of Purcell

High spirits on a feast day in the village

as the Beatles, but an innovation that astonished European composers at the time.

The English tradition of descant singing in intervals of thirds and sixths was probably rooted in rural folk song which could have been heard in the Poulton ale house or around the maypole and might well have been taken up by the brothers at Poulton Priory for sung Eucharists.

As for military skills, we do know that archery practice was compulsory throughout the land, so the Poulton yeomen would have had to put in time at the Butts (at the southern Down Ampney edge of the village) shooting their arrows at straw-filled targets. They probably preferred crossbows for hunting, but for warfare, where penetration, accuracy and rate of fire are paramount, no weapon surpassed the English longbow. General Sir John Hackett, the eminent military historian, has written that the skill required for its effective use took years to acquire, but 'not until the nineteenth century were infantry to be equipped with anything offering a greater sum of advantages'. The Poulton yeomen would also have seen to it that their sons were learning archery skills at a very early age. Bishop Hugh Latimer described how, during the time of King Henry VII, his yeoman father...

> 'taught me how to draw, how to lay my body in my bow...I had my bows bought me according to my age and strength; as I increased in them, so my bows were made bigger and bigger, for men shall never shoot well unless they be brought up to it'.

Archery practice at the village Butts was compulsory in every village

The men of the village were made to practise their archery skills primarily for defence, like a home guard or the territorial army, but some doughty young tearaways may have volunteered for a military adventure or been obliged to go off to Normandy or to Wales to join this battle or that at the request of a local knight. Certainly, tenants were expected to drop everything and go off to war as ordinary foot-soldiers, when required, and there may have been a few Poulton veterans from that army of 6,000* that fought under Henry at Agincourt.

It was probably also at the Butts where the local men and boys played football with a pig's bladder stuffed with dried peas. These football games were rougher than rugger, and players took it for granted that they would end up with broken bones. Although most people associate tennis with Henry VIII at Hampton Court, it is recorded that tennis was being played in the English villages as early as the fifteenth century, and quieter games like backgammon, chess, draughts, dice and cards, were popular at the village ale house. Playing-cards were the latest fashion and have scarcely changed in five hundred years; the kings, queens and knaves on court cards of modern packs are still depicted wearing fifteenth-century attire. The ale house would not have been very different from a traditional village pub today, except that the beer was actually brewed by the women who served it. The other social centre of the village was the Parish Church, which sponsored 'Church Ales', a sort of mediaeval version of the vicarage tea party-cum-church bazaar. Men and women drank ale in the churchyard

Playing draughts in an ale house

and even in the church itself to raise funds for some worthy cause. Trevelyan says that the nave of the church was the 'village hall' for most communal purposes.

The figure estimated by General Hackett in his book The Profession of Arms. Cassell's Dictionary of English History puts the figure at 15,000 men.

During the summers, life was sweet and even the peasants ate well; a little meat and masses of vegetables fresh from the fields. White bread was the fashion of the day, a status symbol, but only afforded by the lords, the more prosperous yeomen and the monks. The peasants had to make do with a coarse black rye bread – but according to the wisdom of today, they were the better off for it. The winter diet was bleak and monotonous for everyone, and consisted of little besides salt meat, bread and peas. The monks had fresh fish, mostly pike or bream, from the Priory stew ponds, and plump pigeons from the Priory dovecote, but by spring nearly everyone was on the verge of scurvy.

April was the cruellest month; the winter supplies had run out and the new crops weren't ready. The primary produce in April was corpses, particularly those of children. The average life expectancy in England was only about forty years, but this reflected the very high rate of infant mortality through malnutrition and susceptibility to disease. In villages like Poulton, people lived longer than town folk crammed cheek-by-jowl in unhygienic tenements, and monks, well fed and closeted in spacious priories, tended to live a full ten years longer than anyone outside the walls. Once someone survived childhood, they had a reasonable chance of enjoying the full biblical life of three score and ten years. Although Chaucer lived to be only sixty in the fourteenth century,William Caxton, in the fifteenth, reached seventy.

Most laymen were still illiterate, but that didn't affect their lives as there wasn't anything much to read in any case – at least not until Caxton got his printing press going in Westminster and brought out his two best-sellers, Chaucer's *Canterbury Tales* in 1477 and Malory's *Morte d'Arthur* in 1485. But even the illiterate Poulton peasant would have been familiar with the *King Arthur* legends, the biblical stories, of course, and the latest exploits of the ballad hero, *Robin Hood*, which captured the imaginations of lords and liegemen alike. They knew these stories by word of mouth and from watching the stagings of the miracle plays by troupes of strolling players who went from village to village, setting up their pageants on the Butts. Poulton was surely on the touring circuit from Cirencester. The actors wore contemporary clothes, with costume accessories to indicate their characters; he who played God wore a beard, a tiara, a white cope and gloves; baddies wore turbans and swore by Mohammed; Mary Magdalene was decked out like a mediaeval tart, and angels climbed up to heaven and down to earth on normal ladders, while blue, red and black devils, often wearing animal heads, dashed about the audience claiming damned souls, to the accompaniment of clattering pots and pans which signified the discord in Hell. On feast days such as Poulton's three-day bash at Michaelmas, or May Day, there would doubtless be itinerant jugglers and minstrels with their hurdy-gurdies, pipes, tabors, psalters and sackbutts, and troupes of mummers and morris dancers 'playing' Poulton before moving on to Down Ampney or Driffield. It added some jollity to village life, even though the monks at the Priory may not have entirely approved.

The English love of dressing up, pageantry and processions could be seen even in a small village like Poulton, where the local archery competition would be excuse enough

Troupes of mummers toured the villages to provide jollity

for the yeomen to dress up as Robin Hood and Little John and lead the villagers in a jolly parade down to the Butts. And those Poultonites with more of a thirst for entertainment could have ridden into Cirencester for colourful tournaments and jousts, wrestling matches, horse races, dazzling displays of banner-swirling and mystery plays produced by the wealthy wool merchants' and clothiers' guilds; no expense spared on a proper raised tableau stage with machinery that could produce startling effects such as 'drawing a ship on to the place of the action'. The big hit of the day was *Castle of Perseverance*, a play that portrayed the siege of man's soul by the Devil, the World and the Deadly Sins. It packed the house at every performance.

This was the beginning of the great English love-affair with the theatre, and these mediaeval performances involved the audience in a way not seen again until the experimental happenings at the Fringe of the Edinburgh Festival.

The English language was changing so fast that the English spoken in the fourteenth century was already incomprehensible to people in the late fifteenth century. Caxton was asked by the Abbot of Westminster in 1490 to translate a passage of 'olde englyshe' into 'our English now usid' and he claimed that it seemed more like Dutch than English. He eventually gave it up as a bad job, saying:

> *'I coude not reduce [translate] ne brynge it to be understonden. And certaynly our language now used varyeth ferre from that whiche was usid and spoke when I was borne'.*

He was speaking of a span of only 68 years, and although the text above shows that he felt free to spell the past tense of *use* two different ways in the same passage, it was Caxton and his printing press that stabilised the language and spelling for the first time.

The canons in the Priory would no doubt have always been fairly adept at reading Latin and could also have read Caxton's books in English when they appeared, for the clergy made a point of being literate when all about them were not, but by now some of the yeomen farmers and local squires were prosperous enough to send their sons off to Eton or Winchester, or to one of the monastic grammar schools, where they were required to speak Latin to one another even whilst at play.

The mediaeval rules of conduct at Westminster School stated:

> *'If anyone who knows Latin dares to speak English or French with his companion, or with any clerk, for every word he shall have a blow with the rod.'*

By the fourteenth century, French was being taught as a completely foreign language, and from late mediaeval school reports, the pupils' efforts to speak it were not much more successful than those of the modern English schoolboy. The translator of the Bible, John of Trevisa, wrote in 1385:

> *'The disadvantage is that now the children of grammar schools know no more French than their left heel, and that is bad for them if they pass the sea and travel in strange lands and in many other places. Also gentlemen have now much left off teaching their children French.'*

It is equally interesting to note that in other respects as well, the mediaeval schoolboy was not unlike today's. The Westminster School rules also set out, in terms that could have been written yesterday by any distraught boarding-school housemaster:

> *'Whoever at bedtime has torn to pieces the bed of his companions, or hidden the bedclothes, or thrown shoes or pillows from corner to corner, or roused anger, or thrown the school into disorder, shall be severely punished in the morning.'*

But the important point is that laymen were now becoming as educated as the clergy, and the position of the Prior and his canons was much diminished.

By the end of the fifteenth century, the Poulton Priory estates were most likely managed by laymen, and the majority of Poulton's fields let out to tenant yeomen farmers. The unpopularity of the monasteries was growing; firebrand academics at Oxford and Cambridge, such as Latimer and Cranmer, were fomenting reform, the fabric of the Middle Ages was crumbling, and a new age was dawning. In time these radical changes were bound to affect Poulton as much as every other hamlet in the Kingdom.

The sons of the yeomen and country squires were sent away to schools. Education was rapidly spreading beyond the clergy and the nobility.

The interior of a village cottage in the sixteenth century

V
𝕿𝖚𝖉𝖔𝖗 𝕻𝖔𝖚𝖑𝖙𝖔𝖓
The Sixteenth Century

By the time King Henry VIII ascended the throne in 1509, England was socially quite unlike her continental neighbours in two important respects: firstly, only England had developed a large, literate and powerful middle class – the yeomen, merchants and local squires that came in all degrees of importance and means – sandwiched between the artisans and labourers on the one level, and the titled nobles on the other. On the Continent there was virtually nothing between a rich, educated aristocracy and an impoverished ignorant peasantry. Secondly, although London was even then the greatest city in Europe and the seat of the Royal Court and Parliament, there was also vast power, wealth and influence in the towns, grand houses, and even villages scattered throughout the country, and the English had already developed a fervour for country life that was unique. Trevelyan tells us that foreigners of the time were astonished at the preference of the English gentry for rural life. 'Every gentleman,' they remarked, 'flieth into the country. Few inhabit cities and towns; few have any regard of them.' Whereas in France and Italy, according to Trevelyan, the Romans had deeply implanted the civilisation of the city, England 'was still in its essential life and feeling a rural community... The place for the squire, whether he were rich or poor, was at home in his manor-house, and he knew and rejoiced in the fact.'

The King relied upon these rural communities for much of his personal support, the Crown's income, and

Shilling of Henry VIII

perhaps above all, to form an army for military adventures. Throughout the sixteenth century there was no English or Royal army as such, but every shire had a militia commanded by the Sheriff, and later in the century, by the Lord Lieutenants, and every villager felt an obligation to train not only in archery, as before, but now in shooting firearms as well. Trevelyan tells us that the self-respect and self-reliance of the English commonfolk was in military training, and this would clearly have applied to Poulton, as William Harrison, a contemporary of Shakespeare, wrote:

King Henry VIII by Holbein

'There is almost no village so poor in England, be it ever so small, that it hath not sufficient furniture in a readiness to set forth three or four soldiers, as one archer, one gunner, one pike, and one billman at the least. The said armour and munition is kept in one several place [sic] appointed by the consent of the whole parish, where it is always ready to be had and worn within an hour's warning.

Militiamen in the time of Henry VIII. Even a village the size of Poulton could provide at least three or four well-trained soldiers.

During the sixteenth century the longbow was being replaced by the caliver, a type of handgun. In a scene from Henry IV (pt. 2) Shakespeare has Falstaff and his side-kick Bardolph recruiting Cotswold village yokels with names like Mouldy, Feeble, Bullcalf and Wart, for the militia, by the authority of their Justices of the Peace. They are not looking for archers but for good shots; 'put me a caliver into Wart's hand, Bardolph,' says Falstaff, and he tests Wart's ability as a shot, which he proclaims...'very good, exceeding good,' even though the Justice claims 'he doth not do it right'. The handguns were in fact very inaccurate for all but almost point-blank range, but in 1595 the Privy Council decreed that bows would never again be issued as weapons of war. The bow was, however, still used for sport. As late as 1621 the Archbishop of Canterbury had the misfortune to aim his crossbow at a buck but shoot dead his gamekeeper instead.

It is very likely that Poulton contributed some soldiers for the army of 40,000 massed by Elizabeth I when the Armada was off the shores in 1588. Still more soldiers from the villages of the shires were being recruited daily when Sir Francis Drake and the weather scattered the Spanish ships and the danger passed away.

The End of Poulton Priory

By the time the founder of Poulton Priory's descendant, Jane Seymour, became Queen, monastic life had fallen into more or less total disrepute all over England. The monks were hated for being harsh landlords, and their vows of poverty and chastity had become something of a bad joke. For many years they had been leading lives of self-indulgence that were secular in all but name, and many lived openly with concubines. The Act of 1536 meant that Queen Jane witnessed the dissolution of most of the smaller monasteries before she died the following year, and had it not been for

Jane Seymour, Queen of England 1536–1537 (Holbein)

a fluke, she would have seen the closure of the Priory her ancestor, Sir Thomas Seymour, had founded. As it happened, Robert Holgate, Master of Sempringham, became chaplain to the King and through his influence, the Gilbertine houses were given a reprieve for three years. John Leland, another chaplain of Henry VIII, who journeyed around the country, visited Poulton, and in his itinerary he wrote:

Vicarage Cottage, built in the sixteenth century, is thought to be Poulton's oldest surviving house. It was, for many years, the home of the schoolmasters. It is now a private residence.

> *'I noted just a little beyond Pulton Village, Pulton Priory, where was a prior and two or three Black Canons. I saw in the walls where the Presbytery was, three or four arches where there were tombs of gentlemen. I think there were buried some of the St Maurs, of a surety one St Maur, founder of it, was buried there.'*

On 16 January 1539, Thomas Lenewood, Prior of Poulton, and either two or three of his canons, depending on which of two

Poulton in 1577

This portion of Saxton's map of Gloucestershire shows 'Pulton' during the reign of Elizabeth I. Ciceter is now also shown as Cirencester, but Ampney St Peter is still called Peteramney and Ampney Crucis is Holiroodeamney. (Original map in British Museum. Copy from Poulton Manor House.)

differing reports is accurate, surrendered the Priory. Their fate is unknown, but it was probably to their satisfaction. Redundant monks were often appointed to secure positions within the church structure as rectors and even bishops, or were at least pensioned off with something approaching a golden handshake. John Sympson, the Prior of the similar Gilbertine house in Marlborough, was given a pension of £10 a year, and one of his canons made rector of East Kennet church. It is highly likely that some such arrangement was made for the prior and canons at Poulton.

At the time of the Dissolution, the Poulton Priory was valued at £20 3s. 2d. The Priory, with all the property belonging to it, was granted by Henry VIII to Thomas Stroude, Walter Earle and John Paget. We know nothing about them or how the transfer affected the village, and we have no record of another rector of St Michael's until 1738, but presumably the church was again under the auspices of the Diocese of Salisbury.

> Think your Country your home, the inhabitants your neighbours, all freinds your children, and your children your own Sowli endeuouring to surpass all these in liberality and good nature.
>
> *Elizabeth R*

Communion with Elizabeth Tudor

The Poulton Parish Church's Communion chalice and paten, which also forms a cover for the chalice, bear hallmarks that prove that they were made in 1569, ten years after Elizabeth I was crowned Queen and pronounced 'Supreme Governor' of the Church of England.

Under Elizabeth, church attendance was made compulsory and absentees were fined, but she had cleverly compromised between the anti-papist stance of her father and various more ardent reformers than he, and the often ferocious anti-Protestant reign of Bloody Mary, her Catholic half-sister. The new Queen's policy of olive branches tossed in both directions was so successful that all but the staunchest Roman Catholics on the one hand and the die-hard Calvinist Puritans on the other could embrace her revised English Prayer Book of 1559 and the new character of the Anglicanism she created – a character that changed remarkably little from that time up until the last few years, when recent Church of England authorities have seen fit to depart from established Anglican tradition in a variety of ways, some of which look set to renew the sort of religious unrest not seen in the English Church since before Elizabeth's time.

Barbara Hill pointed out, in her history of *St Michael and All Angels Church*, that Poulton parishioners today are still taking Holy Communion with the same chalice from which villagers 'drank and thanked God for the defeat of the Spanish Armada'. It gives pause to think of how many sets of lips of Poulton villagers have sipped the wine from this handsome silver cup over the hundreds of years it has served the parish faithful.

The hall marks shown above are stamped on the Poulton church Eucharist chalice and paten. The crowned lion's head shows that the Assay Office was in London, the Lion Passant indicates that the metal is of 'sterling quality' and the letter 'm' signifies that the year of assay was 1569. The symbol of the silversmith also appears on the chalice and paten but is meaningless today as all records of makers' marks before 1666 were destroyed in the Great Fire of London.

The Communion chalice, 1569, still in use at St Michael and All Angels Church, Poulton

The Flowering of the Elizabethan Age

The dynamic creativity, innovation and sheer vitality of Elizabethan England have been long recognised; it blossomed in commerce, in science, in architecture, in exploration, and not least in the arts: music, drama, poetry and to some degree in painting. The music of William Byrd, John Dowland, Orlando Gibbons and Thomas Tallis, the greatest of the sixteenth-century composers, still regularly gets a hearing, not just by elitist ears in concert halls, but on such a popular medium as Classic FM radio, and people who know little or care nothing about music may nonetheless be familiar with such Elizabethan favourites as *Drink to Me Only with Thine Eyes* and certainly *Greensleeves,* which would have been sung in village taverns at the time.

Although the great Elizabethan theatre was centred in London, the popularity of contemporary poets and playwrights was to affect the language throughout the land. It was a grammar school boy from just north of the Cotswolds who led the way in transforming Middle English to Modern. Never mind the power and timeless insight of his dramas or the beauty and inspiration of his poetry, Shakespeare would be hailed a genius were it only for his contributions to the enrichment of the language throughout the English-speaking world. He left us not only with the legacy of hundreds of household words and phrases that have passed through the centuries and travelled across the seas, such as: *what's in a name?, to the manner born, hoist with his own petard, a charmed life, in my mind's eye, band of brothers, milk of human kindness, brave new world, salad days, blood-stained, fancy free,* and the very expression *household word* itself, but he coined countless new words like *dwindle* and *lonely* and indeed *countless*, which no modern speaker, be he in Poulton, Perth or Pottstown, Pennsylvania, could do without – yet which simply did not exist before the Warwickshire Bard put pen to paper over 400 years ago.

The sixteenth century defined the English character in the arts. Left clockwise: A painting of a young Elizabethan man by Nicholas Hilliard (1547–1619), founder of the English school. Thomas Tallis (1505–1585), William Byrd (1539 –1623), Orlando Gibbons (1583 – 1625), three of the greatest of the Elizabethan composers. William Shakespeare (1564–1616) who enriched the English language as no other man has ever done. Trevelyan says 'to understand the Elizabethan mind and character, turn to Shakespeare as the true authority'.

Foods, Fads and Fashions

The Elizabethan interest in and exploration of far away places, not least the American continent, introduced a wide variety of new edible delights such as coffee, chocolate, tomatoes and potatoes, which became so much a part of everyday fare that one now wonders how the English survived without chips, tomato ketchup, chocolate bars, and crisps. Under Elizabeth, strict laws were passed ordering observance of 'fish days', making it an offence to eat meat during Lent, or on Fridays. In 1563 it is recorded that a London woman was pilloried for having flesh in her tavern during Lent, but this had nothing whatever to do with religion and everything to do with boosting commercial fishing, and preventing arable land being turned into pasture to cash in on the almost insatiable English appetite for meat – a national peculiarity that endlessly caused amazed comment from foreign visitors.

As timberlands became depleted, coal was introduced as a new heating fuel, and hearths originally made for wood had to be re-built with cast-iron fire-backs. Another novelty which appeared around the middle of the century was destined to change the English social customs down the centuries – the introduction of tobacco. The New World weed, which had fuelled the peace pipes of American Indians for heaven knows how long, was readily taken up by Europeans and by the end of Elizabeth's reign, smoking tobacco in long clay pipes was widespread throughout the land. In the following centuries, tobacco was to become as associated with the world-wide image of the Englishman as bowler hats, solar topees, tea with milk, and gin and tonics in the tropics; from the snuff boxes of Beau Brummel and the Regency fops to the ubiquitous pipe-sucking of the contemplative Oxbridge don, the unflappable Colonial Governor, the tweedy country squire, and the Chief Inspector of Scotland

Smoking tobacco in clay pipes was widespread throughout the land by the end of Elizabeth's reign.

Yard; from the clubbable milords in velvet smoking jackets discussing world affairs over fat aromatic cigars and vintage port, to the bright young things flashing a silver monogrammed cigarette case – *Virginia on the left, Turkish on the right* – at cocktail hour in Mayfair; from Sherlock Holmes puffing on his curly calabash – as important a prop as his deer-stalker or magnifying glass – to Sir Winston chomping his oversized Havana; from Noël Coward in silk dressing gown with a cigarette holder clenched between his teeth, to the ordinary bloke in the local with a pint of bitter and a Woodbine dangling from his lip.

Not only must the enjoyment of tobacco have been as prevalent in Poulton as elsewhere in England, but the fortunes made from its manufacture were also in evidence in the village: the Poulton Priory estate was bought in 1927 by Major Mitchell with the wealth accrued from his days as Chairman of Imperial Tobacco, and Poulton Fields was for some years the home of Captain Stephen Player, backbone of the local hunt and scion of the family that made one of the most popular brands of English cigarettes, now vanished but remembered by older residents for their long-running slogan: 'Players please.'

James I deplored tobacco

Smoking has been decried from time to time by puritan forces over the centuries, not least by Elizabeth's successor, the dour Scot, James I, who, in 1604, wrote a fierce diatribe against tobacco, but nothing has had the success of the sustained attack of recent years. If, after the best part of four hundred years, tobacco is finally banished from Britain, as seems possible by the ferocity of the modern anti-smoking lobby, future school children may one day read of the existence of snuff, cigarettes, cigars and pipes as an historical curiosity, along with shillings and pence, inches, feet and yards, pints, quarts and gallons, kings and queens, and people once quaintly referred to as ladies and gentlemen. That is assuming, of course, that children will still be able to read.

VI
Jacobean Poulton
The Seventeenth Century

Gradually the horse was replacing the ox as a working animal for cart and plough. The breeding and selling of horses became an important part of Jacobean life, and of course riding was still the primary mode of transport. Much slower was the family 'coch', initially not much more than a cart with roof and leather curtains against the weather, used only for those too elderly, infirm or delicate to ride. Gradually more elaborate and comfortable coaches became fashionable, though they were more expensive and slower than travelling on horseback; in 1658, the stagecoach from Exeter to London took four days and cost forty shillings. Nonetheless, the coaches became more and more popular, so more and better coaching roads were built to accommodate them. The London Road (today the A417), which runs through the centre of Poulton (if *centre* isn't too grand a word for such a small village), became the main route to London from Gloucester and Bristol. These coaching roads attracted new hostelries to provide for overnight guests on long-haul journeys and were more prevalent and more useful than service stops on today's motorways.

The Inns in and around Poulton

We can assume that Poulton would have been served by a selection of inns and ale houses which would have sprung up after the dissolution of the Priory, but we have

A stagecoach in the 17th century; slow, expensive, but fashionable

very little knowledge about them before the mid-seventeenth century. From about 1650 on there is documentary evidence of their names and locations: *the Red Lion, the Packhorse Inn, the Falcon Inn, the Axe and Compass,* a.k.a. *the Carpenters' Arms, the New Inn,* and *the Three Magpies* were all in the London Road in or just out of Poulton Parish boundaries. There is also historical reference to a pub in Bell Lane called *the Bell*, though little is known about it, but we have a mass of legends, many conflicting, about the inn and hostelry for drovers and cross-country riders that was at Ready Token, where the Welsh Way, the ancient drovers' road, crossed the principal road to and from Oxford.

The original structures are still standing, though most have been converted or much modified for use as residential dwellings, but two of the old inns, the Red Lion and the Falcon, have, as of 2012, survived intact and are still serving pints of ale as they have done since they were built over three hundred years ago. The country inn of the sixteenth and seventeenth centuries was a splendid institution with a unique character and reputation for individual attention accorded guests. Fynes Moryson, a sophisticated traveller of the time who, it is said, had 'sampled the wayside hospitality of half Europe', wrote:

> *The world affords not such inns as England hath, either for food and cheap entertainment after the guests' own pleasure, or for humble attendance on passengers, yea even in very poor villages... if he eat with the host or at a common table with others, his meal will cost him sixpence... yet this course is less honourable and not used by gentlemen. But if he will eat in his chamber, he commands what meat he will, yea the kitchen is open to him to command the meat to be dressed as he best likes... While he eats, if he have company especially, he shall be offered music, which he may freely take or refuse. And if he be solitary, the musicians will give him good day with music in the morning... A man cannot more freely command in his own house than he may do in his inn.*

Travellers dining at a common table at a 17th century inn

The innkeeper would 'by obsequious attendance on the guests' discover the routes they would be taking

However Trevelyan tells us that the rural innkeepers and servants were often in league with highwaymen and would, by searching their rooms, take note of what valuables their guests were travelling with, and 'by obsequious attendance on the guest' discover what routes he would be taking. Before the age of cheques and credit cards, travellers often carried large sums of gold and coins to pay expenses or do business along the way. The publicans or staff would then inform thieves, who would waylay and rob the travellers further on down the road. In this way the inn would keep its good name, for no robbery would take place within its walls, but clearly those who gave the tip-off would receive a cut of the loot. Shakespeare, in various plays, depicted this seamier side of Elizabethan/Jacobean inns and William Harrison, his contemporary, said that the system works 'to the utter undoing of the honest yeoman as he journeyeth on his way.' The famous innkeeper's son-turned-highwayman, Dick Turpin, is alleged to have been operating in and around Poulton, particularly at Ready Token, in the early part of the eighteenth century.

The Red Lion

Just to the west of Poulton, on the London Road, is one of the most bizarre little pubs in England. The Red Lion was purpose built in the seventeenth century doubtless to serve the Bristol/Gloucester to London coach trade, and has been continuously operating as a licensed public house from then till now. Amazingly, the Red Lion has had only three publicans in the last hundred and twenty three years; James Wilkins and his son Horace ran it for eighty-seven years, and John Barnard has been mine host for over thirty years. Apart from its historical interest and the quality of its ale, the Red Lion is worth a visit because it is so downright peculiar and charmingly uncommercial. It is listed as one of 32 *Classic Unspoilt Pubs of Great Britain,* and given a three-star rating. Although the house itself is of reasonable size, only one small room to the right of the door is now used. The saloon, which has no bar as such, scarcely seats more than eight or ten guests, and to drink there is more like being in the publican's front room than in a public house. It is certainly not a place to go for a confidential *tête à tête*; all conversation is communal. John Barnard, who, after serving the drinks, will sit down and chat with the customers, runs it as a hobby and on whim. When asked the opening time, he replies with a chuckle, 'Whenever I'm thirsty'. It is too small to be profitable or even to provide a proprietor with a livelihood, so what will become of this eccentric little piece of local history if and when John Barnard decides to give it up, one hates to think.

Outside the Red Lion, 1892. James Wilkins (centre) was the licensee from 1887 until 1959, when his son Horace took over

The Packhorse Inn

Precisely when the Packhorse ceased to be an inn and was converted into a private residence is not really known, but during the reign of Charles II it was a popular coaching inn with extensive stabling, where travelling horses were looked after overnight or exchanged for fresh ones for the continued journey. The site of one of the present bathrooms is known to have been a cock pit, and the adjoining bedroom was formerly a gallery from which guests could watch the cock fights. It is now known as The Old Packhorse House.

Old Packhorse House in the London Road, built as a coaching inn with a cock-fighting pit and gallery. It has for many years been a private residence.

The Falcon Inn

The Falcon was built as a coaching inn and is today the only functioning public house within the village of

The Falcon Inn, with stables on the right, as it was during the early part of the 20th century

Poulton. Like so many Cotswold structures, it is impossible to know exactly when it was built, but the six-foot thick walls are a fair indication of its ripe old age. The Falcon's earliest publican on record was 'Edward Hewer alias Radbourne of Poulton, Innholder' according to his will dated 1751. In 1796, when its publican was John Jeffries, the first meeting of the Commissioners was held at the Falcon to organise the Poulton Closure Award, and it was over a pint of ale there that the exchange of contracts took place for the sale of the *Poulton Manor House* in 1824.

For seventy years of the last century (1905–1975) the Falcon Inn was tended by two generations of the Tanner family.

The Axe and Compass/Carpenters' Arms

Built c.1650, this London Road house, in the heart of Poulton village, has been put to a wide variety of purposes over the past three hundred and sixty some years. It was the Axe & Compass Inn, later re-christened the Carpenters' Arms, and, as the residence of the Harrison / Strafford family for centuries, was also used as a carpenter's workshop, a saddlery, an undertakers, a post office, the telephone exchange, a bicycle sales and repair shop, and a filling station. It was for many years a car repair garage run by Wilf Freeth, but now it is a private house, which, because Freeth thought of himself as a general factotum, he named *Figaro*.

The inn, which was later a post office and a telephone exchange is today a private house

Ready Token

Ready Token House was also built around the middle of the seventeenth century, and has accumulated a mass of mysteries, myths and legends from its original days as a popular inn. It lies at the crossroads of the old Roman

Aerial view of Ready Token House. The inn, built c. 1650, was at the crossroads of the ancient drovers' road called the Welsh Way, and the old Roman road, Akeman Street (seen top right), the northernmost tip of Poulton Parish.

road, Akeman Street, which forms the northern boundary of Poulton Parish, and the much older drovers' road, the Welsh Way, to the east. On the west, it borders Bell Lane, which runs down to the village of Poulton.

At 491 feet above sea level, Ready Token is the highest point for miles around, and it was an important site long before the inn was built. As mentioned in Chapter II – Roman Poulton – there is, in the garden of the house, a well 130 feet deep sunk by the Romans through solid stone to provide water for early travellers and legions of soldiers going back and forth between the Roman colonies of Corinium (Cirencester) and Verulamium (St Albans). Later, Ready Token provided the water supply for all the houses and farms of Poulton. This provision of water for travellers made it an ideal spot to build an inn in 1650.

Not least of the mysteries is the origin of the name itself. One source claims that Ready Token is a corruption from the Celtic word *rhydd* and the Saxon word *tacen*, meaning 'the way to the ford', referring to the crossing-place of the River Coln at Fairford. *Rustic Legends,* a section in the book *The Language of the Cotswolds*, reports a folk-myth that the name was coined by Oliver Cromwell, who arrived at the inn but found all the rooms occupied and therefore exclaimed 'It's ready taken!' The book has the grace to comment, 'Was ever such nonsense heard?' Perhaps Cromwell, knowing the inn was called Ready Token, did make such a remark as a rather feeble pun to milk a Puritan chuckle, but the name most likely pre-dates his arrival there during the Civil War. Other sources claim it was named after a sinister early landlord of the inn named Tom Ready, who, according to legend, would murder guests in their beds and take their money 'if they did not like his ale or didn't drink enough of it'. The inn was certainly popular with travellers on horseback and farmers on their way home from Ciciter market or returning from big fairs at Oxford and Gloucester, with their pockets full of money, and there was widespread contemporary gossip about travellers who stayed at the inn who 'were never seen alive again'. *Rustic Legends* quotes a simple labourer repeating the folk-memory tale of a packman and a 'jewelrer' who both vanished after a night at the inn. For many years nothing was heard of them, 'but about twenty year ago,' said the labourer, 'some skellingtons [sic] were dug up on the exact spot where the old inn stood,' so their disappearance was accounted for. Eight skeletons were indeed found in the grounds. One theory is that they were victims of the Civil War, which will be discussed later. Another that they were murdered by some highwayman, but the most persistent belief was indeed that they were guests at the inn, murdered by the innkeeper as they slept.

The countryside was certainly full of highwaymen and thieves, and riding cross-country was dangerous. Therefore yet another theory of the origin of the name is that when horsemen saw the inn, which was in bleak countryside, standing high, they knew they were at last safe, as it was a landmark or 'ready token' from which to take their position. The last record found about the inn at Ready Token is an announcement printed in the *Gloucester Journal,* in May 1738:

> *This is to give Notice that Thomas Skillin, who kept Barnsly-Inn [sic] for these thirteen years last past, is removed from thence to his own House, the Sign of the Ready-Token Ash, at Ready Token, lying between Fairford and Barret's-Brook [now Perrott's Brook], in the same Road to London as his former House; and between Burford and Cirencester, in the Oxford Road to Bath: It's a new-built House*, with good Stabling, and is pleasantly situated, with a fine Prospect: Where all gentlemen, Ladies, &c. may depend upon meeting with good Entertainment, and most reasonable and civil Usage, from their Humble Servants,*
>
> *Thomas and Susanna Skillin*
>
> *N.B. At the same Place may be had good Wines, good October Beer, and good Herefordshire Cyder.*

* *The 'new-built house' could only refer to refurbishment or rebuilding of some sort, as an inn had stood there for over eighty years before this notice.*

Ready Token House today. The inn was joined up with two cottages in 'butterfly plan' in 1929 by the distinguished 'arts and crafts' architect Norman Jewson*, to make one large residence.

* *Norman Jewson also built Poulton Grange*

Poulton and the Civil War

Between 1642 and 1646 there was considerable fighting in the area of Poulton Parish. In Poulton itself, villagers would have been divided between those who supported Charles I and the Church of England and those who sided with the Puritans and Parliament, but Trevelyan tells us that the division was based on political and religious issues, rather than social or economic conditions. Men chose their sides according to their own independent opinions, although the yeomen and business agrarians more often tended to favour the Roundheads, whereas the old fashioned West Country squires 'who took a more feudal attitude to life and society' were typical Cavaliers. On the whole, according to Trevelyan, rural areas, villages and market towns were more likely to remain Royalist, though this was not true of Cirencester, which sided with Parliament from the start. In 1643, the Royalist forces battled their way into Cirencester and seized the town. In that same year, the thirteen-year-old Charles Stuart, in disguise, would have passed through Poulton on his way from London to Cirencester and thence to the coast.

Cavalier

Sally Adams, who grew up in Ready Token House, wrote about the local legend that says that during the Civil War, a number of Roundheads held out in the inn, but were eventually defeated, killed and buried there in a circle, feet to centre. She states, 'Certainly a large grave has been found and bones taken to the museum'. She also tells of a tunnel that runs from the house to Furzey Farm Buildings and another to Quarry Hill Farm. She says these escape tunnels are still there; 'the entrance is open and steps of earth go down. In the tunnels, children's rib cages have been found, but the main tunnel has collapsed in places and is very unsafe to follow.'

The Puritan, 'the lonely figure with its Bible and the burden of sin' (John Bunyan)

The Gardens of Poulton

Oliver Cromwell

During the period of the Commonwealth, many new varieties of trees, plants and flowers were introduced into England – the tulip, the laburnum, the nasturtium, love-in-a-mist, honesty, and the red maple, among them – and the English developed a passion and tradition for gardening that foreigners have admired for centuries – one national characteristic that survives modernity unabated. Sir Francis Bacon planted the idea into the English psyche that without a garden, 'building and palace are but gross handiworks' and Andrew Marvell, Cromwell's poet-secretary, followed with:

> How well the skilful gardener drew
> Of flowers, and herbs, this dial anew;
> Where, from above, the milder sun
> Does through a fragrant zodiac run,
> And, as it works, the industrious bee
> Computes its time as well as we!
> How could such sweet and wholesome hours
> Be reckoned but with herbs and flowers.

This 300-year-old tradition has produced, in the environs of Poulton, some of the finest gardens and arboreta in England, not least that at Barnsley House, a stone's throw from Ready Token, formerly the home of the late landscape designer and gardening writer Rosemary Verey, and now a country house hotel. But Poulton itself can boast a fine selection of diversely planted and beautifully tended and gardens.

Alma's Cottage in Poulton with a small but exquisite traditional English cottage garden.

Restoration Poulton

In 1663 Charles Stuart would again have passed through Poulton on his way to Cirencester, but this time in triumph as Charles II, the new King of England. With the restoration of the monarchy in 1660 came the restoration of the Anglican Church and the Prayer Book; the theatre, which had been suppressed by the 'religiously correct' bigotry of the Puritans; the patronage of science, which had been scorned; and the respect for Common Law, which had been disregarded and over-ridden. Above all came the return of common sense and tolerance, for the eleven-year military dictatorship of Cromwell and his Taleban mentality had all but extinguished joy from life.

This Bristol coach passed through Poulton on its way to and from London

Medal in commemoration of the Restoration

The Bedwells and Poulton Manor House

The Bedwells were certainly living in Poulton by the middle of the seventeenth century. They were a family of prosperous wool staplers, and Thomas Bedwell, born in 1617, made a fortune during the Civil War. He is on record as being 'the second Lord of the Manor of Poulton'. Clearly the numbering system began again after the dissolution of the Priory, but whether the first new lord was Thomas's father or another, we know not. Nor do we know where the Bedwells were living before Thomas built the present Manor House in 1680, when he was 63 years old. He and his wife Anne and their son Thomas, who was 24 then, were the first occupants of the house. Anne Bedwell, 'after

A typical seventeenth-century country woman

a pious life and a tedious sicknesse, dyed the 25 November Anno 1682', just two years after the completion, but young Thomas's wife, Martha, probably took over her role of running the Manor for her widowed father-in-law.

Old Thomas himself died in 1691, not living long enough to see his grandchildren, Joseph (b. 1696) and Ann (b. 1697), romping about the splendid house he had built. On his death, Thomas Jr. became Poulton's third Lord of the Manor. Inside St Michael's Church there is a plaque *(below)* honouring 'Thomas Bedwell, Gent.' and his wife Anne, and also to the memory of 'their son who erected this monument and dyed the 15th May Anno Dom. 1728 in the 72nd yeare of his age and of Martha, his wife, daughter of Mr Wm. Townsend, who dyed the 15th of March Anno Dom. 1714.' This memorial, and the burial tablet of Francis Bedwell, which had originally been in the old mediaeval church, were transferred to the walls of the new St Michael's and All Angels' Church when it was erected in 1873.

One of two memorial tablets to the Bedwell family, originally in the mediæval church. They were transferred to the interior walls of the new St Michael and All Angels Church.

Jacobean Poulton

Although the Manor House is built in Cotswold stone with a locally-quarried stone tile roof, the architecture is totally different from any other house in Poulton, or the Cotswolds, come to that. The typical look of the Cotswold house of this period is, for example, Jenners (shown below), with its gables and chimneys in rows. Jenners, formerly called The Gables, was probably a farmhouse in the sixteenth century or even before, but the façade is now a seventeenth century renovation, in the style of many other Poulton houses – a style so traditional to the area that houses very similar were still being built in the Cotswolds 150 years later.

Jenners, formerly called The Gables, built in traditional Cotswold style – a style that lasted through the eighteenth century without much change. Jenners is a Grade II listed property. Parts of the house pre-date the seventeenth century.

The Manor House, however, has a tidy, classical box shape, like a dolls house, and instead of gables, it has a hipped roof with projecting eaves which shows a distinctly Dutch influence. Another unusual feature is its single chimney, placed in the very centre of the roof. The classical windows, too, are quite unlike those of other Cotswold houses.

The design reflects the change from the lofty, raftered halls, which were the essential features of the country house from Saxon to Elizabethan times, to a new concept of many smaller rooms for different purposes: drawing room, dining room, library, etc. The symmetrical Manor House has two rooms at the front and two rooms at the back on each floor, a number of which are wood-panelled – a Jacobean fashion that replaced the hanging tapestries on Tudor walls. The house has been preserved, virtually unaltered (and only minimally restored in 1930), since it was built. With its original staircase, panelled walls and broad oak and elm floorboards, it remains as it was – a little gem of the Restoration period.

In 1705, the Manor House was occupied by the Cripps family, who owned the house throughout the eighteenth century. The Crippses were large landowners in this area, and though they have vanished from Poulton itself, there are still Crippses in the area. They are remembered by the ancient barn nearby which is still known as Cripps' Barn, and for their illustrious descendant, Sir Stafford Cripps, the Labour politician so prominent in the Churchill wartime coalition government. For most of the nineteenth century the Manor House was in the Heywood family, although

The Manor House, built in the very centre of the village in 1680, is architecturally unique in the Cotswolds. It is a Grade I listed property.

curiously a Bedwell is shown to have been an occupant in 1866 – possibly through marriage into the Heywood family. Certainly the Bedwell family continued to reside in Poulton, even if their original wool fortune was much diminished. A Mrs Bedwell owned fields in Poulton in 1899, and in 1904 and again in 1906, the church registry shows two Bedwell marriages. Another Thomas Bedwell, born in 1846, was buried in the church grounds as recently as 1916. The fate of the Manor House in the twentieth century will be dealt with in that chapter.

Seventeenth-century Families and Houses

The earliest existing church register of baptisms and burials at Poulton dates from 1695; the baptism of Thomas Bedwell's son Joseph is one of the first recorded. From these records we can see that a fair number of the families who were to feature in village life for years to come were already in residence in Poulton during the seventeenth century: the Adamses, the Hewers, the Tippers, the Bettertons, the Lanes, the Byes and the Moulders. The three church bells today bear the names of these early benefactors: one is inscribed Richard Roberts and William Tipper, 1643; another, Giles Horsewell and Thomas Bye, 1671, and the third, in memory of David Tipper and William Lane, 1736.

This was also the era of the building of so many of the sturdy Cotswold stone houses that still dominate the village. Apart from Jenners and the Manor House, others include: the Old Forge, the Old Farmhouse, Peach and Pear Tree Cottages, nos. 12 & 14 London Road, Southcott Cottage, Edwards' General Stores, Jenner's Barn, Gardener's Cottage, and the House on the Corner. These are all Grade II historical buildings listed by the Cotswold District Council.

The Old Farmhouse, one of Poulton's 17th century houses listed as a Grade II historical building.

A World in a Grain of Sand

Poulton in 1720

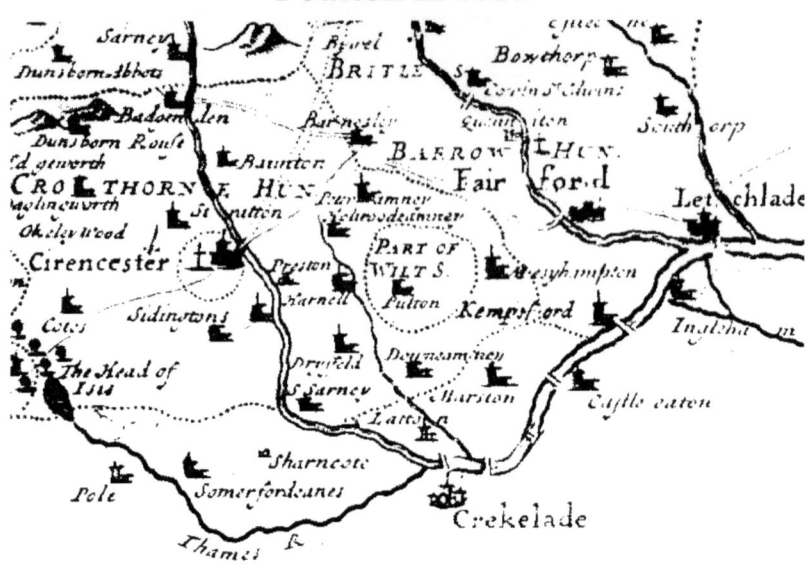

From a map of Gloucestershire by Robert Morden. Poulton is still 'Pulton, Part of Wilts.'

Poulton in 1777

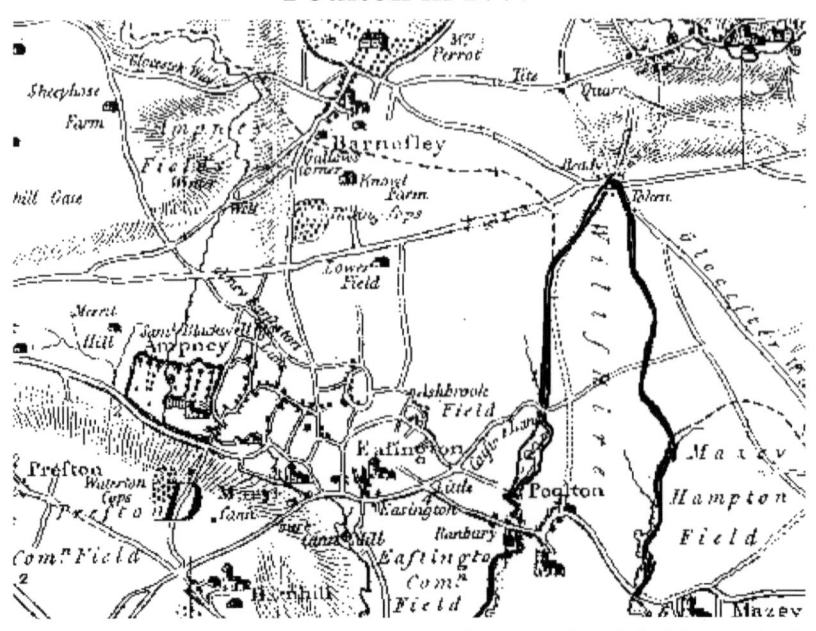

Poulton appears as Poolton, and 'Amney' is now spelt Ampney, though the 'p', mysteriously added, is still unpronounced locally.

86

VII
Georgian Poulton
The Eighteenth Century

The old church register, written in the hand of Richard Adams, churchwarden, lists the first marriage between Henry Boulton and Joan Popworth in 1703. The eighteenth-century families whose amazing fecundity fills pages of the baptismal register include the Griffins, the Wheelers, the Bishops, the Gardners, the Edwardses, the Prices and the Harrisons, along with those families mentioned previously, who continued to be prolific. A few offshoots of these families are still residents of the village at the time of writing.

The Adams family were settled in Poulton by at least 1650, and were still at 'the House on the Corner' 300 years later. From a box of old Poulton deeds, mortgages and indentures of various kinds in the possession of a resident, there is a lease dated 1720 for a house and land by Jane Adams, widow of John, who died in 1713, to Robert Wake for the sum of £6 *2s 6d*. The document, painstakingly copied out by quill on sturdy calf-hide vellum, is still in pristine condition. It begins:

Release of Land in Poulton

THIS INDENTURE made the seven and twentieth day of May in the Sixth yeare of the Reign of our Soveraigne Lord George by the grace of God of Great Britaine France and Ireland King Defender of the Faith in anno dom

1720 BETWEEN Jane Adams of Poulton in the County of Wilts, Relict [widow] of John Adams, late of Poulton aforesaid yeoman deceased, and John Adams son and heire apparent of the said John Adams deceased, by the said Jane, and Richard Adams of Poulton, aforesaid yeoman, the younger son of the said John Adams deceased, by the said Jane of the one part, and Robert Wake now or late of Lower Guiting in the County of Glouc., Taylor, of the other part WITNESSETH that for and in consideration of the sume of Sixe pounds two shillings and sixepence of lawfull money of Great Britaine unto the said Jane Adams... etc.

When it came time for their signatures, we see that although the sons, John and Richard Adams, could sign the parchment quite proficiently, their mother, Jane, could only make her mark. The instance of the husbands and sons being literate and the wives and daughters being unable to write even their own names seems common if not typical of Poulton families of the time. The fact of the matter is that there was very little occasion for yeomen's wives to write, except on legal documents of this sort, and learning the skill for the sake of signing perhaps one or two legal papers during their life no doubt seemed, in the eighteenth century, time and effort unprofitably spent. They got married young, and between the various domestic

The mark of Jane Adams and the signatures of her two sons (actual size) that appear on the vellum lease of 1720.

chores, plus helping with the farm, and producing offspring in sufficient quantity that would guarantee the survival of another generation of the family, there was precious little time or energy left for anything else.

The Adamses, like so many other Poulton families, would often pass on their own names to their children, and it is quite typical that Richard Adams and his wife Rebecca, in the 1740s, named their two children Richard and Rebecca, confusing as that may have been for their home life. As the Bedwells named generations of males Thomas, the Hills favoured Edmund, the Lanes, William, and the Gambles, David, there were in fact six generations of Adamses who named their first-born sons Richard.

The Adams family married into the Jobbins family first in the late nineteenth century, when George Jobbins of Quarry Farm, at Ready Token, married Mary Adams, and then again in the next generation, when their daughter Lavinia 'Doll' Jobbins married Richard William Adams at the 'House on the Corner', which they ran as a steam bakery. It was their son, yet another Richard, who sold up and left the village in 1948, thus ending the 300-year Adams line in Poulton.

Where the London Road meets Cricklade Street, the road to Down Ampney; The House on the Corner (left), was built in the seventeenth century, quite possibly by the Adams family, who lived there continuously until 1948. In the twentieth century it was a steam bakery operated by Will (known as Raggy) and Doll Adams née Jobbins. To the right, Hillside dates from the early eighteenth century. Both houses are Grade II listed properties.

A World in a Grain of Sand

The London Road Turnpike 1727-1879

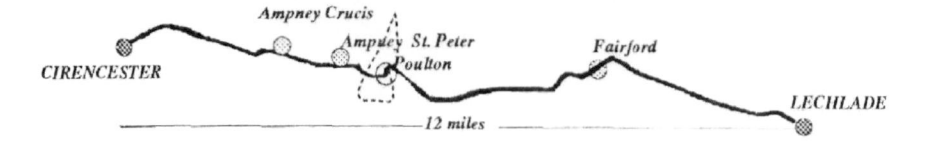

Anno Regni
GEORGII
REGIS
Magnæ Britanniæ, Franciæ, & Hiberniæ,
DECIMO TERTIO.

At the Parliament Begun and Holden at *Westminster*, the Ninth Day of *October*, Anno Dom. 1722. In the Ninth Year of the Reign of our Sovereign Lord G E O R G E, by the Grace of God, of Great Britain, France, and *Ireland*, King, Defender of the Faith, &c.

And from thence Continued by several Prorogations to the Seventeenth Day of *January*, 1726. Being the Fifth Session of this present Parliament.

G   R

London, Printed by *John Baskett*, Printer to the King's most Excellent Majesty ; and *Tho. Norris*, Assignee to *George Hills*. 1727.

Cover of the Act of Parliament which made the London Road through Poulton a turnpike in 1727

The Route to London

From 1698 on, there was a regular mail-coach service from Cirencester to London which passed through Poulton, but by 1720 the London Road had fallen into such disrepair that it was often impassable and it took up to three days to travel the one hundred miles to its destination. If this road was to continue being the main artery from Bristol and Gloucester to the capital, major repairs were clearly necessary, but in the eighteenth century there was no provision for government funds to build or maintain public roads. In 1727 an act was passed through Parliament authorising the London Road to become a toll road between Cirencester and St. John's Bridge in Lechlade. Duty would be charged for every 'Coach, Berlin, Chariot, Calash, Chaise, Chair, Waggon, Wain, Cart, or other Carriage; Horse, Gelding, Mare, Mule, Ass, or any sort of Cattle', that passed, and the received money used to pay for the upkeep of the road. This was the earliest act allowing the erecting of turnpike roads in this area, and the terms and conditions were set out in considerable detail:

An Act for Repairing the Roads leading from Cirencester Towns-End, to Saint John's Bridge in the County of Gloucester.

Whereas the several Highways and Roads leading from Cirencester Towns-End (through the Parishes of Cirencester, Ampny-Crucis, Ampny-Mary, Ampny-Peter, Poulton, Mesey-Hampton, Fairford, and Leachlade) to a Place called Saint John's Bridge, in the County of Gloucester, are, by reason of many heavy Carriages frequently passing through the same, become very ruinous and deep, and in the Winter Season many parts thereof are so bad, that Passengers cannot pass and repass without great danger: And whereas the said Highways and Roads cannot, by the ordinary Course appointed by the Laws now in force (for Repairing the Highways of this Kingdom) be effectually amended and repaired, without some other Provision be made for raising Money to be applied for that purpose: For Remedy whereof, and to the Intent that the said Highways and Roads may with all convenient speed be effectually amended, and hereafter kept in good and sufficient Repair, so as that all Persons may travel through the same with Safety, May it please Your Majesty that it may be Enacted; And be it Enacted by the King's most Excellent Majesty, by and with the Advice and Consent of the Lords Spiritual and Temporal, and Commons, in this present Parliament assembled, and by the Authority of the same, That for the better surveying, ordering, repairing, and keeping in Repair the Highways and Roads aforesaid, it shall be in the Power of the Right Honourable Richard Lord Viscount Gage, of the Kingdom of Ireland; etc.

This is followed by a list of the trustees who were nominated and appointed to put the act in execution, and those named include members of the Bedwell and Jenner families. The trustees were given the power to erect toll-houses and gates across any point in the road between Cirencester and Lechlade, and were authorised to receive the tolls and duties as prescribed by the Act, some of which are as follows:

> *For every Coach, Berlin, Chariot, Calash, Chaise, or Chair, drawn by Six Horses, or Mares, the Sum of One Shilling and Six Pence.*
>
> *For every Coach, etc., drawn by four or more Horses, or Mares, Eight Pence.*
>
> *...drawn by two Horses, or Mares, Six Pence.*
>
> *... by one Horse or Mare, Three Pence.*

For every Waggon, Wain, Cart or Carriage drawn by Five or more Horses, Mares or Oxen (not carrying Corn or any other Sort of Grain, to the Towns of Cirencester or Leachlade [sic], on Market Days there respectively) the Sum of One Shilling:

And drawn by Four Horses, Mares, or Oxen, Eight Pence:, by Three Horses, etc. Six Pence: by Two Horses etc. Three Pence: And drawn by One Horse, Mare, or Ox, Two Pence. For every Horse, Gelding, Mare, Mule, or Ass, laden or unladen, and not drawing, One Peny [sic]. For every Drove of Oxen, Cows, or Meat Cattle, Ten Pence per Score, and so in proportion for any greater or lesser Number. For every Drove of Calves, Hogs, Sheep, or Lambs, Five Pence per Score, and so in proportion for any greater or lesser Number. The Act concludes:

For a Waggon Wain, Cart or Carriage drawn by four horses, the fee at the toll gate was 8 pence

> ... *the Money so to be raised is and shall be hereby vested in the said Trustees; and the same, and every Part thereof, shall be paid, applied, disposed of, and assigned for repairing the Roads aforesaid.*

The Cirencester Flying Coach

The repairs duly got under way, and as the road gradually improved, an enterprising person set up a stage coach to ply from Cirencester to London, taking only two days. Not long afterwards it performed the hundred-mile journey in one day of twenty-four hours. This coach became famous and was known as the 'Cirencester Flying Coach'. In the winter months, however, it took a full two days, and, according to one newspaper report, was said 'not to fly'. By 1800, the Cirencester-to-London run took the old mail coach only fourteen hours, and the ordinary coaches, sixteen hours, and just before the opening of the Great Western Railway they were able to make the coach trip in only eleven hours.

The Turnpike Trust met in coaching inns all up and down the London Road from the Fleece Inn in Cirencester to the White Hart Inn in Lechlade, to decide where to widen the road, where to place the toll gates (one was erected just across the road from the Red Lion), the salary of gate-keepers who towards the end of the century were given a rise to ten shillings per week, and installing 'an Engine for the weighing of carriages' to extract more duty for those carriages that were too heavily laden. As there was then no bridge at Poulton, the little stream called the Ashbrook simply flowed across the road. In 1778 the trustees ordered that 'the Surveyor treat with Mr Dallaway for making a Cut through his Mead for lowering the Water in Poulton Ford.' The London Road was de-turnpiked on 1 November 1879.

Detail from the Isaac Taylor map of Gloucestershire, 1777, showing the turnpike's route through 'the Parish of Poulton' in Wiltshire. 'Poulton Palace' must have referred to whatever remained of the Priory.

The London Road turnpike that passed through Poulton shortened the Cirencester–London coach journey from three days to less than one. It existed as a toll road from 1726 until 1879.

Betty Bastoe, the 'Witch' of Poulton

Elizabeth 'Betty' Bastoe, the so-called 'Witch of Poulton', died in 1796 and is buried at the crossroads, on the corner of Bell Lane and the road to Quenington, which dissects the Parish of Poulton. The spot appears on signposts and maps as *Betty's Grave*. The name first officially appeared on the Enclosure Award of 1796 as 'Betty's Grove', but this was changed to 'Betty's *Grave*' on the first Ordnance Survey map of 1830. Who she was, how she died, and why she was interred at this crossroads is one of Poulton's most lively and disputed legends.

Betty is commonly believed to have lived in the cottage officially listed as no. 10 Cricklade Street, opposite Home Farm. This miniscule seventeenth-century cottage consists of one room only on the ground floor, with ladder-stairs leading to a loft which must have served as Betty's bedroom. The cottage was traditionally part of the Poulton Priory estate, and

No. 10 Cricklade Street, a one up, one down 17th century cottage, believed to have been the home of Betty Bastoe in the 18th century. A Grade II listed property.

the address had nothing to do with its position in Cricklade Street, only that it was tenth on the list of Priory properties. It was bought by the Hill family in 1927 as part of an extensive sale of Priory assets following the death of Major Joicey, and at that time the minute dwelling was occupied by an elderly man, Harry Robins, who paid a rent of £3 per year. Since then it has been officially condemned as uninhabitable, and was used as a workshop by its last owner. Nearly everything about Betty is mythology and conjecture, and there are an incredible number of different versions of her life and death passed down through Poulton folklore. As no research is possible, all the author can do is offer a list of the various legends and allow the reader his or her own fancy:

1. Betty Bastoe was found guilty of witchcraft and was burnt at a stake. Denied a Christian burial, she was buried at the crossroads, as was customary for condemned witches.
2. She was caught stealing sheep and was hanged.
3. She was found guilty of poisoning the man who employed her as his housekeeper, and was executed.
4. She was a gipsy queen, and is remembered and honoured to this day by the Romany travellers. Every year, so say many locals, the gipsies pass by Betty's Grave and place a bunch of plastic flowers on the mound where she lies.
5. She committed suicide.
6. She was the village tart and was caught by the local wives plying her trade to the men working in the fields and was torn limb from limb on the spot.
7. She herself was poisoned by the man for whom she was housekeeper, and years after her death, he confessed the deed.
8. Betty's death was natural and brought about by her accepting a wager that she could mow one acre of corn in a day. She completed the mowing within the time, won her bet, but fell dead of exhaustion and was buried on the very spot where she dropped.

These last two versions do not, however, explain why her body was not taken to the Poulton Churchyard for a normal Christian burial, but the wager legend is certainly one of the most commonly believed, and a Mrs Dicken of Down Ampney was inspired enough by the tale to put it into verse, citing malicious gossip the reason for the crossroads burial:

> Long ago, a country maid
> Too dearly for a wager paid.
> She scythed a field of corn, they say
> Single-handed, in a day.

Success was hers, but don't forget,
She lost her life to win her bet,
For when, at dusk, she reached her goal,
The 'Reaper' harvested her soul.

Whisperers claimed she was a witch.
They put her body in a ditch.
Others doubting how she died,
Spread ugly tales of suicide.

Two unjust reasons thus were found,
To withhold consecrated ground.
Her headstone is of grass and moss,
And intersecting roads her cross.

Rolling fields of corn still wave,
Like restless seas near Betty's Grave,
Until their golden torrent yields
To sheep-shorn turf at Poulton Fields.

There, at crossroads, troubles past,
Betty rests, in peace at last,
And children, superstition free,
Leave flowers there in her memory.

Whether Betty Bastoe was hanged, burnt, lynched, murdered, committed suicide, or died from sheer exhaustion will never be known, nor whether she was a witch, a gipsy, a 'sex worker', a victim or a murderess, but it is true that fresh flowers appear from time to time on the mound at the crossing which immortalises her. Just who places them there is not clear, and this adds yet another element of mystery to the many legends about the dot on the map that will probably forever be known as Betty's Grave.

Betty's Grave, at the crossroads of Bell Lane and the road to Quenington and Coln St. Aldwyns. Fresh flowers are often laid upon the mound to the right of the signpost, which is Betty's final resting place.

The Reverend John Keble

The list of incumbents of Poulton Church shows a gap of about two hundred years between John Cumberworth in the fifteenth century and Clement Headington, who arrived as Rector around 1738. Headington officiated at Poulton Church for over forty years until his death. Beyond that we know little about him, but we have considerable information about his successor, the Revd John Keble, who was licensed to the curacy in 1782 and remained Curate of Poulton for thirty-seven years. His annual stipend was £20 10s., which more or less equalled the revenue of Poulton Priory at the time, and the patrons of the living were then Thomas Ingram, Sir John and Rebecca Bridger and a Mrs Mary Eliot. Ingram and Sir John Bridger were partners in owning large tracts of land north of Betty's Grave.

John Keble was not only responsible for St Michael and All Angels, Poulton, but also had to serve at the church in Coln St. Aldwyns, four miles away, and we gather from his letters that he felt a bit put upon by all the demands on his time, for so little reward. In 1786, Keble wrote that 'the Bishop appointed the Curate of Poulton to preach at Marlborough', which he considered unreasonable considering the value of the Benefice, and in another letter he complained about being made to attend at Gloucester Assizes as a witness: 'I was kept at Gloucester in downright captivity until Sunday morning and then was obliged to set out at 4 o'clock so as to reach home at breakfast time and serve my two Churches afterwards'.

He also wrote that as Curate of Poulton he ought to have attended the Bishop's Visitation at Marlborough, but instead 'had to meet his Lordship at Swindon'. Though sounding a bit miffed, he nonetheless graciously added 'like the rest of the clergy, [I] was much pleased by his affability and politeness'.

The first meeting of the Commissioners of the Poulton Closure Award was held at the Falcon Inn in 1796. One provision was 'to secure to the Revd John Keble, the

Perpetual Curate, an enhanced stipend of £30', which must have mollified the cleric somewhat. Another provision was the allotment to the Churchwardens and Overseers of about 20 acres for furze or fuel in lieu of the 'immemorial privilege of "the poor of Poulton" to cut and take away a limited quantity of Furze from certain parts of the commonable land called the Downs'.

This John Keble is now best remembered for being the father of the famous Revd John Keble, who was an illustrious poet and theologian and, according to Newman, the 'true and primary author of the Oxford Movement', an academic coterie dedicated to restoring Anglo-Catholic ceremony and ritual, upholding 'the apostolic succession and the integrity of the Prayer Book', and rescuing the Church of England from the escalating evangelism of the time. Considering that a number of its chief supporters, including Newman, crossed over to the Church of Rome out of frustration with the state of the Church of England, the situation has a strangely contemporary ring. Keble junior was born in 1792 in nearby Fairford, ten years after his father was appointed Curate of Poulton. By the age of fifteen he had already left the area to join his older brother as a student at Oxford University, but was back again when he was twenty-three, as Curate of St Michael and St Martin's Church*, Eastleach Martin. He later became professor of poetry at Oxford and, in 1827, wrote *The Christian Year*, a book of sacred poems which enjoyed immense popularity throughout England, and was influential in extending the ideals of the Oxford Movement, doctrinally, spiritually and liturgically, throughout the Anglican Community. He also wrote a number of familiar hymns, such as *Bless'd Are the Pure in Heart*. He died in 1866, and in 1870 Keble College, Oxford, was founded in his memory, designed by William Butterfield, the architect of the present Poulton Church.

The Revd John Keble, whose father was Curate of Poulton.

a 12th century class I listed church, now redundant but open to visitors

The Jenners and the Lanes

During the reigns of the Georges I, II, & III, various acts of parliament assured that the enclosure of fields and commons rapidly took place. This was to the advantage of farming efficiency, and equally to the advantage of the great landowners of the realm, but it was at the expense of tenants, yeomen farmers and the lesser rustic squires in communities like Poulton. The Enclosure Acts gave rise in the number of landless labourers who, because labour was plentiful, were in no position to bargain for better wages. Poulton labouring families like the Hewers and the Wheelers, who would previously have had small strips of land or allotments to grow a bit of this and that for their own use, and common land to graze a sheep or two, now found themselves without anything, and they were probably worse off than they had ever been in history.

The smaller landowners could only join in on the new agricultural prosperity by increasing the size of their holdings, and if they hadn't the capital to buy or lease more land, the answer was often to gain it through judicial marriages with other land-owning families.

The Jenners, the Lanes and the Hills were just such families in the Poulton area in the eighteenth century, and it was probably no accident that their offspring found mates from similar families who brought along a dowry of a few fields and houses to add to the joint holdings. So it was that the Lanes married the Jenners, and the Hills in turn married the Lanes, ending up all the more prosperous for it.

The JENNERS left their mark all over Poulton, even though they were originally from Kempsford, a few miles away. Not only the large house that is today called 'Jenners', but the property next door, known as Jenners' Cottage, and the structure still called Jenners' Barn, which has been converted into another residence.
It is widely believed in Poulton that the world-famous Gloucestershire doctor, Edward Jenner (1749–1823), who

discovered vaccination as an immunity to smallpox, was related to this local family. Certainly Edward Jenner was born in Gloucestershire and went to school in Cirencester, but the link with the Poulton Jenners has not yet been established.

The **LANES** of Poulton were originally a branch of the Lane family of King's Bromley in Staffordshire, who held the manor there for centuries. The Lane family, great supporters of the Stuarts, played a prominent role during the Civil War, and a crucial one for the survival of the monarchy. Colonel John Lane was instrumental in saving the life of Prince Charles (later King Charles II) after his defeat at the Battle of Worcester in September, 1651. One account says that he gave the fleeing Charles refuge at 'his seat in Bentley'; another that Colonel Lane spirited the Prince away to the manor house of a friend at Boxwell. In any case, it was the Colonel's sister, Jane, who was the real heroine of the day. She agreed to act as guide and accompany Prince Charles through Roundhead territory to Bristol, where he hoped to find a ship to take him to safety in France.

Charles rode before her on a strawberry roan, disguised as 'Will Jackson', a humble servant to Mistress Jane Lane. They hid for the night at the manor house in Long Marston (now known as 'King's Lodge'). According to a report in Highways & Byways in Gloucestershire, the cook there ordered Mistress Jane's 'servant' to 'wind up the jack' [a device for turning a spit], and Prince Charles had to confess that he was unable to do so, whereupon the cook, amazed at his clumsiness, asked him wherever he came from. He replied that he came from Staffordshire where they did not use jacks, 'and so the matter dropped.' Jane Lane duly delivered the Prince safely to Bristol, and the rest, as they say, is history.

After the Restoration, King Charles II showed his gratitude to Jane Lane by giving her a pension of £1,000, and she received a further sum of £1,000 from Parliament. In addition, the King granted to the Lane family the 'especial' honour of commemorating the event with an addition to the Lane family coat of arms, which the College of Arms describes as 'one of the most famous augmentations in English heraldry'. The book *The Romance of Heraldry* echoes this phrase in their description of the badge of honour: 'Mistress Lane's courageous loyalty earned for her family one of the most notable augmentations known to heraldry, none other than the three lions of England. Two variations of the Lane family coal of arms, showing the three lions *passant gardant*, the strawberry roan bearing between his forelegs the royal crown, and the motto *Garde le Roy* [Protect the King].

The Lane Coat of Arms

Two variations of the Lane family coat of arms, showing the three lions passant gardant, the strawberry roan bearing between his forelegs the royal crown, and the motto Garde le Roy.

They were added as a canton to the Lane arms. The accompanying crest is the faithful strawberry roan, holding a crown in token that he once carried its owner, and the motto is *'Garde le Roy'*. Col. Lane was likewise offered a peerage, but turned it down. John and Jane Lane had a brother William, but whether it was he who was the patriarch of the Poulton Lanes or another is difficult to establish. Certainly the Poulton William Lane (1630-1748) was a close relation, possibly a nephew. It was his son, also William, who married Susannah Jenner in 1740, thus linking these two distinguished families. The Lanes only held forty-five acres in Poulton when they married into the Jenner family, but as a result of this propitious match, they ended up owning thousands of acres in and around the Parish from Verge Farm and Poulton Fields (then called The Firs) to the aforementioned farms, houses and barns known as Jenners within the village proper. They produced five generations of male descendants, all named William Jenner Lane. By the nineteenth century, the Lanes had become the major landowners in Poulton.

Georgian Poulton

The male line of descent of the LANE Family of Poulton

William Jenner Lane III (1839 - 1922), father of Elizabeth and Annie Hill, lived at the Firs (below)

```
WILLIAM LANE (c. 1680 - 1748)
m. Mary Cull
        |
WILLIAM (1714 - 1790)              +5
m. Susannah JENNER
        |
WILLIAM (1743 - 1823)              +4
m. 1) Jane Gardner
    2) Edith Gardner (sister)
        |
WILLIAM JENNER (1776 - 1862)       +7
m. Elizabeth Humphries
        |
WILLIAM JENNER (1812 - 1875)       +3
m. Sarah Waine
        |
WILLIAM JENNER (1839 - 1922)       +7
       twins      m. Elizabeth Walker
        |
ELIZABETH ADA      ANNIE         WILLIAM JENNER (1867 - 1942)   +3
(1865 - 1901)      (1867 - 1934)  m. Mary Florence Stephens
m. Albert Edmund   m. Albert Edmund       |
(Bert) HILL (m. 1887) (Bert) HILL (m. 1907)
                                 WILLIAM JENNER (1899 - 1976)   +1
```

(above) The Firs, a Regency house that was the home of several generations of William Jenner Lanes. (right) As it is now. The house was dramatically transformed into 'Cotswold Tudor' style by the architect Eric Cole in 1939 and now called Poulton Fields, owned for many years by Lt. Col. the Lord Wigram.

103

A Poulton Dynasty: the Hills wed the Jenner Lanes

In 1779, Elizabeth Betterton, daughter of an old landowning Poulton family, married John Hill, and together they produced Poulton's most illustrious family of yeomen farmers, who were based at Home Farm for four generations – from the eighteenth century up to the second half of the twentieth. 'In the old days when families belonged to districts and did not migrate as they do today, the **HILLS** belonged to Poulton,' so wrote an anonymous correspondent in the Standard, when Albert Edmund Hill died. He continued: 'so stable was Mr Hill that he seemed the most enduring thing in Poulton – as enduring as the fields he farmed. So much was he a part of Poulton that he seemed the embodiment of its spirit.'

When Albert Edmund **HILL**, known as Bertie, married two daughters of William Jenner **LANE** in sequence (as William Lane had married two Gardner sisters some forty years before), the Hills acquired new Jenner/Lane property such as the Gables (the substantial house now known as 'Jenners'), where Bertie and his Lane wives lived for nearly fifty years. As well as owning Jenners, Home Farm and Southcott, the Hill family by the twentieth century had

The male line of descent of the HILL family

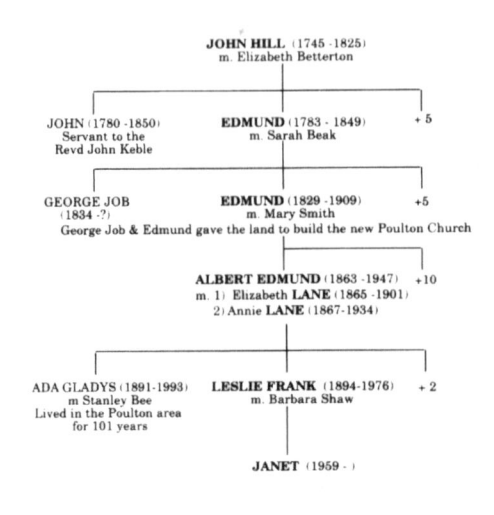

JOHN HILL (1745-1825)
m. Elizabeth Betterton

JOHN (1780-1850) — Servant to the Revd John Keble

EDMUND (1783-1849) m. Sarah Beak   +5

GEORGE JOB (1834-?)

EDMUND (1829-1909) m. Mary Smith   +5

George Job & Edmund gave the land to build the new Poulton Church

ALBERT EDMUND (1863-1947)   +10
m. 1) Elizabeth LANE (1865-1901)
2) Annie LANE (1867-1934)

ADA GLADYS (1891-1993)
m Stanley Bee
Lived in the Poulton area for 101 years

LESLIE FRANK (1894-1976)   +2
m. Barbara Shaw

JANET (1959-)

Edmund Hill II
(1829–1909)

amassed considerable acreage of arable farmland all round the Poulton area and became property owners second only to the Priory estate, from which they leased additional fields.

They were long livers, the Hills; Edmund II, his son Bertie, and his grandson Frank were all octogenarians, and Frank's sister Gladys reached a century. Sturdy yeoman stock indeed. The Hills shared a passion for horses that is legendary, and kept stablesful for pulling, ploughing, hacking, hunting, polo, and racing as well as breeding prize-winners in the show ring. When Edmund II was living at Southcott, he required his meals to be served in the stable adjoining the house so that he could eat in the company of his favourite horse. Since his family couldn't beat him, they joined him by knocking the wall through and incorporating the stable into the dining room, which is how Southcott is to this day. As the Hills owned land both in Wiltshire and Gloucestershire, they hunted with both of the Vale of the White Horse packs, and Bertie was still riding to the hounds well into his seventies.

Edmund II and Mary Hill with nine of their eleven children, c. 1879 (back row) *Hannah, a maid, William, the Hill's Governess, and daughter Mary. Front row: Alice, Edmund II, Emilie, George, Mary (the mother), Albert Edmund (Bertie), Pearcy, Sarah and, far right, a maid.*

The Hills were forever active in Poulton community affairs – the school, the village hall, the Parish Council, and the church. (It was Edmund Hill and his brother George Job who donated the land for the present St Michael's Church.) The paterfamilias of the Hills were referred to as 'The Magistrates of Poulton,' because the villagers invariably took their quarrels and injustices to them for arbitration: 'We be cum t' ask 'ee which be in th' right, zur?' Their case would be duly heard by the senior Hill, and the contesting locals would accept his counsel and judgement without question or rancour, as though the verdict had been handed down by a Crown Court.

The merging of the Jenners, Lanes and Hills: Albert Edmund Hill (Bertie) with his fiancée, Elizabeth Ada Lane, shortly before their marriage in 1887. Elizabeth Ada died in 1901; in 1907 Albert married Elizabeth's younger sister Annie, the twin of William Jenner Lane IV.

Georgian Poulton

A dapper Bertie Hill poses jauntily in the doorway at Home Farm, surrounded by his farm labourers.

The last but one generation of Hills, Frank and his wife Barbara, both died in 1976, and the Hill family's various holdings have all been sold off, including their historical bases Southcott and Home Farm, both Grade II listed properties. The next generation, their only child Janet, left the village soon afterwards, but in 2012 has returned to the area as Janet Crouch, living in nearby Down Ampney.

(left) *Home Farm, an 18th century house that was the seat of the Hill family for four generations.* (right) *Southcott. It was here that the stable* (shown right) *was incorporated into the dining room so that Edmund Hill could eat with his favourite horse.*

107

(above left) *Edmund Hill II's daughter Mary, who married John Titley and brought up eight children at Southcott in Poulton.*
(above right) *Mary Hill, wife of Edmund II, mother of Bertie Hill and Mary (Titley). The Hills, for generations, were most at home on the back of a horse. Below: Bertie Hill's son Frank (Janet's father) gets an early start, assisted by his older sister Gladys, c. 1900.*

VIII
Victorian Poulton
The Nineteenth Century

QUEEN VICTORIA was not born until 1819, but for convenience we shall extend what we are calling Victorian Poulton back to 1800, when there were 306 residents in the village, of which 148 were males and 158 females. In the following seventy years the population was to grow to its all-time high of 499, of which 220 were children under the age of fifteen. It is well known that the nineteenth century was an age of large families, and Poulton's more prolific breeders, like the Hills, the Ashes, the Edwardses, the Wheelers and the Ockwells, scarcely let an annual harvest pass without presenting the vicar with a new offspring for baptism. Mothers who bore from eight to twelve babies were not uncommon, but infant mortality took its toll. Smallpox was still rampant and although Dr Jenner's vaccination technique was discovered in 1796, it was not yet universally practised, and the Poulton Church Burial Register is awash with infants from those same families, who often barely survived their ordeal at the baptismal font. From these records, we can see an interesting pattern: if a baby died, the parents would frequently give the same name to a later issue. Edward and Elizabeth Ash, for example, had twelve children in the space of seventeen years, between 1853 and 1870, and twice christened sons Albert Edward and named two different daughters Fanny Louise. It was also common enough for young mothers to die in childbirth* when they got to number four or five, in which case the widower would quickly remarry and continue producing offspring at the equivalent rate.

* *Now that death in childbirth is rare, women today are outliving their husbands to the extent that widows in the village far out number widowers.*

At the beginning of the nineteenth century there were 59 houses in the village, all but one inhabited, which means that there were, on average, five or six people living in each house. Poulton families not only christened children with peculiarly Victorian names like Fanny, Rhoda, Dinah, Kezia, Cornelius, Uriah, Theophilus, Gabriel, Percival and Bertram, and dredged the Old Testament for Job, Hester, Caleb, Reuben, Isaac, Esau, Eli and Abraham, but also came up with some fairly unusual names, such as a boy named Hulbert Griffin, a mother and daughter both named Thirza Wheeler, two generations of male Ashes christened Worthy, a lady called Wealthy Miller, a carpenter called Samson King Brickwell, a single gypsy woman called Cinnamenti Smith who had her 'base born' child christened Solomon, and the Poulton bailiff, Mr Onesipherus Folbigg, a name that sounds so fictitious that even Dickens might have baulked at using it in a novel.

At the Revd John Keble's retirement in 1819, Richard Martyr was licensed to the Perpetual Curacy of Poulton, and he in turn was replaced by Allen Lechmere in 1829. By the time Victoria was actually on her throne, Henry Cripps, most likely one of the Cripps family so prominent throughout the preceding centuries, was Rector of Poulton. The population was getting close to 370, but only nineteen names appear on the voters' register – most of them from long established families, divided into the gentry, the yeomanry, and the tradesmen. Most of the rest of the population went down in the records as labourers who weren't qualified for the vote until the Third Reform Act passed in 1884.

Two of John and Mary Titley's children, Elsie and Hilda, play outside Southcott.

The Exotic Samblesohns

In the first half of the nineteenth century a tailor, Samuel Samblesohn, born in Poland in 1808, suddenly appeared in Poulton. Why he came to England is unknown, but it is likely that he was a Jewish refugee from one or other Eastern European pogrom. That would not explain, however, why or how he found his way to Poulton, and one can only imagine how isolated he must have felt, for even though England's first Jewish Prime Minister was already a Parliamentarian when Victoria began her reign, one lone Polish Jew in a fairly far-flung Cotswold village 150 or so years ago must have felt like a gefillte fish out of water. Nonetheless, he stayed, married and bred a considerable line of Samblesohns that populated Poulton throughout the nineteenth century.

Samuel, having set up a tailor's shop, married a woman called Elizabeth, and they had eight children, Orlando (1834), Edward (1836), twins Sophia and Charlotte (1837), Minna Sabra (1840), Caroline (1842), Miora (1843), and Adolphus (c. 1845), who, in their time, found local spouses. Whether old Samuel was and remained an adherent of the Judaic faith, we do not know, but Elizabeth was sure to have been a Christian as we can see from the Parish records that some of their offspring were baptised, married and in turn had their own children baptised within the Church of England, and nearly all but old Samuel himself were given Christian burials in Poulton*.

Orlando Samblesohn's wedding to Miss Wealthy Miller was at the old St Michael's Church in 1854, and they, over the next 22 years at Butts Farm, produced ten little Samblesohns. Like his father and brothers, Orlando was a tailor and draper, but in the 1870s he took over the job of village postmaster from Richard Adams – a position that he held until the end of the century. One of Orlando's daughters, Emma, in 1884, married Ernest Tilling, the son of Joseph Tilling, a Poulton farmer and granary owner. Ernest was a grocer and baker, his premises being the present Poulton Post Office and village shop. He was a devout Wesleyan like his father, who had

* *Elizabeth's tombstone in the old churchyard is pictured on p. 239* built the Mission Room for Non-Conformist worship in 1876. In the 1930s it was completely taken over by the Methodists, and Queenie Ball, one of the congregation, said the attendance and enthusiasm warranted holding three meetings in the Chapel every Sunday. Six Poulton Non-Conformists chose to be buried in the Chapel grounds, including the Tillings, father and son.

The old Methodist Mission Room, now a private residence.

By the 1980s the number of Methodists in Poulton had so declined that the old Mission Room was closed down after one final carol service in December, 1988. The gravestones were removed to St Michael's Churchyard, the ground around the Chapel was deconsecrated and the structure sold and converted into a small residence. Quite what happened to the vast Samblesohn family or the thriving tailoring business which came to be called Adolphus Sambleson & Son (the spelling 'Samble*sohn*' was at some point anglicised to 'Samble*son*') can't be fully traced but in checking the Parish register a most

Ernest Tilling, baker and grocer, with his daughter Pearl, the granddaughter of Orlando Samblesohn.

peculiar and dramatic coincidence emerges; the last member of the family to be baptised in the church was the illegitimate son of Anne Sambleson, the then thirty-four year old spinster daughter of Orlando and Wealthy. The baptism took place on 14th December, 1904 – the *very same day* of the funeral and burial of her father, Orlando, who at seventy, would doubtless have been the patriarch of the family. The two disparate services must have made it a momentous day at St Michael's Church for all the assembled Samblesons, and indeed a very busy one for the Vicar, the Revd W. J. Mayne.

Whether the shame of Anne's out-of-wedlock pregnancy was instrumental in hastening the death of old Orlando is a matter for speculation, but the stigma of illegitimacy in a village in those times was considerable. Nonetheless, the Parish Baptism Register shows a fair sprinkling of such cases over the centuries, originally recording the babies as *'base born'* or simply *'bastard'*, but eventually classifying them as a child of a 'single woman' in the politically correct parlance of today. In any case, Anne Sambleson's baby son, christened with the somewhat unusual name *Theo Pinnegar,* only lived for one month, and on 17th January, 1905, some Samblesons must have returned to the church for his funeral and burial.

Another odd fact emerges from the Baptism Register. It shows that almost exactly a hundred years earlier, another unwed mother of the Parish, Mary Palmer, had her baby son baptised on 22nd December, 1805, giving him the name *Thomas Pinnegar.* The name Pinnegar appears in no other Poulton records, and if there hadn't been a hundred years in between the two incidents, one might fantasise that there was an errant roué of that name who made a practice of seducing the spinsters of Poulton Parish. There was indeed a family of Pinnegars living in Down Ampney. It could just be coincidence, or possibly Anne Sambleson had seen the old Baptismal Register and fancied a resuscitation of the name, perhaps out of empathy with Miss Palmer. Or it may have been the vicar's choice. In any case, it is recorded that an Annie Sambleson got married to Arthur Brierly in 1912.

Whether this was the 'fallen woman', who would then have been 42, or another, younger member of the family with the same Christian name can't be established from the records, but we can hope that the saga of Orlando's daughter Anne had a happy ending after all.

Two final Samblesons were buried in 1916; Orlando's brother Edward, at the age of 80, and sister Charlotte, 79, and that is the last trace of the exotic Sambleson clan in Poulton records.

Poulton Becomes Gloucestershire

The Parish of Poulton, after nearly a thousand years of being a Wiltshire island within an alien county, was finally designated by Parliament in 1844 to be a part of Gloucestershire, though it took the cartographers some time to catch up with the fact, as one can see from the portion of a map of Gloucestershire below, published in 1850 by H. G. Collins, London.

In the 1850s, the population of Poulton Parish was 455, of which nearly half were children, and only 25 residents were over the age of 60. Richard Adams, in the House on the

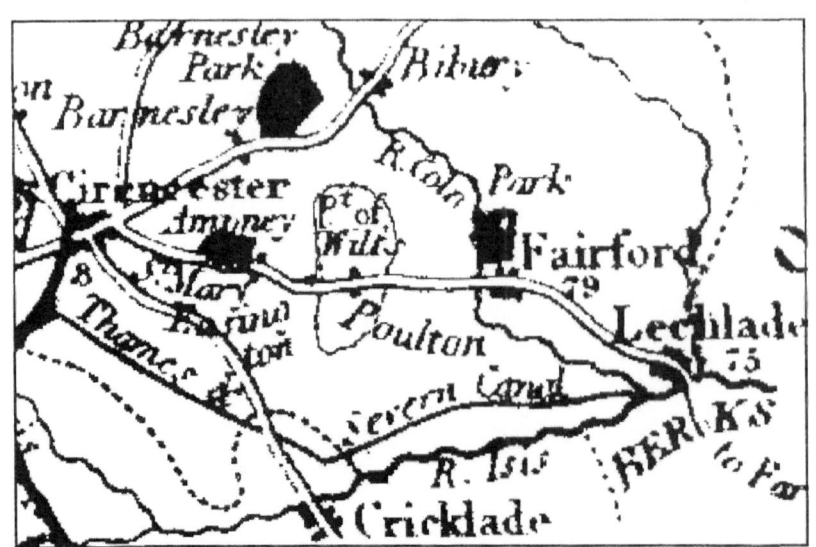

Poulton in 1850, a portion of a map of Gloucestershire

Corner, was the registrar and enumerator for the census as well as being 'receiver of mail', and a maltster. From Richard Adams' list of residents between 1851 and 1863 we can see the variety of occupations within the village: 7 shopkeepers, which included butchers, bakers, drapers, grocers and a coal dealer, 5 quarrymen, 4 cordwainers making shoes and boots, 3 brick and tile makers, 2 tailors, the publicans at the Falcon and the Axe and Compass, a bailiff (the aforementioned Onesipherus Folbigg), a plasterer, a slater, a carpenter, a blacksmith, a governness, a gardener, a drillman, a dairyman, a road contractor, a carter, a schoolmaster, the vicar, of course, and a number of farmers, shepherds, cow men and 39 men listed as labourers. There were also listings of persons as 'landed proprietors' and 'gentry', which included Herbert John Marshall, Esq. at the Priory, Mrs Mary Tombs, a widow at the Manor House, and Richard William Attwood at the Firs. The Vicars of Poulton during the mid-Victorian era were: Edward Daubeny (1845), Mayrick Holme (1848), Thomas Bowstead (1849), William Bartram (1857), and John Rule (1867).

Only during the incumbency of the Revd John Rule did the Rectors of St Michael and All Angels have a residence in Poulton, provided by the Church. There is an old saying that

The Poulton Vicarage, designed by Ewan Christian in 1868   Now a private house

the Church of England vicars are middle-class men who are housed like the upper classes and paid like the lower classes. The truth of this is apparent by noting that while the large, impressive Vicarage was being built in 1868, the stipend of the Curacy of Poulton was still only £30 a year, the same as it was in John Keble's time, seventy-two years before, though the vicar now received a bonus of £10 p.a. from something called 'Queen Anne's bounty'.

The Vicarage was designed by Ewan Christian and according to David Verey, the Cotswold contributor to Pevsner's *The Buildings of England,* it is 'a well-planned house, of stone, with original detail, particularly a nicely proportioned bay window on the west'. It also had a very large garden and field where sporting activities of various kinds took place.

Anyone for tennis? The Revd William Mayne and his family on the lawn outside the vicarage, c. 1894

The Vicars of Poulton who have resided at the Vicarage:

   1868 - John Rule
   1871 - Thomas Daubeney
   1876 - C.W.H. Kenrick
   1886 - J. P. Foster
   1894 - William John Mayne
   1907 - R. H. Barlow
   1916 - D. J. Davies
   1925 - A. J. McMaster Yair
   1938 - C.E. Dodd
   1944 - E. J. Sumner
   1949 - H. S. Hutchinson
   1957 - P. H. E. Tidmarsh
   1966 - J. D. Gott
   1972 - R. H. Nesham

In 1964, a fair amount of the land adjoining the Vicarage was sold off for property development, and a modern Glebe House was built there. The Vicarage itself was sold at auction in September 1984 after the last resident vicar, Robert Nesham, had retired. It was bought by Mr and Mrs John Price, who are the occupants at the time of writing. The Parish of Poulton was amalgamated with five other local parishes and the subsequent vicars have been housed in vicarages in other villages.

Poulton Priory

From the middle of the nineteenth century, the Priory was owned first by Herbert John Marshall, Esq. and later by James Joicey, Lord of the Manor of Marston Meysey, who became a great benefactor of Poulton. The change-over of the squires is documented in an epic poem composed by the then Farm Manager of the Priory, Mr Richard Stevens, whose wife was Anne Edwards of the shop-keeping family. It is worth reproducing the poem in full, not only for its historical interest, but because, in terms of scansion, rhyme and other literary considerations, it is right up there with the odes of William MacGonagall, the prolific Scottish master of Victorian doggerel. It should be with some pride that Poulton can claim its own home-grown MacGonagall.

The Poulton Priory
by Richard Stevens

In 1860 a squire to the Priory came,
and J.H. Marshall was his name
Lots of work he had done, and the money he spent as well
Down in the village it began to tell.

In my remembrance at Poulton there was no squire before,
and many of the inhabitants were very very poor,
After this, things were far more bright
And they could always depend on a good Saturday night.

In the thirty-three years as I can fairly trace,
He spent more in labour than would have bought the place,
Over and above what other farmers had done,
and that spent in the village, it was a grand sum.

When Mr Marshall first to the Priory came.
He lived there a time without a dame,
But after then a nice lady he brought, I am sure,
 for she was always good and kind to the poor.

Two sons and four daughters was the family they had,
to seeing them all leave it was very sad,
after being there thirty years and more
and never forgot the sick and poor.

Now Mr Joicey the Priory has bought,
He is treating the land just as he ought,
He is putting on lots of manure,
Nothing will better that, he may be sure.

Now Mr Joicey, I must say a word to you,
It's not many farmers that will compete with you, The corn
that you spend and lots of hay too,
which no tenant farmer could afford to do.

One thing above all other that would please me,
For to see you take prizes one, two or three,
with your roots and corn and cattle too,
You have got the right land and that you can do.

Now about expense, I must say a word or two,
It's best to be careful in what you do,
For to spend money is an easy thing –
> *You must be careful from day to day*
and see that the balance don't go the wrong way.

And when your balancing day do come,
I think you will find you have spent a large sum,
And to get a return, I wish you may do,
But I am afraid you will not for one year or two.

There is one great advantage that you have got –
Without buying off others you can raise most of the lot,
Your corn and your straw, hay and roots, too,
and put back on the land you'll see what it can do.

There's great pleasure in farming, we know very well
to ride round a farm and see crops looking well,
with your fine stud of horses, good cattle too,
and then you'll find these will be pleasures for you.

Since to the Priory you have come,
You must have spent a very large sum,
Which must have done good to both old and young,
If a tenant farmer had come to the Priory instead of you,
Many of the inhabitants would have had nothing to do.

Now at the Priory such a kind gentleman we have got,
and his deeds of charity they cannot be forgot;
Many a fireplace in the cold winter
> *was warmed and brightened by he,*
and hope he'll live many years at the Priory to be.

The Poulton Cricket Club

James Joicey was a director of the Midland and South Western Junction Railway Company and had come to Poulton from Tanfield, Durham, after buying the Priory Estate in 1890. Perhaps James Joicey's greatest legacy to the village was the formation of the Poulton Cricket Club in 1891. The first game was in a sloping field at Priory Farm on 20th June that year against Ampney United, but the home team was defeated. Poulton's first published victory was in August of the following year, away to Ashton Keynes, who were all out for 24. Joicey was a keen cricketer himself and fielded a Priory team which played against a Poulton Village team. In August, 1896, there is the following report of a Poulton Village v. Poulton Priory match: 'Played at Poulton, a well-contested game resulting in a victory for the village team by 54 runs. Mr J. Joicey kindly provided refreshments and took a catch and got one run.'

James Joicey, founder of the Poulton Cricket Club in 1891

In that same year, Joicey formed the East Gloucestershire & North Wilts Cricket League to try to improve the standard of village cricket. He presented a cup, which that first year went to Barnsley. Alas, Poulton finished at the bottom of the league. From the records we can see that those early days of the E.G. & N. W. League were fraught with problems of one kind or another: in 1897, when Poulton played Castle Eaton, the umpire 'sustained a nasty cut on the head and had to leave the field', then when Kempsford played Poulton, there were certain 'misunderstandings' between the teams, leading to the Poulton Captain refusing to field second innings. The unpleasantness must have somehow been smoothed over as the report concludes 'Mr Joicey kindly gave tea and refreshments'. Later that season the Ampney Crucis team came to Poulton, but only eight players turned up, two of whom were boys. Not surprisingly, perhaps, Poulton won.

The Poulton Cricket Club continued to play at Poulton Priory under James Joicey's patronage throughout his lifetime, and thereafter for the lifetime of his successor, Major Mitchell, with play interrupted only in 1918 and again in 1939, when the opposition came from Germany, which was in a quite different league – and that, for sure, wasn't cricket.

The Priory Mansion

In 1895, James Joicey set about the building of a vast mansion on the site of the old Gilbertine Priory. It was designed by Sir Arthur Blomfield in Tudor-Renaissance style, and was completed in 1897 and a wing was added in 1909 to house in splendour his new Hungarian wife Mariska Christobel and her daughters by a former marriage, whom he adopted, and their governess. During the two years it took to build the mansion, he formed a cricket team from the construction workers to play against his village team, the matches billed as *Poulton Village v. the Mansion.*

The building of Poulton Priory Mansion, which took two years to complete. James Joicey organised the construction workers into a cricket eleven to play against the village team.

The Priory became a focal point for many Poulton activities, sporting and social, as the Joiceys were great stalwarts of the church and benefactors of the village. Apart from allocating the grounds for the Poulton Cricket Club, the Priory was the meeting place for the Rifle Club, to which James Joicey belonged, and he turned one of the Priory barns into a village reading room and a place where various social and educational activities could take place, such as the Victoria League Lecture on New Zealand in 1912, 'illustrated by very fine lantern pictures'. The Joiceys also held an annual Christmas party in the barn for all the children of Poulton. Mariska Joicey made frequent trips to her native Hungary and always brought back bags of presents which she disbursed every year to the village tots: beautiful china dolls for each of the girls, and mechanical toys from Germany for the boys. According to Mrs Hilda Strange, who was born in the village in 1903 and, as a child, attended the Christmas parties at the Priory, this was the highlight of the year for the village children.

An early photograph of the Poulton Priory Mansion, which was enlarged in 1909 to accommodate the two daughters of his new Hungarian bride, Mariska (whom he married in 1908), and their governess. Formerly a village focal point, but current owners have no contact with Poulton.

Poulton School

In 1872, the year the world-renowned composer Ralph Vaughan Williams was born in the vicarage at Down Ampney, a few miles south of Poulton, Mrs. Mary Tombs, a landowning widow who lived at the Manor House from 1861 to 1881, gave to the vicar and the churchwardens one rood of land, a portion of Close Field, for the purpose of building a Church of England village school to accommodate 101 Poulton children up to secondary level.

The services of one of the most eminent Victorian architects, William Butterfield (who was also commissioned to re-build Poulton's parish church), were procured for a fee of only £24, and the construction, using locally quarried stone, was carried out by William Restall for a fee of £403.*8s*. The total cost of the two-roomed building came to £472, of which £50 was granted by the Diocesan Association, £84 from the Commissioners of the Council, and the remainder raised by private subscription.

The school house was opened on 6 January, 1873. The Headmistress, Mrs Kenrick, the Vicar's wife, admitted 84

The girl pupils at Poulton School, c. 1898. Mr Franklyn, the schoolmaster is on the left, and his sister, the infant teacher, on the right. The little girl in the sailor dress is Bertie Hill's daughter Gladys, of Home Farm, who lived to be 101.

The Poulton School Infants Class, 1920

pupils who were divided into infants up to seven years old in one room, and those over seven in the second room. Two days later the Vicar, the Revd Thomas Daubeney, gave a 'Feast for the Scholars'. By February, 1874, the number of children attending had risen to 103. The cost of schooling in that year was a penny per week for infants, two pence for juniors, and

The Old School, originally designed by William Butterfield in 1872, is a private house today. It was the premises of the Poulton village school for 108 years.

three pence for seniors. The dedication of the new St Michael and All Angels Church next door to the school was occasion for the first school holiday, and each child was given a bun. The children were also given a day free to honour the first wedding held in the Church – that of the tailor, Samuel Adolphus Sambleson (old Samuel's eldest son) and Miss Agnes Phelps of Cirencester.

The school celebrated its centenary in 1972. Poulton pupils returned in the school holidays and banged drums, tolled the bell and knocked the walls 100 times.

By law, a village school had to have at least 24 pupils to justify the running expense, and attendance at Poulton finally fell to only 22, as many village children were being schooled privately or sent to the school at Meysey Hampton. In 1980, in spite of vociferous protests, the Poulton school was forced to close – a sad day for the village. The building was sold to Mrs Kitty Arkwright. It was converted into a private dwelling by the architect, Anthony Sanford, who then lived in the Manor House. A later owner of the house, now called the Old School, reclaimed the original school bell from the District Council and mounted it on the exterior wall as a reminder of the 108 years it summoned generations of Poulton's children to learn their three Rs.

The Poulton School classroom in 1936.

The New St Michael and All Angels Church

In 1873, work began on the new Poulton Church on land donated to the Church Commissioners by Edmund and his brother George Job Hill. Sir Michael Hicks Beach Bt. (later Lord St Aldwyn) placed a time-capsule document, written on parchment, in a bottle and buried it beneath the foundation stone. It reads as follows:

> On May 17th in the year of our Lord 1873, the chief stone of this Church, dedicated to St Michael and All Angels, was laid by Sir Michael Hicks Beach, Bt. Member of Parliament, of Williamstrip Park, Gloucestershire. The old Church which is situated about half-a-mile S. W. of this spot, also dedicated to St Michael and All Angels and built early in the fourteenth century, being in ruinous condition, will be taken down and the materials removed and used as far as possible, in building the new Church on this site, which is given for that purpose by George Hill.

[signed]

Thomas Daubeny	Vicar of Poulton
Herbert John Marshall, of Poulton Priory	Churchwarden
Richard William Attwood of the Firs	Churchwarden
William Butterfield of London	Architect
William Restall of Bisley	Builder

In the thirty-eighth year of the reign of Queen Victoria. Population of Poulton 450

The new church was designed by William Butterfield who built the schoolhouse across the way and who enjoyed a national reputation as the architect of many London Victorian churches, which include All Saints (Margaret Street), St

The new St Michael and All Angels Church, completed 1874, as seen from the southwest

Albans (Holborn), and St Matthias (Stoke Newington), The Rugby School buildings, St Augustine's College, Canterbury, and Keble College, Oxford. Although Butterfield, a High-Church Gothic-Revivalist, generally favoured the use of multi-coloured brick in stripes and geometric patterns, in

The interior of Poulton Church, designed by William Butterfield to seat 290 parishioners

Poulton he deviated from what has been called the 'jarring aggressiveness' of his other work and bowed to the traditions of this stone-building district. Keeping the new St Michael's in Early English style, similar to the Priory church, he made use of the actual stones from the original St Michael's as it was dismantled and demolished. The new church, with seating for 290 people, was built at a cost of £2,239 of which £100 was granted by the Diocesan Association, and £100 from the Church Building Society, but over £1,900 had to be raised by private subscription. £200 was given by the M.P., Sir Michael Hicks Beach.

To retain a sense of historical tradition and continuity with the old Poulton Church, various bits and pieces from the mediaeval building were transferred to the new and incorporated into the fabric and design. Two wall memorial tablets to the Bedwell family dating back to 1682 are now situated in the interior, one on the north wall and the other above the vestry door, and two seventeenth-century coats of arms, thought to belong to the Earls of Gloucester, can still be seen on the exterior west and north walls. Also the ancient Mass Clock was built into the new church. The old St Michael's had a full peal of bells which were meant to be used in the new church, but they mysteriously disappeared between demolition and rebuilding, so Butterfield designed a west bellcote for only three bells in two tiers. These bells, as mentioned in Chapter VI, bear the names of the seventeenth and eighteenth-century benefactors.

Coat of Arms, dated 1634, transferred from the old church to the exterior west wall of the new church to preserve continuity.

For those interested in the finer points of ecclesiastical architecture, David Verey in *Pevsner* gives a description of the interior: 'The church consists of a fine, large nave, with a five-bay arcade and north aisle. The windows in the chancel have excellent rere-arches with cinquefoiled heads. The East window and the nearest window on the South side of the nave have, in addition, jamb shafts supported on corbel heads.'

The Church was consecrated and opened in 1874. The first baptism held there was that of John Harrison Strafford who became a saddler, ran the Poulton Post Office, and kept a cycle shop in what had been the Axe and Compass Inn. He was the father of Charles Strafford and Mrs Hilda Strange, about whom you will read more in the following chapter.

Poulton Parish Council

The first meeting of the Parish Council was held in the schoolroom at 7 o'clock on 4 December, 1894. James Joicey of the Priory was in the Chair, and five councillors were elected:

    Richard Carpenter, the blacksmith at the Old Forge
    William Wheeler, labourer
    Albert Hill, farmer
    Joseph Tilling, farmer
    The Revd William John Mayne, Vicar

Joicey was duly elected Chairman, a position he held for the next twenty-some years. The councillors discussed the bad state of the footpaths in the village, and the 'misefficiancy' [sic] of the sewers at the junction of Poulton Street and the London Road, and Messrs. Carpenter and Wheeler had two hundred copies of the following printed, which they then distributed to every household in the Parish:

NOTICE
Poulton Allotments
Numerous complaints having been made as to damage having been done to crops etc. on the above allotments by dogs and those in pursuit of game, such persons are therefore earnestly requested to abstain from such practices, and it is also earnestly desired that all those concerned will do their utmost to stop such proceedings. Notice is called to the following extract from the Poulton Allotments Act: And it is hereby agreed that in case any of the Poor whose names are hereunto subscribed shall be convicted before a magistrate for stealing, poaching, or any other offence, such persons shall lose the benefit of this agreement, and shall forfeit possession of their allotment.

By order of Poulton Parish Council

Councillor Tilling was much concerned about travelling shows pitching up on the Butts (as they had done since the Middle Ages), and it was resolved that a charge of five shillings be made for all entertainment on the Butts and that no performance could take place after ten p.m. nor on two consecutive nights.

For many years the Council meetings were to be concerned with smelly drains, the state of the footpaths and dealing with residents' complaints of one kind or another.

In 1896, new elections were held within the Parish to select future Council members. All the old members were nominated, but there was one new name put forth – that of Mr Charles Herbert, plasterer. The Council minutes record the results of the voting as follows:

>Richard Carpenter 25 votes
>William Wheeler 23
>Albert Hill 23
>The Revd W. J. Mayne 22
>Joseph Tilling 18
>Charles Herbert 0

All the sitting Councillors were re-elected to a man, but the new nominee seemed to have suffered the humiliation of Britain's 2003 Eurovision entry *Cry Baby – nul points*.

Poulton Lights Up

The darkness of Poulton streets had been a subject of some concern and debate since the Parish Council first sat. In 1897 the councillors met with thirty rate-payers and voted to implement the Lighting and Watching Act of 1833, with plans for the installation of eight oil street lamps to be strategically positioned in the village just close enough so that one could be seen from the other. Four lamps were paid for by James Joicey and four by subscription of parishioners.

The rejected Council nominee, Charles Herbert, now put himself up for the job of lamplighter but, as before, received not a single vote; a labourer, appropriately named Thomas Poulton, was elected. His pay was set at seven pence a night, and it was decided that the lamps were to be lit from 14th October until the 15th of March, except when there was a full moon 'unless an extra dark night occurs'.

Cricklade Street looking north up to Poulton House. The street lamp on the left is in front of 'Betty the witch's' little one-up, one-down house.

The eight large lamps were first lit on 3 December, 1896 and illuminated Poulton for nineteen years. Councillor Ernest Tilling supplied the oil at seven and a half pence per gallon, and the total cost for the street lighting worked out at £6.10s.0d. per year.

THE POSITIONS OF THE EIGHT POULTON STREET LAMPS IN 1897

In 1915 the street lighting was discontinued partly for wartime economy and partly for fear of attracting German dirigibles. The lamps were never lit again, and were dismantled in the 1920s. Although the Parish Councillors have frequently considered some form of lighting, Poulton's streets remain perilously dark.

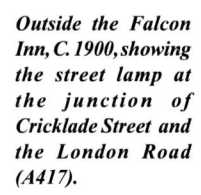

Outside the Falcon Inn, C.1900, showing the street lamp at the junction of Cricklade Street and the London Road (A417).

Poulton Celebrates Queen Victoria's Diamond Jubilee

As part of Poulton's commemoration of Queen Victoria's Diamond Jubilee in 1897, a bench, to be forged in metal, was commissioned. There were several blacksmiths in Poulton during the nineteenth century, but most prominent were the popular farriers Richard Carpenter, the councillor, and his son Ben, who lived at what is now called the Old Forge, and it is most likely that they produced the existing bench as they were certainly inspired by the historic event.

The official Jubilee portrait of Queen Victoria.

The 1897 Victorian Jubilee bench (left) *now stands by the War Memorial, opposite the village shop, and is still seating well after 115 years of Poulton bottoms.*

A companion bench will be forged to commemorate the Diamond Jubilee of Queen Elizabeth I I in 2012.

The Old Forge, for many years known as Horseshoe Pillars. This seventeenth-century house in the London Road was the home and workplace of the blacksmiths, Richard and Ben Carpenter.

A World in a Grain of Sand

To celebrate their Queen's 60 year reign, the father and son farriers, of their own volition, erected two immense horseshoe pillars by the gates of the forge in London Road. These pillars, 'formed of 5,600 horseshoes weighing four and a half tons,' became so famous that postcards were printed depicting them, and Poulton suddenly became a tourist draw of sorts.

Richard Carpenter, the village smithy, at 62

UNIQUE LANDMARK IN GLOUCESTERSHIRE.

Pillars formed of over 5,600 horseshoes, weighing 4½ tons, made to commemorate QUEEN VICTORIA'S DIAMOND JUBILEE, by Mr. RICHARD CARPENTER, BLACKSMITH—who is seen standing between the pillars —at POULTON, GLOUCESTERSHIRE, about mid-way between Cirencester and Fairford, on the London Road. The letters on the rail stand for . . .

BENJAMIN CARPENTER, (Son of the Architect of the Pillars.) **REGISTERED SHOEING SMITH.**

No one remembers just how long they stood at the entrance of the house that was then for many years called Horseshoe Pillars, but if they survived until the outbreak of World War II, they certainly would have been melted down for scrap iron then. Today Richard Carpenter's once-celebrated creation is only remembered through aging photographs and postcards such as the above that are now collectors' items.

The Bizarre Tale of Ben Carpenter, 'the Jolly Bachelor'

While Richard Carpenter's wife Emma lay dying in 1890, her twenty-five-year-old son Benjamin made a deathbed vow to his mother that he would never marry so long as his father was alive. Following her departure from this life, the widower and his bachelor son were meticulously looked after at Horseshoe Pillars by a housekeeper, Miss Emily Powell, who had been with the family since 1884. It appears that young Ben also made 'a sort of joint will' with this housekeeper, promising that if he died first she was to retain the house, the Carpenters' seventeen acre farm, and his two farriery businesses, one at Poulton and one at Fairford. If, however, she predeceased him, all her property would be left to the young blacksmith. Miss Powell was eleven years Ben's senior and the reasons for this arrangement are not known, but apparently Miss Powell, described as 'masterful', was like a second mother to Ben, and ruled the household with a will of iron.

Old Richard Carpenter died in 1920 at the age of 88. Eighteen months later, by what seems a most extraordinary coincidence, both Miss Powell and Ben Carpenter died on the same day in May, 1922; she, at 68, passed away in her sister's arms early in the morning, and he, aged 57, died at 3 o'clock that very afternoon.

Cheery, good-natured Ben Carpenter had been known in the Poulton area as 'the jolly bachelor' and his coffin was borne to his grave by 'a selected band of Cirencester bachelors'. When they were half-way between the house and the village churchyard, the funeral procession was suddenly halted by an unknown thirty-seven-year-old woman who, to the utter amazement of everyone present, announced that the deceased was no bachelor. Indeed she had been the lawful wife of Ben Carpenter for the past eighteen months.

The secret Mrs Carpenter, a total stranger to Poulton, had met Benjamin Carpenter nearly fourteen years prior to his death. She was then a twenty-three-year-old governess and had often brought her charges to the forge to watch the young 'open-featured' smithy at work. The tale of their rustic courtship and clandestine marriage was reported by one newspaper as: 'This Wessex secret wedding romance is all in the style of Mr. Thomas Hardy's *Life's Little Worries*, as well as in a Hardy setting.' The widow, a lady of considerable romantic propensity herself, described in her own words how love was sparked off over the anvil:

'We stood for many hours watching the swing of his hammer; and the children were always specially enthralled by the sparks that flew out of the forge in all directions. Ben stole my heart away, unknown to me. My heart would leap with joy when I saw his big burly frame standing within the portals of the shop. He made no sign of his love during those days but would tell me of his ambition to be a farmer when he had saved enough money at the forge. So the months passed in a sweet dream...he had the manner of a gentleman, my Ben...his charming little ways and his forethought were irresistible. He used to make me up fresh bouquets and garlands of the hedgerow flowers every morning. Sometimes he would pick me a basket of fresh fruit.

Ben has told me since those far-off days that he fell in love with me when I first stood with the children in the door of his shop. "There and then," he declared, "I determined that if ever I was free to marry, I would win you for my wife."

One day when I was out walking alone, I met Ben on the summit of Ranbury Hill driving past in his cart. We stood and chatted together, he sitting in the cart and I standing against the wheel looking up at him. Suddenly our conversation stopped dead. The world seemed to swim round and the only thing I clearly remember of that day was how he leaned over the cart and kissed me. It was there on the summit of the hill that he first kissed me and told me of his passionate love; and it was on that same spot that I met his coffin on the way to the grave a few days ago.'

The events from the first kiss to the interruption of the funeral procession is what makes the story so bizarre. According to reports, Ben Carpenter explained about his vow made to his mother not to marry in his father's lifetime, so 'the dark, vivacious woman' became his fiancée for the next twelve years, until old Richard finally went to meet his Maker. During this time she had taken a post as a governess for a Hampshire family and contact with her lover was apparently limited to an exchange of passionate *billets doux* – his to her, endlessly complaining of the 'cruel separation' and picturing the days when they would finally be together – hers addressed to him in care of a hotel in Cirencester, where he used to call for them when he was in the town on business. He hid all the letters, along with various presents from her, in an outhouse on the farm away from the prying eyes of the sternly disapproving Miss Powell.

After his father died, Ben did indeed marry the governess, but he was so in awe of Miss Powell, who had made it clear that she would never suffer Mr Carpenter to bring another woman into the house, that he insisted on keeping the marriage a secret from her – and from the world. After a week's honeymoon in Scarborough, the wife returned to her duties as governess and Ben returned to Poulton to continue his life as a bachelor blacksmith, farrier and farmer. The hotel in Cirencester remained the receiving station for the love letters, as it had been for years.

'I suppose I ought to have insisted on my rightful position and gone to his home when we were married,' said Mrs Carpenter, sadly, after the death of the husband she had never lived with, 'but I did not like the thought of turning Miss Powell out after she had been there thirty-eight years, and my husband was a man who was all for peace and quietness and did not want a bother. We know she could not live long [Miss Powell had had a heart condition for some years] and we thought as we had waited so many years we could wait a little longer, and should be all the happier for having considered her.'

Eighteen months after the wedding, Mrs Carpenter was suddenly summoned from her distant post by a telegram informing her of her husband's death. Just who, at this point, was in on the secret and was able to track the governess down in Hampshire was never made clear, but by dropping everything she was able to arrive in Poulton in time to put in her dramatic surprise appearance and leave all the locals dumbfounded only moments before the interment.

The story provided a feast for the more sensational of the national newspapers of the day, and though this was before the days of chequebook journalism, Mrs Carpenter was not shy of giving the sort of 'exclusive' interviews for which the tabloids now pay handsomely. The Sunday headlines shrieked:

'SECRET BRIDE TELLS HER OWN STORY'

'MY LIFE, MY LOVE'

'FIRST KISS WHERE SHE MET THE FUNERAL'

'ROMANCE BEGUN AT THE VILLAGE SMITHY'

'TWO LIVES' BAR TO WIFE'S RIGHTS'

In prose more purple than poignant, one paper gushed:

> 'If time is the true test of love, then this forlorn and broken-hearted widow, who now sits alone in the Horseshoe Pillars – the home of her lover, from which she has been baulked for fifteen years – is love's own child. For single-hearted devotion, pure, unselfish love, long-suffering patience, and an almost quixotic forbearance of the whims of the sick old housekeeper who barred her way to a long deferred bliss, Mrs Carpenter is surely without a peer in the annals of reality or fiction.'

Miss Powell's death, only hours before Ben Carpenter's demise, meant that the lawful wife only just squeaked through as the beneficiary of the house, the farm, and the businesses. As it turned out, however, it made no difference whatever.

When the estate was administered, it was discovered that Ben Carpenter had mortgages and outstanding debts that left his estate in the red by some £560, so the poor woman ended up with nothing, and Carpenter's creditors, after a sell-up, only received *13s. 4d.* in the pound. As for the inheritance arrangement with Miss Powell, provided by the 'joint' wills, Ben Carpenter's widow was indeed entitled to all the housekeeper's assets; Miss Powell's total estate amounted to £14.*7s.10d.*

One final and rather sinister twist is suggested by a press report in which a journalist makes a fairly clear insinuation that Ben Carpenter's untimely death, which deprived the couple of the marital bliss they had dreamt of together, may have been due to something other than a cruel turn of the wheel of fate. He wrote:

> *"Was it purely a tragic coincidence that Mr Carpenter and Miss Powell, his housekeeper, should die on the same day within a few hours of each other?" is the question agitating the villagers of Poulton... The doubts of the villagers are further aggravated by the statement made to me by this same witness, and in circulation all over the countryside, namely, that the last words Miss Powell spoke to her sister, in whose arms she died, were: "I would rather see him dead than bring that other woman in this house."*

MEN ABOUT THE VILLAGE
What Poulton gents were wearing c. 1900 *(from the Hill family scrapbook)*

IX
Poulton in the Twentieth Century

We can learn about the twentieth-century life of the village not only from research, but from the actual mouths and memories of the older villagers who were either born here or came to Poulton in the first half of the century. The author was privileged to be able to hear the first-hand accounts and reminiscences of such long-time residents as Mrs Freda Baylis who, at 91, was then Poulton's most senior resident* and had been in the thick of village life for 58 years; Mrs Hilda Strange née Strafford, born here in 1904, daughter of the village postmaster; Janet Crouch née Hill, last of the line of Jenners/Lanes/Hills – for centuries the most prominent farming land-owners in the area; Margaret Thorne, whose parents and grandparents between them ran the Falcon Inn for most of the century; Des Jobbins, who married into the large Jobbins family; John Ash, a farmer, whose prolific family has featured in Poulton history for generations; as well as Frank Pitt, Reg Adams, Queenie Ball, formerly Queenie Little, and Joan Lavin née Gardner, who as children were all pupils at Poulton School and remained in the village all their lives.

Frank Hill in 1900 (son of Bert and father of Janet)

From the turn of the century up to the outbreak of the Great War, Poulton was a quiet, cosy, undisturbed rural backwater of just under 400 residents.

*1993

Outside John Tanner's Falcon Inn in the early 20th century. The horse bus that took the Poulton Cricket team to their matches is probably being driven by Tommy Little.

In 1901 Poulton mourned the first war casualty from the village, Sgt George Wheeler, 27, killed in the Boer War at Standerton, South Africa. Alas, there were many more Poulton Fallen to come in this century of wars.

Much of the village life centred around the new St Michael and All Angels Church, and the church registers and the annual parish reports for those years continue to be awash with the same family names: Ash, Luckett, Edwards, Hill, Gardner, Adams, Ockwell, Jobbins, Strange and Strafford.

The century began with the arrival of a new vicar, R.H. Wilmot, but by 1907 the Vicarage had a new resident, the Revd C.H. Barlow, who was clearly a live wire in the community. Church attendance warranted up to four services on a festive Sunday plus a full service on Thursday evenings, but for Barlow even that was not enough. In the 1908 Vicar's Letter to the parish, he 'calls attention again' to his daily intercessory prayers for the sick and the church's work abroad at the 'dinner hour' between noon and one o'clock. This seems to have been something of a non-starter, however, as the following year he wrote, rather ruefully: 'I have not had many requests for the prayer referred to, nor have I seen the Church much used for private devotion,' however, being the plucky Christian he obviously was, he added: 'but it is

Poulton Street (aka the London Road aka the A417) looking south, in the early 20th century. The old Post Office is on the right. The present Post Office and shop is across the road on the left.

not the course of true faith to cease to hold up higher ideals even if they are not practically conformed to, and I would once more call attention to the fact that I make it a practice to offer intercessory prayer in the Church most days between 12 and 1 o'clock.' Alas, he bemoaned the lack of attendance at these daily prayer sessions every year for the next six years, but no quitter he, and even in his letter of 1914, after complaining that 'the Church is not fully appreciated when it is only looked upon as a place where services are held', he re-affirmed his determination to carry on with the daily midday litany even if, like Eleanor Rigby's friend, Father McKenzie, 'no-one came near'. Nonetheless, St Michael's had enough local village support to maintain for many years a full church choir and operate a Sunday school, had an active Parents' League and Mothers' Union, a Bible class conducted by the Vicar's wife, a 'Girls' Friendly Society', a youth club called 'The Band of Hope and King's Messengers', and a Young Men's League of some twenty members, recent school-leavers who combined matters spiritual with a bit of youthful fun and games – badminton, lawn tennis and football – on the Vicarage field.

Bert Hill religiously kept the audited church accounts, and Hilda Strange's grandfather Charles, and John Ash's grandfather George were faithful churchwardens for years.

It was all go at the Vicarage in those days: cooking classes were held in the Vicarage kitchen, along with lectures on first aid and nursing, and in 1910 Mr Barlow writes that although he did not consider it a part of the duties of his office, he was pleased to have organised a number of village socials – 'pleasant recreation for young people' – throughout the year, and he describes one such entertainment as being 'a most interesting magic-lantern lecture upon John Bunyan given by the Revd W. H. Careless' – the Edwardian version, one assumes, of a teenage rave. Barlow also writes: 'Nor have I found it anything but a pleasure to be Secretary of the Rifle Club which has been very successful in its matches with other clubs, having lost only four of eleven matches,' and the sharp-shooting vicar then added, sniffily, that on three of those occasions the opponents *used special sights.*'

On 22 June 1911 St Michael's was crammed to overflowing for a service to commemorate the coronation of King George V and the parishioners 'listened attentively' while the entire Coronation Ceremony, which was simultaneously taking place in Westminster Abbey, was read out to the congregation. That night, Poulton celebrated with a massive bonfire and fireworks.

Mrs Hilda Strange, at 90, vividly recalled her childhood in the village. Hilda was born in the house that is now called Figaro in the London Road, the youngest of the three Strafford children. This house was then the post office, run by her parents, Mr and Mrs John Harrison Strafford, and though it had been many things before, including the coaching inn called the Axe and Compass, and later, the Carpenters' Arms, the property had been owned continuously by her family for over two hundred years. Although 'Jack' Strafford was officially the village postmaster (taking over the job from Orlando Sambleson), he was primarily an excellent saddler, so his wife, and later his daughters, did most of the post office work to allow Jack to get on with making high-quality saddles and harness repairs for the gentry and huntsmen.

'We had the most lovely childhood in Poulton,' said Hilda Strange, with more than a touch of nostalgia in her voice. 'My older brother Charlie and my sister Edith and I used to play in our beautiful orchard behind the house.' She laments that the orchard was cut down and the land sold off to property developers to build a number of modern houses in a new development called Elf Meadow – not whimsically named for the little people who might have dwelt at the bottom of the Strafford's garden but, typical of the late twentieth century, prosaically named after the Elf petrol station that shared the plot of land. 'There have been many changes in Poulton since I was a girl...and not all of them for the good', sighed Hilda Strange.

There was, of course, no mains water in the village, so nearly every house had a well, but additional water could be

The Strafford family, l to r: Edith (Mrs James, 1902–1970) lived all her life in Poulton; Charles (1898–1960), who became a war hero; John Harrison, known as Jack (1875–1951), the saddler and postmaster; his wife, Emily Kezia (1878–1939); and Hilda (Mrs Strange, 1904–1996)

Poulton children dance about the Maypole in the school gardens at Englands in the early 20th century

fetched from the spring at Stoney Pool, and during droughts the villagers used to queue up at the pump there. Between 1906 and 1911 James Joicey put in a system of pipes to procure running water from a private supply at Ready Token to his mansion and Priory Farm, and incidentally to his tenants at Jenners Farm and Vicarage Farm, for whom he provided the water free of charge. For the right to lay the ten miles of pipes under various fields, he agreed to pay the landowners an annual sum of 2s.6d. The windmill that pumped the water still stands in the fields at the Priory, though its sails have long since gone.

Poulton's links with the outside world, which in the early part of the century meant not much more than Fairford and Cirencester, were provided by Busby's of Fairford who ran a horse-drawn bus service stopping at Poulton en route to Cirencester once a week (Busby's was still in business as a garage on the Poulton side of Fairford in 1994), and Tommy Little, a carrier from Poulton, who ran a little brougham horse bus into Cirencester and back on Mondays, Wednesdays and Fridays. The post came from Fairford, the nearest railway line, and letters were addressed to 'Poulton, Fairford'.

The schoolmaster at Poulton school (where the Strafford children and Tommy Little's son Des went), was now a man called Philip Franklyn, an ex-St Paul's chorister who sang in the Poulton church choir and was very well liked by the older children whom he taught, but he had a dragon of a sister who looked after the infants and gave them a good thumping when they misbehaved. Hilda Strange recalled that caning was common. As some of the children lived a couple of miles or so away at Ready Token and Poulton Grange, Des Little would drive his father's brougham to fetch them every morning, then put it away and attended the school himself. When the school day was over, he would get the horses out and take the children home again. Those children who went on to grammar school in Cirencester mostly had to cycle the five miles each way, though some were lucky enough to be taken in by pony and trap. Boys and girls were strictly segregated and, said Hilda Strange, the girls were forbidden even to speak to the boys and could get into 'a lot of hot water' if caught socialising with the opposite sex.

The London Road, at this time called Poulton Street from the bridge up to the junction with Bell Lane, and thereafter called the Fairford Road, was unpaved until the 1920s, and Cricklade Street was just a dirt path with grass growing down the middle right up until World War II. South of the Butts it was used only for coming and going to the Priory or to the church at Down Ampney.

Hilda Strange admitted that most of the villagers were really very poor in her childhood and life was certainly not easy, but one got the strong impression talking to her that there was in Poulton, and no doubt in all the villages at the time, such a sense of community and family that people could be made extraordinarily happy by the smallest and simplest of pleasures. She recalls the tradition of *'the Saturday penny'*, which the children received from their parents and sometimes their grandparents, and what a treat it was to go to Edward's General Stores in Cricklade Street and choose the sweets the Saturday pennies would buy!

In 1913 Hilda Strange's grandfather, old Charles Strafford, built a house for himself in the London Road on the site of, and incorporating a part of a derelict old cottage. In those days no planning permission was needed and the house was built without any plans or official documentation of any kind. The house was called Dorian and was the home of Mrs Freda Baylis. When she bought the house in 1935 from Charles Strafford's son Willie, he was forced to get sworn statements from various villagers that he actually owned the house as the property had never had any deeds.

Poulton during the Great War 1914–1918

War broke out on 2 August 1914, and most of the able-bodied Poulton men, grand and humble alike, went off to the front; ninety-five in all, which represented more than a quarter of the entire village population. These included the postmaster's son (Hilda Strange's older brother, Charlie Strafford), aged 17, who joined the Royal Navy Air Service and became an ace pilot; Alec Tanner, the son of the publican

Poulton youths Bert and Percy Ockwell pose in front of the Falcon Inn before going off to war in 1914. The Ockwell brothers were lucky to come back home in one piece. Over a quarter of Poulton's soldiers were either killed or wounded. Far left, Margaret Tanner (1868—1939), the publican. Far right, old Charles Strafford, the builder (Hilda Strange's grandfather).

of the Falcon Inn, James Joicey from the Priory, who was made a Major; Bert Hill's son, Frank; and many relations of present or recent Poulton residents: the late Queenie Ball's father, Al Ash, as well as her future first husband Des Little; Dorothy Griffin's father and uncle, Percy and Bert Ockwell; Joan Lavin's father and uncle, Frank and Albert Gardner; Frank and William Edwards, sons of the family that ran the General Store, and a whole collection of relations of John Ash, who, at the time of writing, still farms many a Poulton field.

Of the Poulton casualties, Alec Tanner was the first, wounded at the Mons retreat, and was back in Poulton by December, hailed as a hero. Des Little suffered severe head wounds in battle. By an extraordinary co-incidence, the military ambulance that scooped him up off the battlefield was driven by Frank Edwards from Poulton who, taking one look at the gaping hole in the soldier's forehead, said 'That's the end of Des Little.' Fortunately it was not. Des was taken to the field hospital where his skull-wound was

Des Little (right), recovering in hospital from his head wound, is visited by his brother Hector, c.1918.

opened up with a circular saw and underwent an operation that saved his life. His wife Queenie said when Des returned to Poulton, he still had a hole in his forehead large enough to set an egg in it. Over the years, the indentation diminished, but it was visible for the rest of his life.

Some twenty years later, the army surgeon who had performed the radical operation, Professor Jefferson of the medical faculty of Manchester University, got in touch with Desmond Little to find out if he had suffered any long-term disability as a result. He hadn't – in fact Queenie testified that it never bothered him right up to his dying day, age 83.

In 1915, Poulton instituted a penny fund to buy tobacco for the soldiers, and the school children are on record as contributing one pound. The school girls made socks, mittens and mufflers for 'Fighters from Poulton at the Front'. In that year, Lance Sgt Arthur Miller, aged 20, became the first Poulton School old boy to be killed in action, but tragically there were many more to come.

In 1917, Poulton school held a memorial service for two more ex-pupils killed in action: Sgt Charles Turner and Sidney Strange. By the time the war was over, the total had risen to eleven wounded and fifteen killed – those dead being about fourteen per cent of all those from this one village who had served King and Country.

Philip Franklyn, the Poulton schoolmaster and sign writer in his spare time, made up a large Roll of Honour to place in the school. Reg Adams recalled being sent to Cirencester on his bicycle to buy the needed art supplies – sticks of charcoal, India ink and paper – to make the Honour Roll, and various boys were given the job of going to every house in the parish on their bikes, verifying all the facts Franklyn had put down about the Poulton soldiers. Even so, there are one or two omissions, but the product of his labours hung in the school until it was closed in 1980. It was then moved to the Village Hall, where it remains today.

ROLL OF HONOUR OF THOSE FROM POULTON WHO SERVED KING AND COUNTRY IN THE GREAT WAR

(Based on Mr Franklyn's original, plus discovered amendments and additions)

(w) wounded in action (p) taken prisoner (✟) killed in action

Adams, J.H. (w)
Aldridge, William(✟)
Ash, Al, A.
Ash, Cecil Edwin (✟)
Ash, Edward R.
Ash, Frank (✟)
Ash, Fred J.
Ash, Worthy
Bishop, James
Booth, Walter
Booth, Wilfred
Chester, G.J.
Cook, Fred (w)
Cook, Percy
Cooper, Norman
Edwards, Frank
Edwards, William H.
Falconer, Alan
Fitchet, Bert
Gardner, Albert E.
Gardner, Frank (w)
Hartshorn, Ernest
Hartshorn, George
Herbert, James
Herbert, T.E.
Hicks, William
Hill, Frank
Hobbs, Thos. Wm. (w)
Hobbs, A.
Iles, William
Jackson, Fred

Jackson, John
Jobbins, Henry
Jobbins, Oscar
Johncey, Ernest
Johnson, Styles
Joicey, James
Little, Chris
Little, Desmond (w)
Lock, Ino (w)
Luckett, William
Mason, Edward
Miller, Alan R.
Miller, Reginald (✟)
Mills, Charles
Niblet, Ray (p)
Ockwell, Bert
Ockwell, Percy
Painter, T.I.
Palmer, William (✟)
Poole, Charles (w)
Pooley, R.
Priest, Thomas
Risby, Arthur (w)
Robins, Albert
Robins, D.T.
Robins, Frank (w)
Robins, Henry
Robins, James
Russell, Alex. G. (✟)
Selwyn, Tom
Selwyn, William

Skinner, Arthur
Skinner, Daniel (✟)
Smith, Charles (p)
Smith, John
Smith, Louis A.
Smith, William
Staples, Frank
Strafford, S. Charles
Strafford, Wm. N.
Strange, Frank
Strange, Sidney (✟)
Stratford, Sid (✟)
Stratford, Wal (w)
Strickland, T.A.G.
Swinford, Fred
Tanner, Alec (w)
Tanner, William
Taylor, William J.
Thomson, J.A. (✟)
Thomson, T. (w)
Tilling, Fred
Trotman, Vic
Turner, Charles (✟)
Turner, Reuben (w)
Waine, Raymond W.(✟)
Waine, W.O.
Wakefield, Ino
Wakefield, William
Weaver, Harold
Wheeler, Arthur
Wheeler, Fred. G. (✟)
Wheeler, Wm.G. (✟)
Winders, Jos.

A stone tablet was placed in the Poulton Parish Church which records the names of those 15 young men from the village who never returned.

Charlie Strafford, a Poulton School old boy, was awarded the D.F.C. *(Distinguished Flying Cross)* in 1918 and his sister Hilda Strange, then aged fifteen, was taken up to London by her mother to see her brother being presented with the medal by King George V at Buckingham Palace. As we shall see, this was just the first of many distinctions Charles Strafford, the village's most distinguished war hero, was to receive.

Charles Strafford, Poulton's World War I air ace, taking off in his flying machine

After the Armistice

A stone Celtic cross was erected in London Road as a memorial to Poulton's dead. It is here that wreaths of poppies are placed on Remembrance Sunday every November.

In spite of the loss of so many of Poulton's sons, life went on after the war much as before. At this time an enormous number of houses and fields around Poulton were owned by the Priory Estate, though the farmlands were let out to tenant farmers, mostly from the two oldest farming families of Poulton, the Ashes and the Hills. The cottage dwellers paid their rents of between £6 and £10 per annum to the Priory, though the Land Tax, which averaged between 2s. and 3s. a year, was paid by the Joiceys.

At the War Memorial, the Revd A.J. McMaster Yair, Vicar of Poulton 1925–1938, conducts a Remembrance Sunday service for the Poulton Fallen. On the left is Reg Adams, and on the right is Tom Poulton, the lamplighter

The Poulton Cricket Club resumed six months after the end of the war, and games continued against local rivals. The Poulton XI, however, ran into a spot of bother playing against Cirencester Grammar school, when rain stopped play at 76-0 against Poulton, mostly the work of a sixteen-year-old schoolboy who had scored sixty-one runs not out when the game was called off; a humiliation had the lad not been Walter (Wally) Hammond, one of cricket's all time greats, who captained the England team just eight years later.

Wally Hammond in 1918, the lad who went on to captain England.

The Poulton Bus

Queenie Ball remembered riding in Tommy Little's horse bus when she was a young girl in the 1920s, but couldn't remember at what point he moved with the times and acquired a small motor bus. According to Freda Baylis, he had some problems adjusting to the horseless variety of transport, and whenever he wanted to stop the motor bus, he would call out 'Whoa', instead of applying the brake.

Tommy's son Desmond helped his father with the bus business, driving it from Poulton to Cirencester twice a week day and three times on Saturday (fare: one shilling seven pence single). On Thursdays, when it was early closing in Cirencester, Des would take shoppers to Swindon or Cheltenham. There were very few private cars in Poulton and on Sundays the Poulton bus would take otherwise-immobile villagers to seaside resorts like Weymouth or, more popular still, Weston-Super-Mare. It cost ten shillings, left Poulton at 8.30 in the morning and returned at about 6 p.m.

The Littles, father and son, were very obliging and did all sorts of commissions for villagers, from specialised shopping to, according to Freda Baylis, taking a few bob to back a winner at Ascot or the Cheltenham races, as they were also the village bookmakers. Queenie recalls that one Monday in 1940 the two of them stopped at the chemists in Cirencester so that Des could pick up a prescription for a villager. When he got back aboard the bus, he said to his father: 'It's already four o'clock. We'd better hurry back.' There was no reply, and he realised that his father was dead. Thus did the driver of the Poulton bus die in harness.

The Poulton Manor

The Young family had owned the Manor since the end of the nineteenth century. In the 1920s a bachelor named Edmund (known as Squire Young) was living in the house with a housekeeper, Miss Janet Hawker. Squire Young, who had an identical twin brother named William, had the reputation among the local children of being a tyrant, chasing them off his land if they were caught trying to nick apples from his orchard. He died in 1925, leaving the Manor House to Miss Hawker, an act of generosity perhaps beyond the usual employer/employee relationship. After his funeral, Miss Hawker, who didn't wish to remain in Poulton, packed her bags and went to live with her sisters in Lechlade. Almost at once, the Poulton children stormed the orchard of the vacant house to feast fearlessly on the previously forbidden fruit. The shock they received sent them screaming to their homes in terror, reporting that Squire Young's ghost had appeared in the orchard and had given chase. It was, of course, Edmund's twin, William, who had dropped in to keep an eye on the place. Over the next few years the property became derelict as Miss Hawker neither sold it nor ever returned to Poulton before her death in 1930. She left the house to her sisters.

Because of the neglect, this elegant house was in a state of considerable disrepair when Mrs Nancy Cartwright bought it for £1,000 and she had it completely restored before she and her daughter Diana took residence in 1932. Nancy Cartwright founded the *Poulton Choral Society* and became its conductor. She took conducting lessons from Sir Malcolm Sargent and in time the *Poulton Choral Society* became famous throughout the Cotswolds. In 1938 it won citations in five different categories in a competition at the Gloucestershire Countryside Music Festival, held that year in Cirencester, and won another five citations in 1939 when the festival was held in Tewkesbury.

Major Change at the Priory

It was in the late 1920s and early 1930s that so many changes in Poulton took place. In 1926, Major James Joicey died at the age of 65, leaving an estate worth £188,000. He requested 'no hearse, coaches or black horse or any sign of mourning whatsoever' and the cremated remains of this keen horseman were sprinkled in Ready Token Cover, a little copse across the Welsh Way from Ready Token House and a favourite meeting place of the V.W.H. Hunt. There is a moss-covered stone marking the spot and bearing only his initials, J.J., and those of his wife Mariska Cristobel, M.C.J, on the back. On the front of the stone, now barely legible, is a verse from *When I am Dead* by Christina Rossetti (1830–1894) which reads:

> *When I am dead my dearest*
> *Sing no sad songs for me,*
> *Plant thou no roses at my head,*
> *Nor shady cypress tree,*
> *Be the green grass above me*
> *With showers and dewdrops wet,*
> *And if thou wilt, remember*
> *And if thou wilt, forget.*

The copse belonged to Poulton Priory, and James Joicey left it to the Charity Commission in perpetuity. After legislation it now belongs to Ready Token House and the grave is meant to be maintained in accordance with the oath taken by the owner.

Major Alexander Black Mitchell, with the proceeds of a handsome golden handshake he had received from being the Chairman of the Imperial Tobacco Company, bought Poulton Priory from Mariska Joicey in 1927, and at that time,

Major Alexander Black Mitchell

probably to pay off death duties, the Joicey estate sold off 195 acres of local farm land and some fifteen to twenty cottages at auction. These included a few largish holdings such as Butts Farm (70 acres) and Betty's Grave Farm (65 acres), as well as the barn which was later to become the Village Hall, and the surrounding land which is now the children's playground in Cricklade Street, and Vicarage Farm, which was bought by Bert Hill and included the tiny seventeenth-century cottage where Betty Bastoe, the so-called *Witch of Poulton*, was said to have lived. Major Mitchell however was still the principal landowner in the parish and had made a deal with the Joicey estate to retain the shooting rights on all this land for twenty-one years thereafter, paying the sum of £30 a year, which was distributed to the purchasers in proportion to their acreage.

Mitchell, like Joicey, was a keen cricketer and was delighted to continue the tradition of the Poulton Cricket Club playing their matches on his land at the Priory. He was president of the club until he died in 1972, when his son Ian took over. The cricket team throughout the first half of the century relied on much of its talent and support coming from generations of old Poulton families, and the club's lists of players and officers are sprinkled with such familiar names as Edwards, Ash, Jobbins and Adams.

Major Mitchell was also a polo enthusiast and created a private polo field at the Priory which he kept operational right up to World War II. After the war, he gave the polo grounds to the Poulton Cricket Club, which has proved to be one of the finest wickets and grounds in the country.

The Great Poulton Water Row

When Major Mitchell bought the Priory in 1927, the sale included the water supply from Ready Token to the Priory mansion, Priory Farm, Jenners Farm and Vicarage Farm. Mitchell, however, 'obtained for his own use a more convenient water supply', so authorised Joicey's estate to dispose of it; thus the Poulton Water Supply was sold to Mr Aubrey Price, grandfather of John Price, a long-time Poulton resident. He continued to furnish piped water to the aforementioned farms, but in 1929 the Poulton Parish Council proposed to extend this mains water to all the village by getting the District Council to buy the supply 'at a reasonable price' from Mr Price, hoping Mr Price would be reasonable..

Normally the Parish Council meetings are pretty routine affairs, dealing with complaints about the state of footpaths and road surfaces, a call for more litter bins, etc. – worthy but dull – and generally received with a consensus of agreement in the parish. The mains water proposal, however, caused an unholy row in the village as it meant that everyone would have to pay for it in higher rates, whether they wanted the water or not. Some did, many did not, and the village was deeply divided.

Mrs Annie Thomas, who lived at Southcott and was Poulton's representative to the Rural District Council, was all for it and got a healthy majority vote of twenty to four in support of the proposal at an Extraordinary General Meeting of the Parish Council. Other members of the Council, including Mr William (Bill) Edwards, the blacksmith son of the shop-keeping family, and Mr William Luckett of the Old Farmhouse, were dead against paying higher rates for the purchase and upkeep of the system when they had perfectly good wells of their own. They got up a local petition against the purchase and sent it to the District Council.

Councillor Annie Thomas YES! to water

The ensuing battle was curiously redolent of some of the Parliamentary Question Time exchanges that entertain the nation from time to time. Bill Edwards claimed that the Parish Council vote was unfair because only 24 parishioners had turned up; he claimed the meeting had not been properly advertised. 'Very few knew about it,' he complained. 'Nonsense,' replied Annie Thomas. 'The notice

Councillor Bill Edwards NO! to water

The New Inn, an ale house at the corner of Bell Lane. Run by Fred and Elizabeth Morse in the 1930s, it offered overnight accommodation for cyclists. It finally closed in 1958, and is now a private residence.

was duly posted and everybody knew about it. If people do not come to a meeting, they have no right to go against the decision afterwards.'

The battle raged. 'Poulton is one of the best watered villages in the country – plenty of wells of good water within two yards of their doors,' thundered Councillor Edwards. Annie Thomas answered that 'in view of the very dry weather we have experienced, I believe that the greater number will be very grateful indeed [for the mains water supply] after running about fetching water when their wells run dry.' Wasn't public health an important issue here? Edwards' views were: 'I firmly believe that the majority of parishioners prefer to drink from a clean well than from rusty pipes. I should like to add that our village has got a good many old age pensioners from 65 years to 85 years, and even 90 years. I think that speaks for itself.'

In the end a compromise was proposed by an offer from the District Council to foot some of the pumping and upkeep expenses, and raise a loan to cover the purchase (at £625) from Aubrey Price. The opposition was apparently satisfied, the proposal was carried, and Annie Thomas was delighted, saying she thought the people of Poulton had rather changed their views and she did not think the Council would have any more petitions.

Houses were eventually equipped with cold taps, so the water had to be heated on a furnace and carried to the bath, which was often upstairs. In 1937, the Baylises had a hot water system put into their house. This was so rare even then that an expert had to come down from Cheltenham to install it.

The sewage problem in the village was a major concern of the Parish Council for decades, and the minutes of its meetings are filled with reports of blocked drains, stinking ditches and overflowing septic tanks. Over the years, the problem became more and more acute as all the sewage from the houses was finding its way down to Stoney Pool, which became fetid, and the spring there was depleted to a trickle due to bore-holes dug elsewhere in the area. Freda Baylis recalled that by the time she arrived in the village in 1935, the stench from Stoney Pool was appalling and deemed a serious health hazard. First her husband and then she became Parish Councillors and were instrumental in getting the District Council to drain it and fill it in. Many years later, a group of council houses were built on the site of the pool, and one of the recent inhabitants claimed that some nights she heard a child crying, the ghost of a young girl who had been drowned in Stoney Pool many years ago.

Poulton Electrified

Electricity arrived in Poulton in 1934, though the power supply was limited. Each house was allowed three, but *only* three sockets for light bulbs. Freda Baylis, who moved into Dorian the following year, recalled the terrible dilemma of having to decide which three rooms were to be favoured with electric light. She applied to the authorities for an electric cooker but was refused on the grounds that there was already one 'high-voltage' appliance in the village, meaning a small electric cooker at the Old Forge. As it was, everyone in Poulton knew when it was in use because the light bulbs all over the village would suddenly go dim the minute the cooker was switched on. The rest of the villagers had to do all their cooking on a grate, which was fairly limiting. Freda Baylis and her husband used to visit their parents' homes in Droitwich and Kimerton at weekends so that they could use their ovens to stockpile as much cooked food as possible to bring back to Poulton for the following week. At Christmas, the villagers used to take their turkeys to one of the local bakers to have them roasted in his ovens overnight and collected the following morning. After three months, Mrs Baylis persuaded the powers that be to put in a transformer so that she could have her own electric cooker. It only cost £15, but she had to go to Birmingham to buy the right sort of saucepans as Cirencester shops only sold huge thick ones for solid-fuel stoves.

A Village Hall for Poulton

Any village meetings or social events had to be held in the school house, the Vicarage or the Priory barn until 1932 when Major Mitchell bought an old barn in Cricklade Street. He gave it to the village, along with enough money to convert it into a proper village hall. Queenie Ball, who looked after the hall for many years, was a girl of eleven at the time and remembered the bestowal as the most exciting addition to the village. She says that from the time the work was completed until after World War II there was an event of one kind or another in the hall nearly every night. Dancing was particularly popular, live music provided by a piano, and a number of the older Poulton residents recalled spending their teens two-stepping the evening away, thanks to Major Mitchell's generosity. It is, of course, still to this day a major facility in the village.

Poulton Shops, Services and Provisions

Poulton, up to World War II, was still a completely self-supporting community. Alfred Edward's General Store 'stocked everything,' although Joan Lavin remembered that Edwards kept provisions under his bed next to his chamber pot, which today would guarantee him being closed down pronto by a zealous Health and Safety Officer. But then that would doubtless have been the fate of all the village food shops of the time, yet everyone who got past infant diseases seemed to live to a ripe old age. Gladys Hill, born at Home Farm in 1891, lived until 1993, deprived for 101 years of the benefits of EU health and safety regulations. There was a choice of local pubs – the Falcon Inn, where the Tanners pulled the pints for most of the century, and the New Inn, run by Fred and Elizabeth Morse, offering accommodation for cyclists as well as ale. There were two bakeries – the House on the Corner was still a steam bakery run by Will and Doll Adams, and Fred Ash's grocery shop doubled as a bake shop, making what Freda Baylis describes as 'the most delicious doughcakes' on the premises of today's post office.

Fred Ash had worked in this shop when he was a lad. The story goes that Ernest Tilling, the proprietor, an upright teetotal Methodist, disapproved of young Fred's blowing his entire wages, judged to be around 10s. a week, on beer at the Falcon Inn every Saturday night. Tilling said to the lad: 'I'll not be paying you a wage for the next ten weeks. Then I'll give you the whole lot all at once and you can do with it what

The village shop has served Poulton for well over 100 years. Started by the Tillings in the 19th century, it was taken over by the Ashes in the 20th century. (left) Fred Ash's son Len, c. 1970. Since Len Ash, the shopkeepers have been Stuart and Liz Russell 1985 to 1998, Sue and Rob Rootes from 1998 to 2012 followed by David and Deborah Fowles, pictured above.

you like.' It's hard to imagine an employer getting away with such a thing today, but thus did Fred Ash learn the virtue of saving and was eternally grateful to his boss as he continued saving his wages and eventually was able to buy the whole shop lock, stock and barrel when Mr Tilling died in 1909. Fred also took Tilling's place on the Parish Council. Fred's son Len continued running the shop right up to 1985. Fred Ash's half-brother George also kept a provisions shop in what is now called Gardener's Cottage, which formerly extended right out to the London Road (or Poulton Street as it then was called). He and his family lived above the shop but George used Jenners Cottage next door as a slaughter house-cum-butcher shop. Jenners Cottage is one of the very few houses in Poulton that has a cellar, and it was there that George hung the meat after slaughtering the beasts in what is now the back garden. He made home-made sausages, home-cured bacon, and meat pies which he sold along with Sunday joints from a hatch in the side of the house (which is still visible today). Incidentally, George Ash's son, Owen, married Fred Ash's daughter, Marjorie. The product of that all-Ash union was the farmer John Ash of Knapp Farm in Bell Lane, who must be about as native Poulton as anyone can get.

George Ash, the butcher (1871-1942), with his son Owen, behind Jenners' Cottage where he had his slaughter yard, c. 1908. He was famous for his home-made meat pies and sausages.

Adolphus Sambleson & Son had vanished by World War I, but William Johnson tailored all through the war before becoming an insurance agent in the 1920s. It is curious to note how many villagers listed a wide variety of occupations which they either practised simultaneously or consecutively over the years. After the war Harry Jobbins, the bachelor brother of Doll Adams and Alma Jobbins, ran a taxi service and a tailor's shop in one of the three little cottages that, when put together, became the Round House. He made superior hunting coats and riding breeches, and no doubt his customers included the hunting/riding gentlemen farmers like Major Joicey, and later, the Mitchells and the horsiest family of them all, the Hills. Although Harry had living quarters upstairs, Des Jobbins remembered that, in his later years, he more often than not spent the night sleeping in a chair in the scruffy shop below. Margaret Thorne, the publican's daughter. reported that Harry used to be in the Falcon every night, and being a man of few words, would just rattle his glass on the table when he wanted more beer.

His brother Sam up at Betty's Grave Farm was a stonemason and builder, but later took up farming when he developed silicosis from the stone-dust. He was also a habitué of the pub, but his wife Lizzie disapproved and devised a plan to scare him out of drinking so much. One night as he was coming home from the Falcon, she jumped out at him wrapped in a sheet and went 'whoooo!' to give him a proper fright. Sam, brooking no nonsense from a ghost, bashed her severely on the head.

Poulton Street aka London Road, looking towards Bell Lane, c. 1937, showing Jack Strafford's petrol pump outside the old post office on the left, today's post office on the right

With the advent of motorised transport, Jack Strafford put in Poulton's first petrol pump outside the old post office, and switched from saddle-making to the more lucrative business of bicycle sales and repairs. Reg Adams remembered that petrol in 1929 cost $1s.6d.$ a gallon, which is more or less seven and a half pence now. Mrs Strafford sold knitting wools and oddments in the post office, which also housed the first telephone exchange. It was, of course, manually operated and

Poulton on Wheels

Poulton villagers were more mobile after World War I. Above left: *Farmer Owen Ash cuts a dash in his touring car, while Reg Adams' wife Cissie, and Iris Selwyn* (above right) *make tracks on a motor bike.*
Below left: *Fred Ash, the grocer who had learned to save, and his daughter Marjorie, arrive by car at Poulton Church for her wedding with Owen Ash in 1934.* Below right: *Dossie Tanner, escorted by her brother Bob, leaves the Falcon Inn to be driven to Poulton Church for her wedding to George Malden in 1932.*

their daughter Hilda recalled there were just eight private telephone subscribers in Poulton. Alfred Edwards' brother Bill, the blacksmith and boot repairer who had waged verbal war with Mrs Thomas over the water proposal, also became the village postman, famous for reading all the post cards that arrived before he did the rounds on his bicycle. It was common for him to tell Mrs Ash or Mrs Adams all about their sister's operation or their cousin's trip up to London before he handed them their morning post, the source of the information.

Postmaster Strafford's half-brother, Willie Strafford, was the village undertaker as well as being a carpenter – coffins a speciality. The stairs in the house known as Figaro were made by him, using coffin wood. In addition to Willie's father Charles, and Sam and Oscar Jobbins, there were several other builders in the village, including William Luckett at The Old Farmhouse, who, as well as being a carpenter, painter, wheelwright and haulier, supplied the village with wallpaper and distemper.

Fresh milk in churns was delivered daily by Fred Leach from Ashbrook Farm in a pony and trap which stopped outside the Luckett's house. The villagers would take their own jugs out to the cart and Fred would ladle out the required pint or quart to fill the jug. There were, of course, plenty of farmers in and around Poulton, but everyone in the village had an allotment in what is called Lot Lane; some retired men used to spend the entire day on their allotment, relying on their wives to bring them their meals.

Poulton also had its own full-time road man who worked from the small structure that is now the bus shelter. Mrs Baylis says the London Road was, in those days, immaculately kept up.

Don't Make I Too Grand

Billy Weeks was a scruffy old codger who drove a team of oxen and lived on his own in one of the oldest cottages in the village, which stood next door to Freda Baylis's house, Dorian. (This cottage was pulled down by the Council and the site is now occupied by a modern house called Leo.) Apparently old Billy was never known to venture into bathwater nor clean, wash or tidy any part of himself or his house. The cobwebs in his cottage, according to Mrs Baylis, hung from ceiling to floor like stalactites. He was, in her words, a bit simple, and had a hard time looking after himself, so Freda Baylis used to take him meals from time to time – but, she points out, 'always on a cardboard plate. It was like that'. She recalls that one night old Billy hammered on her door in panic, crying out 'The Devil a' come to Poulton, and he is in my 'ood pile. I've seen his eyes shining,' and begged Freda Baylis's husband to get him out. Mr Baylis grabbed a stick and went along. The devil that 'a' come to Poulton' turned out to be nothing more diabolical than a neighbour's black cat which Mr Baylis chased away from the terror-stricken old man's woodpile, and Poulton was saved.

Billy Weeks had a sister who lived at Honeycombe Leaze, a good two miles from the heart of Poulton. Every morning of her life she walked that distance in to Fred Ash's bakery and bought one loaf of bread, and then, as she walked the two miles home, she crumbed the entire loaf all along the way to feed the birds, arriving back at Honeycombe Leaze empty-handed.

When Billy Weeks became seriously ill, the Baylises had a difficult time trying to persuade him he must go into hospital because he thought he would have to pay. He finally agreed after they bribed him with chocolates. Before the ambulance came to fetch him from his squalid dwelling, Freda Baylis thought it a good idea to put a clean pillow case on the bed where he lay. To this modest concession to rudimentary hygiene, Billy rose in protest: 'Don't make I too grand, or they will think I've got money and charge I.'

The Silver Jubilee Seat

Poulton celebrated King George V's Silver Jubilee in 1935 with flags flown during the day and lights in the windows at night. The Parish Council gave a dinner for the Old Age Pensioners and presented mugs to all the children at a laid-on tea. A Jubilee seat was presented to the village but this gave the Parish Council headaches for years to come – firstly, because they couldn't agree where to put the wretched thing... initially placed outside Jack Strafford's garage, then moved outside the Falcon, then taken down to a grass verge near the bridge... (not to be confused with the 1897 Queen Victoria Diamond Jubilee bench by the war memorial) ... but secondly, it was forever being damaged due to road accidents or teenage vandalism. In fact Poulton seems to have been plagued with so-called 'bad boys' in the late 1930s and there were endless complaints to the Council about lads riding their bicycles through the village without lights after dark, and other bouts of unruly behaviour and the use of 'bad language'.

In 1940 some of these rowdy Poulton youths picked up the Jubilee seat for a lark and dumped it outside Mrs Cartwright's wall at the Manor House and in doing so broke the pins that held the seat. Police were called in and the culprits were hauled into the Fairford Magistrate's Court and made to pay for the damage. The blacksmith, Bill Edwards, was usually employed to put right the various mishaps with this ill-fated Jubilee seat, but on this occasion he took so long getting round to it that the Parish Council lost their patience and sent it off to Fairford for repairs. Heated discussions about this infernal bench went on in the Parish Council meetings for an incredible *fifteen* years, but no one now seems to know where it is or what has become of it.

Blue Quar – the House that Joan Built

In 1936 Miss Joan Esmond-Matthews, an attractive twenty-five-year old woman, and her older cousin, Miss Phyllis Auden, a first cousin of the poet W.H. Auden, searched the Cotswolds for the perfect spot to build a house for the two of them to share. They were sufficiently charmed by Poulton to purchase a field called Blue Quar adjoining the then uninhabited Ashbrook Lane, off Bell Lane.

Joan Esmond-Matthews

Miss Esmond-Matthews aged 25, at work building Blue Quar single-handed, on her home-made ladder, October 1936.

The amazing plan these two young women had in mind was for Miss Esmond-Matthews to build the house by herself from scratch, while Miss Auden looked after their animals and did the cooking in the caravan that was to be their living quarters during construction. Feminine independence came early to Poulton, indeed.

On 8 October, Miss Esmond-Matthews drove the first nail into what was to be her new house, which she christened *Blue Quar* after the name of the field.

Without any training in architecture or experience in construction, she designed and built, single-handed, a timbered nine-room, two-storey house, and was able to move in a mere seven weeks later. She built it without the aid of a spirit level, plumb-line or set-square. Her tools, nearly all of which she bought at Woolworth's in Cirencester, consisted of a saw and brace, two chisels, two hammers, a screw driver, a spanner, a plane and a pair of pliers. Even the ladder she used, she had made by hand herself.

'I saw no reason why a house should be any more difficult to build than a dog kennel,' she told the press, who viewed her work with amazement. (Her unique accomplishment was widely reported in the national papers, articles appearing in *The Daily Mirror, The Daily Express, The Field,* etc.)

First she drew out on paper the plan for the nine-room house: drawing room, dining room, library, three bedrooms, a bathroom and kitchen on the ground floor, and on the first floor, a small spare room, linen room, storeboard and

Miss Esmond-Matthews and Miss Auden (shown right) *moved into the nine-room house just seven weeks after work began.*

saddleroom. She then set about to erect the framework, put up the walls, and tile the roof with cedarwood shingles. She panelled the inside walls in a variety of different woods, left for the most part unstained in their natural state (oak floors, walnut panelling in the drawing room, satiny pink natural mahogany in the dining-room, honey-coloured birch in the library, hall, kitchen and bathroom, silver ash in the two main bedrooms, and teak in the spare third bedroom). Finally she put in the casement windows and built the chimney. She worked eleven hours a day, from 6 a.m. until 5 p.m. No-one gave her any instruction or as much as handed her a nail.

The builder at rest in her walnut-panelled drawing room

There were, of course, mishaps. No sooner had she erected the framework than gale-force winds rose up towards evening and tilted the structure two inches out of the straight. In order to save the house, Miss Esmond-Matthews worked all night righting the structure with the aid of a car jack. Later, during a particularly wet and cold November, the rungs of her home-made ladder would ice up frequently, and she once slipped and tumbled off the roof.

Although the local authorities had accepted her basic building plans, they compelled her to bring in professional workmen for the plumbing and electrical wiring. By the end of November, she and Phyllis were able to move from the caravan into their new house, and by Christmas they were able to entertain friends for a house party.

Two years later, in 1938, Joan Esmond-Matthews married Philip Cole of Manor House Farm, Poulton. They had what was, for Poulton, a rather grand wedding in the Parish Church with full choir, 'Master D. Gamble in attendance as page.' The groom appeared in the expected formal tail-coat attire, but the bride must have given the more conventional guests a jolt by coming down the aisle on the arm of her brother swathed not in white but entirely in gold – a gold dress with a gold tunic-type top tied with a gold sash, covered by a gold veil topped with head-dress of gold leaves – not quite

Philip Cole and Joan Esmond-Matthews were married at Poulton Parish Church in 1938. The bride wore gold.

what bourgeois wedding tradition decrees, but then this was the same rugged individualist who built Blue Quar single-handed, and she clearly had a mind and style of her own.

Joan and Philip Cole adopted a son, Charles (given the surname *Esmond-Cole*), and they lived at Blue Quar together with Phyllis Auden and a herd of Jersey cows (which Joan herself had bred) for some years before moving to Devon.

Charles Esmond-Cole became a farmer in Devon, keeping the same herd of Jersey cattle that his mother bred in the field of Blue Quar. He reported that his parents divorced, but Phyllis Auden continued to live with his mother until Joan died in 1969. Although she never built another structure of any kind again, her plucky spirit stayed with her to the end. Throughout her life she had regretted never having learned to drive, and after contracting terminal cancer and knowing she had only months to live, she signed on for driving lessons and managed to pass her test first time before dying.

On Christmas Eve in 1972 the then owners of Blue Quar returned from a shopping expedition in Cirencester to discover their house in flames. As it was made entirely of wood and there was no mains water in Ashbrook Lane, they could do nothing but watch their house and all their worldly possessions go up in smoke. Mrs Freda Baylis reported that the roar of the flames could be heard all over the village, and in a short time Blue Quar was no more. But the village rallied to the cause with generosity and true Christmas spirit; the Vicar, Desmond 'Father' Gott, put the distraught couple up at the Vicarage, and everyone in Poulton immediately donated enough furniture and household equipment to them to furnish an entire empty house in Cirencester that was soon found for their interim accommodation.

A new modern house was built by Oscar Jobbins on the site, but it retained the name Blue Quar, a reminder of the remarkable and legendary achievement of the 25-year-old Joan Esmond-Matthews, the plucky lady master-builder of Poulton.

Poulton During World War II 1939 – 1945

Freda Baylis, founder of the Poulton Women's Institute and active in the Women's Voluntary Service (W.V.S.) during the war, wrote an account of how the village coped with the dramatic changes of wartime life:

> 'By order, all windows had to be blacked out at night, in case of air raids. People were using old rugs, blankets or anything dark and heavy. The shops did a good trade in blackout material, often still damp from the dyes.
>
> Within a few days a London school was evacuated to Poulton, and children were billeted on all the houses in the village. These children had scabies and were all very uneducated and backward. I was allocated the school mistress, and they used the Village Hall for lessons. After some months (during the period known as "the phoney war") they all drifted back to London and I was then asked to take in a Polish lady, Madam Podoska, and her little son George.'

[In 1941 the Poulton school roll totalled 70 children: 47 from Poulton, 2 evacuees from Eastbourne, 13 from Willesden and 8 unofficial evacuees.]

The Poulton Dad's Army

> 'The men of the village too old for active service formed the Local Defence Volunteers, known as the L.V.D., which later became the Home Guard. They all wore arm bands, but it was some time before they had any ammunition or uniforms, and most had never handled a weapon of any sort. The L.V.D. had to remove all sign-posts and immobilize all petrol pumps from garages and farms in their area, and when there was an air-raid alert they all went out on duty, including one old soldier who had actually been in the Boer War. Major Mitchell of Poulton Priory

was the Officer in Charge, with my husband (who held a commission in the 1914–18 war) as Sergeant. They did marching and rifle drill, and for some who did not know their right from their left, my husband made them tie a hankie round the right arm'.

The Women's Voluntary Service

'The women of the village joined the Women's Voluntary Service, and our first job was to go daily to the Council Offices in Cirencester where we were issued with special indelible ink to fill in the identity cards, without which you could not get a ration book for food; one I remember filling in was for someone called Bill Billio, of Upper Up, South Cerney. Some people were reluctant to sign their names, as they were hardly able to write.

You could only get rationed food from the grocer or butcher with whom you were registered; in Poulton there were two of each. The weekly rations per person comprised about 6 ozs of meat, 2 ozs of butter and margarine, 2 ozs of cheese and 4 ozs of sugar. Little squares were cut from your ration book. The children also had sweet coupons. I used to post these through the letter box of the sweet shop and collect what was available once a month.

Nothing was wasted; Miss Hill held wartime cookery lessons for the village at the school, and the Women's Institute taught the villagers how to preserve fruit, how to make cakes mixed with cold tea as a substitute for eggs, how to make something new from something old, and how to turn dustbins into improvised field cookers. The country people gathered rose hips to make syrup, allocated to infants to supply Vitamin C, and horse chestnuts to manufacture glucose.'

[In 1942 alone, records show that the children of Poulton School collected 1,791 lbs. of rose hips and 2 cwts. of horse chestnuts.]

'People were surprisingly healthy, because although we had no imported fruit such as oranges and bananas, we all had to eat more vegetables to fill up. It was surprising the number of people in Poulton aged between 80 and 90.

My most important task was to help fit gas masks for the 440 residents of Poulton. These were of three sizes, and had to fit securely round the face; not an easy job for men with beards and side whiskers! Naturally the children were frightened by these great ugly snouts, so I told them that Father Christmas was only coming to children who had gas masks. Babies were issued with a sort of large plastic pillow case. We also had intensive first aid classes in the evenings.

The next task for the W.V.S. was to make a list of all the wells in the village, for fire fighting, in case of air raids and if the water was turned off. For this we were issued with stirrup pumps. Almost every house in Poulton had a well in use; only about half the houses had mains water from Ready Token. This supply proved sadly inadequate when the evacuees came.

The Women's Land Army

One good lady in the village, Miss Burnett [the late Peggy Burnett, who lived in Manor Cottage until her death in 1992 and had a room at the top of the Manor House during the war] *organised the Women's Land Army in this area of Gloucestershire.*

They wore a khaki uniform with breeches and did all the usual farm work such as milking, haymaking and harvesting. This was an alternative to working in a factory for all eligible single women.'

The Mother of All Winters

Mrs Baylis well remembered the nights of 27th and 28th of January, 1940 when rain fell on the frozen earth and built up into a sheet of ice, inches thick, which covered everything. She wrote:

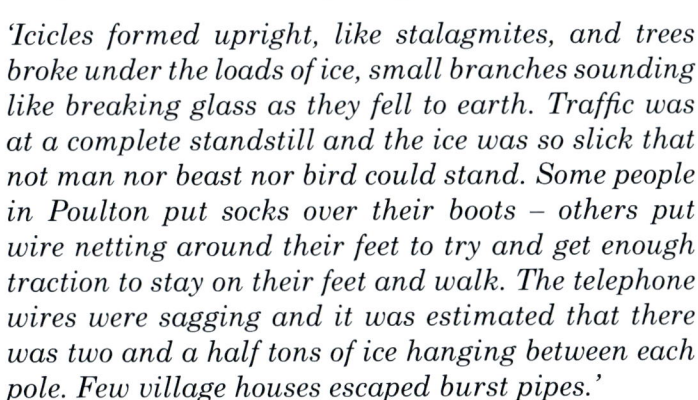

'Icicles formed upright, like stalagmites, and trees broke under the loads of ice, small branches sounding like breaking glass as they fell to earth. Traffic was at a complete standstill and the ice was so slick that not man nor beast nor bird could stand. Some people in Poulton put socks over their boots – others put wire netting around their feet to try and get enough traction to stay on their feet and walk. The telephone wires were sagging and it was estimated that there was two and a half tons of ice hanging between each pole. Few village houses escaped burst pipes.'

Fortunately Poulton has seen nothing like it since.

The S.A.S. in Poulton

The Strategic Air Service ran a training course in Poulton. Mrs. Baylis here recounts their effect on the village:

'They camped out all over Poulton and had to fight mock battles and things like that. They had bazookas and had to live on concentrated rations which were in a little tin about the size of a cigarette packet to which they added water and that had to last them the week of their course. They got very hungry, and if they saw a bread

van they used to ask the children to get some bread, adding the caution: "but don't let anyone see you".

One of the things they were trained to do was to take over a house at night. It was nothing to find them sitting down in your house after they'd broken in. They wouldn't tell you ahead of time and they did it very quietly. Nancy Cartwright's daughter, Diana, who lived in the Manor House, was terrified out of her wits when she came home one night. To hear her tell it: "the rhubarb rose up and met me". It was, in fact, one of the S.A.S. men lurking in the garden, but she couldn't tell as he was so camouflaged under the rhubarb.'

According to Mrs Baylis, each button on their uniform unscrewed and contained something of practical use inside; one would be a compass, another contained a terminal pill to facilitate suicide as they were never to be taken prisoner; if one of their comrades was wounded, they were pledged to finish him off. At that time they had to be over forty and without family connections, so there was no one to grieve for them. As Mrs Baylis says: 'They were expendable'.

Menace from the Air

Poulton was surrounded by targets for enemy bombers: besides the military air base at Fairford, there were airfields at Down Ampney (which had the troop-carrying gliders used for D-Day and Arnhem), Kemble, and the most important one at South Cerney, a training unit for officers of the RAF. Brize Norton and Rissington were not far away, and there were also two small aerodromes at Rendcomb and Ablington, plus the Gloucester Aircraft Factory and a munitions dump in the woods at Chedworth – all probable targets.

In spite of air raids in the area, day and night, Poulton itself was only bombed once. A stick of bombs landed in Bell Lane, which removed roofs and blasted the chimneys off several bungalows, but caused no casualties. It was Oscar Jobbins who was called out to repair the damaged houses. Mrs Baylis believed that the German planes mistook the crossroads there for the one near the Down Ampney air base, and adds: 'The biggest nuisance was from *butterfly* bombs – incendiaries dropped on fields of crops, hoping to set fire to and destroy growing corn. We had a lot of those around Poulton.' There were also several air accidents. In 1942, an RAF Avro Anson crashed near Poulton and its crew of five were killed. In 1943 two Airspeed Oxfords from the South Cerney air base collided directly above Poulton, one crashing in the field behind Manor Farm House, the other in Ampney Crucis. The pilots of both were killed.

An Airspeed Oxford trainer flying over Poulton collided with another 'Oxbox' as these planes were affectionately known, and fell into local fields. Both pilots died in the crash.

Over-sexed, Overpaid and Over Here

By 1942 the U.S. Airforce had arrived in strength and the surrounding area was swarming with 'Yanks'. Mrs Baylis recalled that their jeeps raced along the narrow roads, causing many mishaps. 'One overturned outside my house, and I had five Americans laid out in my lounge. They would not accept even a cup of tea because they had been told we were so short of food.' Mrs Baylis tells of a dance that the locals put on for the Americans in the Poulton Village Hall; '...and what did we give them to eat? Beetroot sandwiches!' she replied with a shudder.

'They soon made friends with the local girls, with their traditional gifts of chocolates, chewing gum and nylons. For most of the girls it was their first introduction to nylons.'

The Poulton School Journal of the time states that American troops supplied eleven pairs of Wellington boots to the village children who lived the furthest distance from the school, and on 26 November, 1942, U.S. Thanksgiving Day, an American Officer stationed at Fairford came to Poulton to tell the school children about this important American national holiday. The entry for that day reports: 'The children gave three cheers for England's ally whose soldiers had arrived in England in great numbers.'

Tragedy at Poulton Priory

Major Mitchell's eldest son, Michael, a Lieutenant with the Coldsteam Guards, had lost a leg in combat in Italy. After recovering, he was posted to Wellington Barracks in London, and his family in Poulton arranged to join him for a service at the Guards' Chapel, held on 18 June, 1944. A few days before that date Major Mitchell's wife, Vera, had taken the train up to London to join their daughter Janet, a nurse, who had been given 24-hour leave. Major Mitchell was hoping to join them for the service, but his taxi to Swindon station got held up and he missed the London train, so he returned to the Priory. In time he was to learn that a doodlebug flying bomb had scored a direct hit on the Guards' Chapel during the service and that his wife, daughter and eldest son had all been killed. Only his younger son Ian survived, as he was in the North Sea at the time serving in the Royal Navy. The Mitchells had long been much respected and loved benefactors of the village – they had replaced the Joiceys as 'the royal family' of Poulton, and the tragedy was deeply felt by every one of the villagers.

Four days after the tragedy, Major Mitchell arranged a memorial service at the Parish Church with the help of the Vicar, the Revd C. E. Dodd. The church was decorated 'in floral masses of blue, white and gold' and filled to the brim with mourning parishioners. Miss Brown played the organ and Nancy Cartwright from the Manor conducted the choir.

Major Mitchell later commissioned the brothers Webb of London to make a three-panelled stained glass East Window for St Michael and All Angels as a memorial. This window above the altar portrays St Michael and St Gabriel flanking the Virgin Mary and Jesus. One panel, dated 1946, is signed with Geoffrey Webb's trademark – a spider's web – in the corner, and another panel by his brother Christopher employs St Christopher as his mark. It is meant to be among the finest windows of its kind. A plaque recounting the Guards' Chapel tragedy is displayed on the north wall of the church. Amazingly enough, the Mitchell family provided the only casualties Poulton suffered throughout World War II.

Poulton Digs Deep

One of the important wartime activities was mobilising the villagers to contribute whatever they could to the war effort. The W.V.S. promoted the National Savings Fund and found volunteers for blood donations. One way they raised money for War Savings was to hold sales of their surplus clothes at the Manor, and they were paid in Savings Stamps. Poulton School gave a concert in 1942 in aid of the National Savings Fund and collected £10, but in 1943, during Wings for Victory Week, the children raised £537 *17s. 0d.* to invest in National Savings and for this the school received a Certificate of Honour from the Air Ministry. Queenie Ball at the Post Office collected money to sponsor a submarine, and the village was given a citation testifying to the success of the significant Poulton fund-raising and sponsorship of Submarine P31.

Poulton Detects D-Day

In spite of the intense secrecy surrounding the greatest invasion in history, the Poulton villagers saw it coming days in advance. Mrs Baylis said there was an air of expectancy building up: 'there was a sudden urgent request for blood donors, and bus-loads of sailors (what was left from HMS Hood) passed through Poulton on their way to Fairford to paint foot-wide stripes on all the planes to distinguish them in battle.' All the roads around the aerodrome were sealed off for three days before D-Day, and Mrs Baylis, who went to mass in Fairford the Sunday before, recalled seeing swarms of airmen coming out of the Catholic Church there, dressed in full battle gear, with a dagger strapped to their right leg. Queenie Ball was another villager who predicted the invasion. One of her jobs at the Post Office, where she worked throughout the war, was to operate the three petrol pumps in the London Road. The American army based locally rented two of these three petrol pumps, and Queenie related that some days before 6 June, she was rushed off her feet filling up a convoy of American military vehicles that formed a seemingly endless queue down Poulton's stretch of the London Road. Queenie guessed correctly there could only be one reason they all wanted petrol at the same time. When D-Day came, Mrs Baylis said she saw dozens of planes arising from Down Ampney well until dark, towing troop-carrying gliders behind them. She remembered that there were some empty piggeries just out of Poulton, on the Down Ampney Road, which were being used by girls of the Signal Corps. It was from there that the signal was sent out to begin *Operation Warlord.*

The Inspector General of the Royal Air Force

Charlie Strafford, Poulton's air ace of World War I, assumed even greater eminence in World War II. As Air Commander Stephen Charles Strafford C.B.E., D.F.C., he was assigned to Control Operations in 1940. In 1942 he was made Head of British Air Planners and Combined Chief of Staffs in Washington D.C.

In 1944 he was appointed Chief of Operation and Plans for the Allied Expeditionary Air Forces, and was made an Air Vice Marshal. For his illustrious contribution to the succesful outcome of the war he received the *Croix de Guerre,* the *Légion d'honneur* and was awarded a C.B. *(Companion of the Order of the Bath)* to add to his already impressive collection of gongs. The Poulton School gave all the children a one-day holiday to celebrate the success of their illustrious former pupil. After the war, Charles Strafford was promoted to Air Marshal and made Inspector General of the RAF. He died in 1966.

Air Marshall Stephen Charles Strafford, C.B.E., D.F.C.,C.B., the Poulton Postmaster's son.

The First Lord of the Admiralty

Lord Cilcennin was born James Purdon Lewes Thomas in 1903, the son of Mrs Annie Thomas, the previously written-about District Councillor for Poulton, and the brother of Miss Joan Thomas, who was an active and ardent supporter of village institutions most of her life. Jim Thomas, after his early years at Southcott, the Thomases' house in Cricklade Street, became a distinguished Conservative M.P. and in the 1930s was *Secretary of State for Colonies*. When Churchill formed his wartime government, he appointed Thomas *Lord Commissioner of the Treasury* and *Parliamentary Private Secretary to the Secretary of State for War*. In 1943 Thomas became *Financial Secretary to the Admiralty*, and in 1951 James Thomas was appointed *First Lord of the Admiralty*. He was ennobled in 1955 as 1st Viscount Cilcennin and died in 1960. In 1964, Joan Thomas gave the Poulton Parish Church a new high altar in memory of her distinguished brother. When she herself died in 1973, the Lady Chapel in the church was dedicated in her memory, and furnished with hassocks embroidered by her friends.

Lord Cilcennin né James Thomas, First Lord of the Admiralty; son of Annie Thomas of Southcott, Poulton

Elizabeth, Lady Clarke

The late Lady Clarke was possibly the most colourful character in Poulton's recent history. 'Not just colourful,' said Diana Peters, a great friend and confidante of Liza Clarke during her Poulton years. 'She was positively *magnetic*.'

'What a character', wrote the well-known 1950s journalist Nancy Spain, in an interview with Elizabeth Clarke, published in the *Daily Express*, adding: 'She had an air of austerity, of authority, of fanaticism, which was contagious.' Lady Clarke lived in the Old Forge in Poulton until her death at the age of 73, and those villagers who remember her in her heyday all have vivid memories and anecdotes to supplement the legend she left behind, not least her alleged exploits during World War II.

Born Constance Elizabeth Gibbs at the tail-end of World War I, she was the daughter of a London solicitor whom she adored, and a mother whom she could never get on with. During her childhood, her father fell victim to financial disaster and had to give up his practice and move the family out to Camberley. According to her son, Stephen Langton, the young Elizabeth so loathed the suburban environs that she developed a hatred of pine trees and rhododendrons that lasted to the end of her days.

Liza Langton in her early twenties, c. 1941

When she was seventeen, a great tragedy finally destroyed her family life; she asked her handsome brother Henry, whom her mother doted on, to drive her and two friends to Maidenhead for an evening's dancing. On the way back, the car struck a tree with such force that her brother and one of her friends were killed. Her mother held Liza forever responsible for his death because the spree had been her idea. The burden of the blame was insufferable, and at eighteen she was only too happy to escape Camberley by marrying John Langton, a young man with considerable charm and wealth, who whisked her off to a pleasant life of bridge, riding, tennis (she had played at Junior Wimbledon), golf, and rounds of parties. By twenty she was a mother, comfortably off and well looked after, but it was the outbreak of war that provided the opportunity to indulge her heady spirit of adventure, or possibly fantasy. What follows is her own account: In 1940, after hearing the reports of the disaster at Dunkirk, the twenty-two-year-old Liza left baby Stephen with nanny (her husband was already away, serving at Aldershot with the Grenadier Guards) and set off together with a friend to cross the Channel in the Langtons' small power boat. Some miles out to sea they came across a returning paddle boat which had taken a direct hit from a German bomber. It was bringing British soldiers, some of whom had been wounded, back from the beaches of France and was sinking, jettisoning its human cargo into the sea.

Liza naturally went to their aid and picked up as many survivors as her little boat would hold. Overloaded, the boat plodded slowly back towards the English coast, a sitting duck for the German plane that spotted them and dropped another bomb. It missed its target, but exploded so close-by that the swells caused the boat to keel over, leaving everyone clinging to the upturned hull. They were eventually rescued from the sea by a Royal Navy destroyer and taken back to Dover.

No sooner was she back in dry clothes than the intrepid Liza and friend decided to have another go. As her own capsized boat had been abandoned at sea, they 'borrowed' a stranger's launch after dark and cast off for France in the blackness of night. They managed to locate and pick up a number of straggling British soldiers on the beaches of Dunkirk, but on their return to Dover in broad daylight the next day, they were met by the harbour police who promptly threw the pair of them in jail for pinching the launch. The soldiers whom they had saved made such a row that the police eventually had to release them and allow them to return to London.

One might think that was quite enough wartime adventure for one young mother of a baby son, but there was a great deal more drama, danger and derring-do to come. Although Lady Clarke, after the war, never revealed details and rarely talked to anyone about her wartime career, even to her own children, she did document many of her hair-raising experiences in a book written while in hospital in 1956 as part of post-trauma therapy. Presumably for security reasons, it was published under an assumed name, Elizabeth Denham. Whether all the tale is true is a matter for conjecture, as it is now impossible to verify details, but her version of the events was this:

The cloak and dagger boys in London, it appears, had got wind of Liza's plucky Dunkirk crossing and recruited her to be an undercover agent. She was trained in ciphering, wireless transmission, and explosives, kitted out with false identity papers and French clothes from beret to knickers, and spent the next three years secretly being shuttled back and forth from England into the Cognac region of German-occupied France for periods of time that ranged from a fortnight to a month.

Her official wartime job was training military chauffeuses for the Motor Transport Corps, a sort of up-market ATS. When she disappeared from work and home at various intervals for reasons officially explained as suffering 'a recurring virus', neither her colleagues in London nor her nanny apparently ever guessed the real reasons behind these abrupt and mysterious absences. Coming and going in the dead of night on military planes landing in French farmers' fields, fishing trawlers and rubber dinghies rowing out to submarines hovering off the coast, her 'special duties' included transporting money and explosives to the French Resistance, co-ordinating with them to arrange safe passage home for British soldiers who had escaped from POW camps and RAF airmen who had been shot down behind enemy lines, instructing the Resistance in British secret codes and radio communication with London, and the use of high explosives. Though she admits that she was terrified, she took part in Resistance forays to blow up German military convoys and equipment, and on one occasion, had her ribs crushed in a premature blast.

The risks for a young Englishwoman behind German lines in wartime were obviously immeasurable, and her clandestine adventures and close shaves were pretty hair-raising, but she survived enemy detection again and again until that one fateful day in 1943: Liza, looking for all the world like an ordinary French working girl, had just crossed a street in a small town in southwest France when she was accosted by a German Military Policeman demanding to inspect her papers. This was a fairly common occurrence and she remained cool, knowing that her forged identity papers were impeccable. Although her French was faulty and less than fluent, the Germans' attempt at the language was a good deal worse, so they were never able to detect her foreign accent or mistakes. On this occasion, however, the German soldier suddenly shouted at her 'Why did you look RIGHT?' She had no believable answer. An instinctive reflex action from a lifetime of crossing roads in England had cruelly betrayed her.

The game was up. The soldier marched her into the occupation headquarters to face interrogation by a German officer who, twigging at once that she must be a British agent working with the Resistance – 'You are too tall for a French woman' (she was in fact 5 feet nine inches tall) – commanded her to put her hands upon his desk, whereupon he took a heavy ruler and methodically broke each and every finger of both her hands. In excruciating pain and terror of what was to come – prolonged torture, perhaps a firing squad or, at the least, a forced-labour camp – she was dragged off and locked away for further grilling. With her crushed and swollen hands, she was unable to manage any ordinary human functions during the time she was captive. Clarissa Mitchell was perhaps the only person with whom Lady Clarke ever discussed her war years. Liza once told her the only way she could keep her sanity in this agonising situation was to keep walking back and forth from one wall of the small cell to the other, like a caged animal. For this reason, says Clarissa, Lady Clarke never again got into a swimming pool, as swimming lengths was too painfully reminiscent of this experience.

In a daring raid a couple of nights later, her Resistance colleagues used her explosives to blast their way into the German headquarters and, in the pandemonium that followed the explosion, managed to

Elizabeth Langton, as she then was, dressed for her 'cover' job in the Motor Transport Corps during the war years.

rescue her. After some days, with her hands in splints and a price on her head, she made her way to the coast in disguise, carrying a borrowed French baby whose blankets covered up the bandages on her fractured fingers. At a pre-arranged spot on the beach, a Royal Navy ship picked her up in the dead of night and ferried her back to England.

After such a harrowing and agonising experience, it is hard to imagine that once her hands had healed, she had the guts and *sang-froid* to return to occupied France yet again – this time to Paris, straight into the cocktail bar at the Ritz, which was filled with high-ranking German officers. She had gone back to find and try to save an English agent who had been her working partner since her first mission and with whom, to read between the lines, she was perhaps in love. He was now on the run, a victim of an intensive manhunt by the German command. She tracked him down in his Parisian hiding place, and they got as far as Bordeaux before the colleague was recognized by the Gestapo and was mowed down in the streets in a hail of bullets. Once again Liza Langton somewhat miraculously managed to give them the slip and got back to England.

The traumatic memories of all she had witnessed continued to haunt her long after the war. Clarissa Mitchell says Lady Clarke suffered 'a persecution complex' to the end of her days – paranoia apparently being a lifetime affliction common to nearly all ex-spies. Nancy Spain, in her Daily Express interview, reported, 'She [Lady Clarke] wouldn't lunch with me: she said she didn't trust me. Indeed I could see she trusted no one.' Nonetheless, her son Stephen reckons that for a true adventuress like his mother, 1940 to 1943 were probably the happiest and most fulfilling years of her life. From the French Government she received the Médaille de la Resistance, the Croix de Guerre, the Légion d'honneur, and the right to vote in French national elections. What honours she received from the British Government is not quite clear, but Stephen Langton remembers that, as a schoolboy, he was left in her car outside Buckingham Palace while she popped in for reasons she never explained.

Her post-war life was bound to be an anti-climax and, like her childhood, her later years were not without a certain amount of turbulence, drama, and distress. She divorced John Langton in 1947 in order to marry Humphrey Clarke, the squire of Bibury. Clarke was equally obliged to obtain a divorce from his American wife in order to marry Liza.

By Humphrey Clarke, Liza gave birth to a second son christened Orme Roosevelt, after Humphrey's father, Sir Orme Clarke Bt., and his mother, who was the American heiress, Elfrida Roosevelt, a member of the family of the U.S. presidents, Teddy and Franklyn Delano. Upon the death of his father, Humphrey inherited the baronetcy and Liza, for some years, revelled in the role of Lady of the Manor, which, according to all reports, she played superbly, opening fetes, throwing tennis parties, hunting, shooting and helping to run the large estate. In time, however, Sir Humphrey's philandering became unbearable and Lady Clarke, being a proud woman, cut her losses and bailed out of the marriage. In 1952, she came to live at the Old Forge in Poulton with her two sons and a splendid old cockney retainer called Gertrude Wadhams who, according to son Stephen, was the only person ever who could get away with ticking off the formidable Lady Clarke. He recalls 'Waddy' telling his mother, on more than one occasion: 'That was a f***ing stupid thing to do...', finishing the sentence with a slightly sarcastic, 'milady!' The London-born Waddy so disliked the countryside that she never ventured beyond the garden of the Old Forge.

At Poulton, which Lady Clarke referred to as 'Piggy Poulton' (with affection and a predilection for alliteration rather than intended disparagement, says her son. A reference, no doubt, to the aforementioned piggery), she made her presence keenly felt in a number of ways; although eminently 'grand', she always kept a common touch and it has been said that she was eternally kind to the villagers and was always ready to drop everything to help anyone in need. Her resolute sense of *noblesse oblige* kindled her passion for community service and she relished dreaming up new schemes intended to benefit the less privileged of the village, particularly the young.

The Revd Robert Nesham, then Vicar of Poulton, recalled her 'good works' weekends when she would round up all the lads of Poulton and march them out into the countryside for a working party to remove the ivy from trees. She would provide a splendid picnic lunch, doubtless with a flask of tipple for herself and the vicar, and they all sat around a campfire like so many boy scouts clustered about a rather prepossessing Brown Owl, elegantly attired. Whether the youth of Poulton enjoyed these outings or not was neither here nor there; apparently no one ever dared refuse Lady Clarke her will, but by all accounts, the young people in the village held her in great esteem and affection.

Diana Peters, who once lived next door to Lady Clarke, tells of the time when Liza's Jack Russell, Tompy, killed a dozen or so of her chickens. Diana, furious, slung the corpses on the porch of the Old Forge. No apology was forthcoming, but the chickens, plucked, cleaned and ready for the pot, appeared the next day on Diana's front doorstep. Not a word about the incident was ever uttered by either party.

Liza Clarke, who has been described as a handsome, rather masculine lady, was always beautifully turned out, with a preference for crisp white shirts, cashmere cardigans and magnificently tailored tweed pleated skirts, and Clarissa Mitchell recalls that she wore a diamond clip in her hair, which had been a gift from one gentleman admirer or another. She had a string of ardent suitors over the years and received not only gifts of jewellry but several proposals of marriage. Her son always felt she was on the brink of accepting, but she never married again.

For many years she served as a highly controversial, singularly outspoken, but dedicated Gloucestershire County Councillor, and would spend two or three days a week at the Shire Hall to impose her indomitable will on the cowering councillors, but if she ended up getting her way over most things, many were well worth the getting; as *Chairman of the Special Needs Committee* she tirelessly campaigned for facilities for the disabled and bludgeoned the Council into granting the land for Clarissa Mitchell's Seven Springs Adventure Playground for handicapped children. Furthermore, she managed to by-pass months of bureaucratic red tape to get it done in record time. According to Clarissa, she strode into the office of an officer of the County Council and asked him if he had signed the paperwork necessary for granting the land. He told her he had not, and furthermore it would be some weeks before he could get round to it as he was extremely busy with other matters. With this, Liza Clarke locked his office door, popped the key down her crisp white shirt, and said, 'You no doubt have a wife and children you would like to get home to see tonight. I have no one to get home to. Before I came in, I made sure my dog had a good pee and was locked in the car and now I am prepared to wait here until the papers are signed, even if it takes until midnight.' The stunned captive bureaucrat apparently concluded the paperwork in minutes.

Over Liza Clarke's ample bar at the Old Forge was the notice *Work is the Curse of the Drinking Classes,* and she was was known for her generously-proportioned martinis. It was rather unfortunate to say the least that during the time she held the position of *Chairman of the Gloucestershire Safe Driving Committee,* she was herself convicted of drunken driving and banned from the roads for a year. The circumstances were amusing enough to make the story worth repeating; apparently, after a dinner party in Tetbury, Lady Clarke was driving home in her Jaguar when she became aware that a car was following her, very close and with its lights up, so she opened the throttle and sped straight to the door of the Cirencester Police Station to complain about the nuisance pursuing her. The officer in charge was obliged to point out that it was in fact a police car that had been following, nay, chasing her, for rather good and possibly obvious reasons. She was found to be over the limit, but remained so convinced that she was in the right that she elected to go to the Crown Court and be tried by jury. According to her neighbour Diana Peters, the jury was extremely sympathetic and would possibly have let her off if the judge hadn't instructed them otherwise.

Liza Clarke's book, called *I Looked Right* was well reviewed by Nancy Spain, who wrote 'I think her story is one of the most moving I have ever read,' and it was serialised in the *Daily Express*. Curiously enough, Liza, at the time, never mentioned writing the book to her sixteen-year-old son, Stephen, and he only learnt about its publication, serialisation and the attending press publicity about his mother from a fellow schoolboy at Eton.

I Looked Right sold well enough to require a second edition, but the book is now out of print. It might seem a natural subject for a heroic wartime film, and in fact ITV did make a programme called *Wish Me Luck*, based on the book, but for some absurd reason the producers neglected to consult Lady Clarke herself and blithely altered any factual details they fancied. So remiss was the television company that she would not even have known about the transmission had it not been for the Revd Robert Nesham drawing it to her attention. According to him, she was not best pleased with the programme nor by the actress who portrayed the Liza Langton heroine, and reportedly she sniffed indignantly: 'How dare that woman wear my clothes!'

Lady Clarke with her eldest son Stephen Langton in 1986

Twenty years after the Clarkes were divorced, Sir Humphrey was out with a shooting party on what has been described as the warmest, sunniest January day the Cotswolds has ever known. Clarke had his gamekeeper reload his shotgun and then, surrounded by all his friends, he suddenly announced, 'It's the end of the shooting season, and now it's the end of me!' and with that, turned the gun onto himself, and, to the horror of the assembled guests, he calmly blasted his life away.

Lady Clarke lived in Poulton for 38 years until her death in 1991. About a year later her younger son Orme, always the apple of his mother's eye, tragically followed in his father's footsteps by taking his own life in the identical manner, employing his mother's shotgun. The ashes of Orme and his mother Elizabeth Clarke are buried in Poulton.

The ashes of Lady Clarke and her son Orme, side by side in the Poulton Churchyard

Murder most foul on Poulton Bridge

Ernest Wood, 55, known in the village as Dick, lived with his wife Ellen, their three children, and their lodger, Wilf Lafford, at Ranbury Cottages, on the road towards Cirencester. Both Wood and Lafford were farm workers and Lafford, 28, had been a lodger at the Woods' cottage for four years. Though the two men had originally been good friends, their relationship had begun to curdle in 1941. Wood was a popular regular at the Falcon Inn, and would spend the evenings smoking his pipe, downing a quantity of pints, and reminiscing to anyone who would listen about his younger days as the driver of a brewery dray with a team of grey horses. On the Monday evening of 25 August, 1941, he went to the Falcon at nine o'clock as was his custom. His lodger, Lafford, arrived about five minutes later, but the publican, George Maiden, testified that neither man spoke to one other during the course of the evening. Lafford left at about ten and Wood at closing time, which was then ten-thirty.

The following day Alec Tanner, the publican's brother-in-law, was cycling to work and found Mrs Wood in the road in a distraught state. Dick hadn't come home that night and his cloth cap had been found on Poulton Bridge, which spans the little stream known as Ashbrook. Alec Tanner and Albert Clack, who lived in the Ranbury Cottage adjoining the Woods' cottage, went to the bridge to have a hunt. Tanner first found Wood's pipe, and then spotted a pool of blood on the verge. In the nearby ditch, he discovered Wood's lacerated dead body under a pile of freshly cut hedge trimmings. Wood had obviously been the victim of the most savage assault. Tanner called in the police, who set up their murder investigation HQ at the Falcon Inn.

After a post mortem, the pathologist reported that Wood had been hacked to death by a hedge cutter, which was found about 100 yards from the body. The blade had inflicted nine serious wounds: one had broken Wood's arm, another had pierced his stomach and kidney, but the fatal wound had slashed his head, making a gash some 12 inches long that had gone through the bone and three inches into Dick Wood's brain. The lacerations, the pathologist said, were the result of a furious and prolonged attack.

At first, when Lafford was charged with the murder, he told policemen 'I won't say nothing at all,' but he later confessed in a statement that reads:

'I murdered Mr Wood for kicking up rows indoors with him and his wife, and coming home drunk at

Poulton Bridge, which goes over Ashbrook on the A 417 to Cirencester and referred to as 'Pultons Bridge' as early as 1603, was the scene of Wood's murder. The Old Manor Farmhouse (centre) *was then called Bridge House.*

nights. He goes to bed and can't sleep and won't let anybody else. He has been carrying on some long time, so I made up my mind to wait for him, which I did, and murdered him.'

At his trial, neighbour Albert Clack's wife, Maisie, testified to overhearing a quarrel between Wood and Lafford, which ended with Wood telling Lafford to clear out, adding, 'but wait until morning,' to which Lafford replied, 'Yes, and you wait till the morning!' Both men, according to Maisie Clack, 'used bad language.' Wagging village tongues however linked the murder with an alleged affair between Mrs Wood and the lodger, though no evidence of a romantic involvement was ever mentioned publicly.

The defence admitted that there was no doubt that Wilf Lafford had committed the dreadful deed, but argued that the accused did not realise what he was doing at the time of the frenzied assault, and that there was a good deal of insanity in his family. Indeed, his mother had been in the Cirencester Public Assistance Institution 'as a person who was mentally deranged', and his sister and half-sister were both at Stoke Park Colony for Defectives.

After retirement, the Foreman of the jury announced that the prisoner was found guilty but insane at the time of the crime. The Judge ordered Lafford to be detained at His Majesty's pleasure and Lafford 'walked calmly from the dock.' John Nunn said he still sweats at the memory of Wilf Lafford taking him for walks when he was a child.

At Wood's funeral in Poulton Church, the Vicar, Mr Dodd, said it was hard to believe that Dick could have met with such a tragic and untimely death. One floral tribute read: *'With very happy memories of the hours he spent with his friends at the Falcon.'* Wood's employer, Mr MacTaggart of Ranbury Farm, remarked 'Poor old Dick! He was a good man. Only a humble farm worker, Dick was yet a perfect gentleman'.

Hit-and-Run at Hartwell Farm

On the night of 1 June, 1943, a Sgt Eric Rosser of the RAF was found lying in a pool of blood 'very seriously injured' on a dark roadside in Warwickshire. Near his unconscious body were bits of a broken car number plate with the letters 'DF' and the number 7. An intensive nationwide search led police enquiries to Hartwell Farm, Poulton, the home of Captain Robert St Vincent-Parker-Jervis whose damaged car number plate ADF 847, happened to be missing the very letters DF and the number 7. Captain Parker-Jervis was a well-known local toff, heir to Viscount St Vincent and a relation of a famous admiral, Sir John Jervis, Earl of St Vincent, who served with Nelson.

The Crown prosecuted, and in court Parker-Jervis admitted that yes, he had been driving along that very road that very night and yes, he had seen something lying in the road that he thought 'to be a tree branch'. According to his somewhat fanciful testimony, he stopped his car and discovered it to be a body, but claimed that Sgt Rosser had been knocked down *by some vehicle previously* and told the judge, Lord Justice Mackinnon, that he had taken 'all possible steps to acquaint the police and RAF authorities.' His efforts to acquaint anyone, or even call an ambulance, didn't seem to be on record anywhere, and surely it was the gravity of the offence and the gentility of the court which, at this point in his testimony, curtailed cynical laughter or derisive hoots. His Lordship, not surprisingly, found Parker-Jervis's explanation 'unsatisfactory'. In fact, the judge concluded from the evidence that not only had Parker-Jervis hit the poor fellow and knocked him down, but that his car had then actually dragged Rosser's body along the road some fifty-nine feet. Sgt Rosser survived, just, but had to be discharged from the RAF. Capt Robert St Vincent-Parker-Jervis, found guilty, was compelled to compensate Eric Rosser 'for the loss of services' by paying all of £172. *3s. 1d.* with costs. Some compensation, you might think! But that was not the last to be heard of this 'well-known amateur steeple-chase rider and owner', as the papers called him, who was clearly better off on a horse than behind a wheel.

When Colonel Lennox John Livingstone-Learmouth returned home from military service in France, he discovered that his wife Pamela, daughter of the Honourable Lady Howard of Thornbury Castle in Gloucestershire, was not in residence keeping the home fires burning in his London flat. In fact he discovered that no sooner had he been posted abroad in the service of King and Country, than Pamela had hot-footed it to the Cotswolds and had spent the last of the war years at Hartwell Farm in Poulton in the intimate company of none other than that famous rider Capt. Robert St Vincent-Parker-Jervis. The distressed Col Livingstone-Learmouth divorced Pamela in 1945 on the grounds of adultery, citing Parker-Jervis as co-respondent, and was given the custody of their child and awarded costs against his wife and her posh Poulton lover, which one hopes came to more than £172. *3s. 1d*. A year later the Captain married the ex-Mrs. Livingstone-Learmouth, but the cuckolded Colonel had been, in a manner of speaking, yet another victim of a Parker-Jervis hit-and-run.

Fowl Play

In 1946 our friend Captain Parker-Jervis was back in the news again, but this time in a different role – not as a defendant, but as prosecutor – pressing charges against a Poulton lad of 23, Private Ralph Adams of the REME, for stealing five sacks of barley from his field at Hartwell Farm, valued at £10. Pte Adams was also accused of stealing 550 lbs. of potatoes, valued at £1. *17s. 6d*. from another farm in Ampney Crucis and admitted the thefts after the tyre tracks found in the field matched those of a two-wheel trailer discovered at Adams' house in Poulton. In a Cirencester court, Pte Adams told the magistrate that when he came back to Poulton on leave he read that potatoes were likely to be rationed and 'as they at home had but few' he took the 5 cwt sacks 'on the spur of the moment'. As for stealing a half a ton of barley from Parker-Jervis, Adams told the court that 'it was intended to feed the fowls.' The young soldier then added that he 'did not realise that he would not require so much.' The Bench decided to bind him over for two years in the sum of £5. As a footnote, in 1949 Capt. Robert St Vincent-Parker-Jervis was called before the Stewards of the National Hunt Committee and was disqualified from hunting under the National Hunt rules and from riding in point-to-point steeplechases. Fancy that! Disqualified from riding but *not* from driving.

Capt. Robert St Vincent-Parker-Jervis well out of the saddle, and well out of favour with the racing/hunting authorities

A New Mistress at the Priory

After losing his wife, eldest son and only daughter in the London blitz, villagers claimed that Major Alec Mitchell went into a deep depression and scarcely ever left the confines of his Victorian mansion, though his son Ian responded to this by saying that due to shortages at the end of the war, everyone's social life was much curtailed and that his father 'like every one else lived a very quiet life; any social evening was restricted to the nearest of neighbours'. In any case, by 1946 he was venturing down to Poulton House for bridge evenings, which his friend Lord Banbury organised specially, it has been said, to get the Major out and about again.

Also living in Poulton at the time was Mrs Violette Worsley, whom contemporary villagers described as being a merry widow with a large wardrobe of fashionable frocks and a shrewd eye for self-improvement. Mrs Worsley found her way into the Priory and eventually into Major Mitchell's heart which, according to local gossip, was via his bedroom. They were soon engaged and this liaison certainly kept

Poulton tongues wagging. Perhaps because the villagers had been so fond of the first Mrs Mitchell, they may have been prejudiced against this woman whom they saw as a gold-digging adventuress, but certainly she was not a contender for any popularity contest in Poulton. Throughout the duration of their engagement, so the author was told, she was charm itself, and enchanted all the Major's friends, but the moment that little gold band was fixed on her finger, and she was the second Mrs Mitchell of Poulton Priory, the veneer of niceness eroded with a vengeance. Said one villager: 'The fact that Violette Mitchell's first husband had actually committed suicide during their honeymoon just may speak for itself'.

Ian Mitchell, the Major's only surviving heir

Queenie Ball told the story of Major Mitchell coming to see her shortly before she married Des Little. 'What would you like for a wedding present, Queenie?' he asked. 'A set of chairs, perhaps?' Queenie was touched by his generosity. Later Violette Mitchell came in to the post office where Queenie worked, holding a very ordinary glass vase. 'Here's your wedding present', she said ungraciously, and slammed it down on the counter so hard that Queenie feared it would shatter.

Gracious is not a word that springs to many lips when speaking of the second Mrs Mitchell. In fact someone close to the Mitchell family said 'I've never met anyone who liked her.' People felt she made life hell for the Major's son, Ian, who was a young man of twenty when she took command of the Priory. Sources close to the family reported considerable conflict between son and stepmother; for whatever reason, old Alec bought Ian a house near Tetbury, seeing him at odd times when Violette was away.

Major Mitchell died in 1972. At the reading of his will, the gathering was stunned to discover that he had left the Priory not to Ian, as everyone expected, but the whole kit and caboodle went to Violette. According to widespread Poulton legend, the Major had revised his will in the last few months of his life when, by all reports, he was not compos mentis. Not only did the former Mrs Worsley get the Priory estate, but apparently every stick of furniture and all the Mitchell family heirlooms. According to one member of the Mitchell family, Ian asked Violette if he could at least have his mother's writing desk for sentimental reasons. Violette told him that it had strangely disappeared and she couldn't imagine what had happened to it. Sometime later Ian Mitchell was a guest in the house of a distant relation of Violette and behold, there was his late mother's writing desk – a gift to them from Violette. It's said that Violette in fact gave Ian nothing of his family's possessions, and when she put them up for public auction Ian was compelled to buy back some of the items he had grown up with. The dealers who also attended the auction apparently knew of the sad situation and magnanimously withheld their bids on those lots that Ian specially treasured.

Violette Mitchell, it is reported, had promised Ian she would leave what remained of his father's possessions to him when she died, but in fact she left everything to a very distant relation of hers. The older Poulton villagers who knew and thought so highly of the Mitchell family expressed sadness that Ian was cut out of Poulton Priory which, they felt, was his birthright.

Poulton Pilot Sets New World Record

Eric Greenwood (*left*), the chief test pilot of the Gloucester Aircraft Company was living at *Ranbury Farm,* Poulton, in 1945 when he broke the world's air speed record, flying that company's latest jet, *The Meteor,* at a speed of 603 m.p.h.

Fresh Blood in Post-War Poulton

After the war, the village welcomed a flow of new settlers who added a certain amount of distinction and colour to the drab post-war years. A considerable number of new residents were eminent military figures; others were distinguished in a variety of other fields, but in any case, these years saw the balance of Poulton life swing away from the agricultural community it had been for centuries to the far more cosmopolitan and diverse village it is today.

Dr R. Edgar Hope-Simpson and his wife moved from Cirencester to Packhorse House, Poulton in 1947, where they remained for thirty years. Dr. Hope-Simpson set up a small research group in Cirencester to study common infectious diseases such as influenza, shingles and the common cold, working closely with Peter Higgins, a consultant who also lived in Poulton. During his years in Poulton, Dr Hope-Simpson published numerous articles in the world's most prestigious scientific journals and travelled the world lecturing on his 'sometimes controversial and provocative ideas'. In 1992 he published a definitive work: *The Transmission of Epidemic Influenza*, which *The Lancet* reported to be 'a classic... the crowning achievement of a brilliant and modest man.' Hope-Simpson, however, considered his discovery of the cause of shingles in the 1960s to be his single most important contribution to medicine. In September, 1993, R. Edgar Hope-Simpson, OBE, was given an Honorary Fellowship of the Faculty of Public Health Medicine and was recognised as the world's foremost authority in the field of epidemiology. When the author went to see him, he had recently suffered ill-health and had undergone major surgery, which he described with great good humour, saying: 'I went into hospital with a colon and came out with only a semi-colon, but that's still a lot better than a full stop.'

Dr Edgar Hope-Simpson, OBE, who lived at Packhorse House for thirty years.
Photo: Abbey Studios

Naval Commander John Mackay came to live in Poulton with his wife Marjorie in 1947, the same year that the Hope-Simpsons arrived. Mackay's father, who lived at Cann Court down the road at Ampney St Peter, was a principal landowner in this area and in Poulton owned The Malt House, which was let to two elderly ladies, Mrs Lister and Mrs Alexander; The Paddocks, where a Miss Stevens lived; Packhorse House, which he sold to the Hope-Simpsons; and Ranbury Farm, where his son, the Commander, and Mrs Mackay settled. Dr Hope-Simpson reported that the whole village would quake from tremendous explosions in the fields around Ranbury Farm. The cause turned out to be Commander Mackay dynamiting dozens of trees he wished to get rid of to clear the fields. His widow told me that they didn't think anything of it at the time as the Commander, with his military background, assumed that using explosives was the normal way of dispensing with unwanted trees.

The Strange and Suspect Death of Mrs Gassor

Mrs Gertrude Gassor, aged 31, lived in the post-war years with her husband Benjamin Gassor, a painter and decorator, at Green Close, Poulton, which was then called Gable Cottage. One Tuesday evening at 7.30 p.m., Mrs Gassor sipped a glass of home-made wine, and then at 9.30, after her supper, she drank a cup of cocoa. According to her husband, she complained of feeling unwell soon after they had gone to bed. 'It must have been either the home-made wine or the cocoa,' he told her, but according to his testimony at the inquest, she had replied '*It was the stuff in the jar.*' She died an hour later, just as the doctor arrived from Cirencester. Death was attributed to poisoning by sodium nitrate, a toxic substance that causes methaemoglobinaemia which turns blood chocolate brown, turns skin blue and can dispatch an imbiber in minutes. The doctor said it was used, so far as he knew, only for industrial treatment of skins. Benjamin Gassor testified that he found a jar of sodium nitrate in the house after his wife's death.

Miss Alma Jobbins lived in the small house next door to the Gassors, which is today still known as Alma's Cottage. She was the sister of Harry Jobbins, the tailor, and of Lavinia (Doll) Adams, the baker's wife, who lived across the road in The House on the Corner. Alma had left Poulton at a youngish age, had worked as a civil servant in London until retirement, and had only recently returned to the village. In London she had moved in theatrical circles, and she often entertained artistes of various kinds at her cottage in Poulton. One frequent weekend guest was the BBC radio comedian Nosmo King, well known for the legendary derivation of his professional name from the NO SMOKING sign that ran across the doors of railway carriages, which, when opening, separated the notice between the second O and the K.

At the inquest into Mrs Gassor's bizarre death, Alma Jobbins, as the Gassors' only close neighbour, became a key witness, and was called into the Coroner's court in Cirencester to be questioned about the relationship between Benjamin and Gertrude Gassor. She gave evidence that Mr and Mrs Gassor, so far as she knew, seemed happily married and there were no outward signs of marital discord.

Where had the industrial poison – *the stuff in the jar* – come from? It appears that Gertrude Gassor herself had

Green Close, as it was when it was called Gable Cottage, where Gertrude Gassor met her strange death beneath its roof. It has since been modified and modernised.

sent a note to Boots the Chemist's in Cirencester asking for 1 lb. of sodium nitrate. Before they got round to filling the order, she wrote to the chemist's yet again requesting the substance, so the manager of Boots, assuming that there was some urgency, had it delivered to Poulton by carrier. Why had a housewife ordered a toxic industrial chemical? Why had Boots supplied it without questioning the motive or application? And how did Mrs Gassor get the dose that dispatched her within an hour? Was it in the wine? The cocoa? Was it suicide? An accident? Or ...   A report on the internet says it is possible to kill someone by lacing his or her drink with as little as 2 grams of sodium nitrate which can cause death within a few minutes

The jury returned a verdict of insufficient evidence to show the reason why the poison was taken, but the foreman added a rider complaining about the easy manner in which it was obtained. Quite so, but the real answer to the strange death of Gertrude Gassor of Gable Cottage will doubtless never be known.

The Evolution of Poulton House

It is fairly common that the old houses of Poulton have been considerably altered and added to over the years. In this century, with the dwindling demand for farm labour and decreasing importance of agriculture altogether, many of the old farm buildings – barns, stables, tallets, malt houses, granaries and labourers' cottages – became redundant, so were joined together and/or converted into larger houses and additional living quarters for non-farming families. These alterations, of course, affected the value of the property as much as did the changing economic conditions in the country in general. The history of Poulton House is typical.

In the 1920s, what is now called Poulton House was a smallholding farm referred to as The Barn, owned by the Adams family, with their steam bakery at The House on the Corner next door. The dwelling was a typical Cotswold 'cross-passage' house, that is, the farmhouse and the barn had been built as one structure, separated by a passageway between them. There was an exterior door at each end of the passageway, one opening out onto Cricklade Street, and the other to the farmyard and stables behind.

Adams sold the barn, farmhouse, cottage, stables and land in 1926 for £360 to a widow, Agnes Chard, and it

Poulton House in 1930, when it was called 'the Barn'. All the right-hand half was still an old barn when this photo was taken by its then owner, Squadron Leader Aubrey Rickards. The barn was incorporated into the house in the 1930s, and an annexe for servants added to the left of what was an old 'cross-passage' smallholding farmhouse. below: Poulton House after the conversion. The farmyard was terraced and the garden landscaped by Mrs Campbell in the early 1950s. The author and family have lived there since 1986.

was never to be a working farm again. Mrs Chard in turn sold the house in 1930 for £400 to Squadron Leader Aubrey Rickards, OBE. It was during the 1930s that the 'front' door to the street was sealed off, and the walls of the cross-passage taken down to incorporate house and barn into one residential unit. The barn was converted into additional bedrooms and reception rooms, and an annexe was built on to the main house to provide servants' quarters, thereby nearly trebling both the size and the value of the property. The Barn, newly christened *Poulton House* in 1937, was sold as one residence for £1,100. The purchaser was Mrs Helena Rankin of Cirencester, who apparently bought the house as a wedding present for her son John, an Army Captain, and his fiancée Olivia Stanley, and they lived there during the war.

By 1946, the value of Poulton House had increased to £8,000, the price paid by the young, newly married peer, Charles William Banbury, son of the first Baron Banbury of Southam, also Charles William, who had been killed in action in World War I, and father of the present Lord Banbury, yet another Charles William (known as Bill), who owns the Coln Galleries in Fairford and Cirencester

Lord Banbury sold the house in 1949 to Lt. Col. Frederick Maule and his wife, Isobel, for £8,700 and she sold it a year later to the Honourable Mrs Duncan Campbell, who was to live in Poulton House for the next twenty-five years, before passing the property on to her son, Air Vice-Marshal Ian Campbell, CBE, who was in residence until 1986.

Florence Evelyn Campbell, like her good friend Lady Clarke, was a high-profile village character who left a legacy of amusing legends behind. Mrs Campbell was cut from the same cloth as those indomitable no-nonsense British ladies who used to stride around the Empire from Kisume to Rangoon on their own, armed only with an umbrella and an unwavering sense of rectitude. 'An old-fashioned battle-axe,' the late Revd Robert Nesham called her, but quickly added 'Felicite (his wife) and I adored her.' She apparently always spoke fortissimo 'like a squiress talking from the top of a horse,' said Nesham. Stephen Langton, Lady Clarke's son, describes her as a hail-fellow-well-met, who would accompany a hearty 'Good to see you, boy, have a drink,' with a mighty, manful slap on the back. He jokingly refers to her as Mrs. Drunken Campbell. Her notorious vocal projection caused a certain amount of amusement. Robert Nesham, who was the Vicar of Poulton for ten years, recalled the Sunday service when the whole congregation was startled to hear Evelyn Campbell's very audible gasp to her daughter-in-law. 'My God, darling...the blackberry pie!', and sent son Ian's wife scampering back to Poulton House to extract the pastry from the Aga.

At other times her megaphone voice caused her friends acute embarrassment as she had a habit of walking with them down the street giving decidedly unflattering views of various villagers, inevitably just as the subject of her disdain would be coming up the street in the opposite direction, well within earshot. This, however, didn't seem to faze the old girl, who was never timid about expressing her opinions, or tearing a strip off anyone who displeased her. The most frequent victims of her displeasure were the various vicars of Poulton, often for being too long-winded in the pulpit. If a sermon went on for more than ten minutes, Mrs Campbell would ostentatiously look at her watch, then rise from her pew, stumble past her row of worshippers, and march back to Poulton House to baste her Sunday joint. If, when she returned to the church, the vicar was still droning on, he was sure to get an earful of Campbellian deprecation on the porch steps after the service.

Worse was to be meted out if the vicar had employed one of the modern 'rites' services instead of sticking to the traditional language of the *Book of Common Prayer,* and there was hell to

The Hon. Mrs Duncan Campbell c.1970.

pay if she disapproved of the sentiments expressed from the pulpit – which was invariably the case when the sermon came from the poncey, pretentious Revd J.D. Gott, who was appointed Vicar of Poulton in 1966.

Poulton in the 1960s had an ex-military and war veteran residency that was extraordinarily large in relation to its total population of not much more than 300: Major Mitchell at the Priory, Major Sanford at the Manor, General Arkwright at Jenners, Major Lanyan at Butts Farm, Major Meredith at the Old Manor Farmhouse, Colonel Fisher at Jenners' Cottage, and Lt. Col. the Lord Wigram at Poulton Fields, to name but a prominent few. How peculiar then that the Diocese of Gloucester, in its wisdom, selected for

L. to R.: *The Revd H.S. Hutchinson, Vicar of Poulton 1949-1957; the Revd F.H.E. Tidmarsh, Vicar of Poulton 1957-1966; the Revd J. Desmond Gott, Vicar of Poulton 1966-1972*

this curacy Desmond Gott – a man whom they must have known was a fervent pacifist. As if that weren't irritant enough in a village full of old soldiers, Desmond Gott, a 'he-never-married' bachelor who had ensconced his parents at the Vicarage, also proclaimed anti-hunting views to his new parishioners, many of whom were farmers. If they themselves didn't actually ride to the hounds, and some did, at least they supported fox-control and the village's historic links with the V.W.H. Hunt. A still further annoyance was this new vicar's propensity to swan about the Vicarage and the village in a cassock, wishing to be addressed as 'Father Gott', which was considered a rather precious affectation for a rural village parson. At Down Ampney, where he was also Rector, they proved a more deferential lot and were happy to call him 'Father', but Poulton would have none of it. Lord Wigram told the story about the churchwarden, Mrs Miles, ringing up the Vicarage to discuss the following Sunday's service. The phone was answered by Desmond Gott's father.

'May I speak to Mr Gott, please,' she asked.

'This is Mr Gott,' replied the old man.

Mrs Miles then began asking about the service, but was quickly interrupted.

'You want to speak to *Father* Gott,' said Mr Gott Senior.

'No, no' replied Mrs Miles, 'I don't want to talk to Mr Gott's father, I want to speak to Mr Gott.

'This is Mr Gott.'

This sort of music hall or *'two Ronnies'* routine went on for a bit, until Mrs Miles finally said, in desperation: 'May I *please* speak to the Vicar.'

To be fair, not everyone disapproved of Desmond Gott. Queenie Ball said he was very well liked by the Methodists and she spoke very fondly of his mother – 'such a nice lady'. Unfortunately it was his own flock at the Poulton Parish Church who found him so unpalatable, and the attendance was seriously decreasing even before his amazing performance at Matins one Remembrance Sunday. The church was decorated with the traditional red poppies of Flanders' fields, as was customary for this solemn November occasion, and the faithful, including many war veterans, had gathered in good time to observe the annual two minutes of silence to remember the fallen, at precisely eleven o'clock. But where was the Vicar? At one minute before eleven, the pacifist Gott swished into the church and called for Churchwardens Owen Ash and Reg Adams to remove all the *Remembrance Sunday* decorations.

'I will not conduct a service so long as those poppies remain in the church,' he told them.

Owen Ash, who had lost a few relations in World War I, was, according to reports, close to tears, arguing that it was a hallowed tradition. Gott would not repent, and during the time the reverential silence should have been maintained, 'Father Gott' was bustling about supervising the clearing out of all 'symbols of war'. His service, perhaps needless to say, did not incorporate any reference to the two wars, traditional prayers for those killed in action, or the singing of the hymn *O Valiant Hearts,* written for the occasion by General Arkwright's cousin, and sung on this day in most other churches throughout England. Indeed, the subject Gott chose for his sermon that day was *'The Harvest'*.

This particular service emptied the pews at the Parish Church for many a Sunday to come. Lt. Col. the Lord Wigram defended continuing church attendance in Poulton by arguing in a loyal soldier's terms: 'Even if the C.O. is rotten, you have to stick by him because he's still the C.O.'

Lord Wigram's military ethic didn't for a moment wash with Mrs Campbell. So contemptuous was she of Desmond Gott that she abandoned the Poulton Church altogether in favour of services in Bibury until Gott was moved on to a parish in Cheltenham, where, acording to his successor, Revd Robert Nesham, he got up to the sort of News-of-the-World hanky-panky in the vestry that landed him a stretch in the slammer.

Before long, however, Mrs Campbell had her quarrels with the vicar in Bibury as well. Her son Ian told about a scene in Charlie Barnett's, the expensive fishmonger's that was then in the Cirencester Market Place. Mrs Campbell was ticking Charlie off about charging such extortionate prices for his cod's roe just as the vicar of Bibury came into the shop. Mrs Campbell had harboured considerable objections to the vicar's previous Sunday's sermon and had no intention of letting it pass without comment. Mid-sentence, she wheeled round to the cleric and trumpeted: 'Don't go away, Vicar. I'll deal with you in a moment,' then turned back to finish her diatribe on the price of fish.

'But her bark was worse than her bite,' said her son, and this is borne out by many who had dealings with her, including John Ash, who said that though 'she didn't suffer fools gladly' and would speak her mind without pandering to anyone's sensibilities, she would usually end up amiably offering the victim of her tongue-lashing a whisky and soda.

Mrs. Erica Mary Sanford says there was never anyone kinder, particularly to the village young, whom Mrs Campbell would often entertain for dinner at Poulton House as a way of getting them together.

She was a fanatical gardener, and it was she who designed and put in the impressive terraced gardens and specimen trees at Poulton House. When Major Mitchell died, Mrs Campbell offered her lovingly-tended garden as a site for the annual village summer fêtes, which for many years had been held at the Priory. Everyone in the village was welcomed.

In 1972, when Gott was replaced by Robert Nesham, Mrs Campbell happily returned to the Poulton Parish fold. Nesham had a long military background and was a Major before being ordained. Like Mrs Campbell's son Ian, he had spent much of the war in a Prisoner of War camp (he must have been the only vicar in England at that time to have a scorpion tattooed on his forearm). Here was a vicar of whom she could approve.

According to Nesham, she would command him and his wife Félicité to come to Sunday lunches on occasions of her choosing, and would use the opportunity to air her strongly-held views about matters diocesan as well as parochial. Her *bête noire* at the time was the then Bishop of Gloucester, whose left-wing posturing and politicking she abhorred. Over the Sunday joint she would wheel round to Nesham and bellow, 'Vicar, do you agree or do you not that the Bishop of Gloucester has no business whatever praying for rain in order to ruin the test match between England and South Africa?' Nesham let it be known to her that he had no intention of being dragged into siding with her against his employer. 'All right then, Vicar,' she replied, accepting Nesham's neutrality, 'but I shall continue to give you my views about him nonetheless.'

At one of these after-church lunches she told Nesham he must do something about the children's playing field opposite Poulton House (which had been a gift to the village from Sir David Gamble of Poulton Manor, in the 1950s). She complained that there were no nets for the goal posts so that footballs kept getting kicked into the road, which was a danger to the children. Nesham said he was powerless to do anything about it. 'What do you mean, *powerless?*', she thundered, 'You are the *Vicar*, aren't you?' Nesham pointed out that the playing field was administered by the elected Parish Council, not the church. Mrs Campbell pointed out she had already been down the bureaucratic route and found the Councillors unable or unwilling to deal with this complaint.

'Look here, Vicar,' said Evelyn Campbell, 'I'll buy one net if you buy the other.' Settled, and the playground goal posts soon had nets. (NB the nets have since vanished, and footballs again are kicked into Cricklade Street, which now has far more traffic than then).

Mrs Jack Shrive told of the time Mrs Campbell came into Edwards' General Store wearing a yellow garter around one leg. As she was leaving, Mrs Shrive asked her what it was for. 'Oh, thank you for pointing it out, my dear,' replied Evelyn Campbell in her booming voice. 'It's to remind me to buy a pound of sugar.'

In 1972, at the age of eighty, Evelyn Campbell suffered a fall in her house and broke her hip. It is said that she crawled over to the telephone and rang up everyone with whom she had social engagements for the following weeks to re-arrange lunches, teas, drinks and dinners. Only when her diary was duly in order did she phone for an ambulance to take her to hospital. Mrs Sanford said that the very day Evelyn Campbell returned from hospital, she nipped round to see if the old girl needed any help and found her out in the garden, clinging to her walking frame with one hand, while digging over the herbaceous border with the other. Needed help? Indeed not!

Evelyn Campbell was famous in the village for being the most appalling driver and had a long history of ramming her motor into various objects, both stationary and moving. On one occasion, according to her son, she ploughed into a car belonging to an RAF officer from Brize Norton. Surprisingly, the damage to her own car was minimal, but Wilf Freeth, who ran the Poulton garage where Elf Meadow now is, pronounced the officer's car a total write-off. Aware that the accident had been entirely her own fault, and fearing that yet another crash would place her insurance if not her driving licence in jeopardy, Mrs Campbell quickly said to the officer, 'Look here. Have mine!', and she handed the bemused man the keys to her own motor car and walked home. It was left to her son Ian, when he learned of the give-away, to buy her a replacement.

In 1975, Mrs Campbell moved to a flat in Preston. Before leaving Poulton, she gave a farewell party in her beloved garden to which she invited everyone in the village. Florence Evelyn Campbell died in 1978 at the age of 86, and Robert Nesham conducted a memorial service at Poulton Church, commending her kindness, humour, and her forthright defence of those standards she held to be of value. She was, by all accounts, a tough old bird and it was spot-on that the selection for the opening hymn was *'Fight the Good Fight.'* Her son, Air Vice-Marshal Ian Campbell, lived in Poulton House until the author and his family bought it in 1986.

September Romance for Queenie

Life-long Poulton resident Queenie Ball, who has been mentioned and quoted throughout this chapter, first married Desmond Little in 1950 and they enjoyed 31 happy years together. Des, who was 23 years older than Queenie, died in 1981, and after ten years of living alone, Queenie married her next door neighbour, Les Ball, 72.

Queenie and Les became engaged on Queenie's 70th birthday, in 1991, and they were married in the Poulton Parish Church three months later, after an interlude of high romance that fuelled an article in the popular national magazine, *Woman's Realm.*

Des and Queenie Little at their wedding in 1950. They enjoyed thirty-one happy years together.

Queenie told the reporter, Rebecca Gooch, 'Someone once told me when older people get married it's just for companionship. That's rubbish! We're proof that love can bowl you over at any age.'

The full-page article that appeared in *Woman's Realm* tells the story of their courtship in terms that can only be done justice by allowing Ms Gooch, Queenie and Les Ball their own words:

Love thy neighbour

'Wearily, Queenie Little pulled the curtains in her neat little sitting room. The clock on the mantelpiece said four, but it was already dark outside. Her heart sank. Another solitary evening in front of the television stretched ahead. It had been nine years since the death of her beloved husband Desmond. She'd learned to live with her grief but not the loneliness... "I'd pray for the hours to pass so that I could go to bed. It seemed my life was over. I was just waiting to go."

"Move house," her concerned doctor urged. But something told her to stay...

After retiring, gardener Les [Les Ball had been a gardener at Poulton Priory] moved into a bungalow next to Queenie's...sometimes when he was working in the garden he would see Queenie pegging out her washing. They would exchange a polite hello, then go their separate, lonely ways. Then, one drizzly day in September, Queenie was in front of her garden when the front door slammed shut...she was locked out. "Mr Ball, this damsel's in distress – can you help?" pleaded Queenie. Les managed to open a window for her to clamber through, but as he climbed back down the stepladder, their arms brushed. An electric tingle surged through their bodies.

"It was an extraordinary sensation," smiles Les. "Even after I'd gone back indoors the tingle was still there."

Soon they were spending evenings together... "One day we even had a dance

Queenie and Les Ball   Photo: Peter Stone

Queenie Little got locked out of her house and opened the door to a beautiful friendship

around the sitting room. It was wonderful" smiles Queenie. "I thought how lucky we were to be such good neighbours." She never imagined she was slowly falling in love with the "boy" next door.

On Remembrance Day Queenie cooked Les lunch. As she cleared away, gathering up all his courage, Les kissed her cheek. Queenie felt an unexpected thrill. "I went into the kitchen to wash up feeling quite shaken. I felt like a teenager. I really didn't think those things happened to older people." Les knew they did. He was in love with the kind, caring Queenie; she made him feel young and happy again.

On the way [home] he was struck by a sudden thought. "This is daft. Why am I walking up and down this path every day when we could be together all the time?" So the next day when he delivered Queenie's paper, he popped the question. Queenie was dumbfounded. "Wait until Valentine's Day" she said, and spent three weeks wondering what to do.

"Then one night as I stood in my nightie in the cold, peering through the window to check if Les had got back from a darts match safely, I thought, why have I left my warm bed? Why am I worried about him? Then I knew I loved him."

On Valentine's Day Queenie accepted Les's proposal. "Now I know why I felt I shouldn't move. Fate had something wonderful planned – and he moved in right next door!" **❞**

In 1988 Poulton won the Bledisloe Cup for being the best kept village in Gloucestershire. Poulton's senior resident, Mrs Freda Baylis, 91, then President and founder of the Poulton Women's Institute, accepted the award, which included £100 which was used to plant roses in the rose garden near the Post Office.

X
Poulton in the Twenty-First Century

Poulton has probably changed more since WWII than in the previous two or three centuries, and these momentous changes have taken place within the lifetime of a few elderly residents who will have seen the village changing so dramatically before their very eyes. Needless to say, Poulton reflects the changes that have taken place all over the Western world, both for better and for worse. It is certainly a far more prosperous and physically comfortable community than it was at the end of World War II, but in those days villagers could go out leaving their doors wide open without the slightest fear of intruders or theft. Even with all the modern security devices and alarms and Neighbourhood Watch, houses in the village are burgled every now and again. Poulton Church in the 1980s had a spate of out-of-village visitors who walked off with various items under their arms, including a table, and many in the village still remember the armed robbery at the Poulton Post Office in 1992; in 2009 the church's lawnmower was stolen from a locked shed, and there has been a spate of daytime burglaries at the time of writing in 2012.

The rise of private transport has made life a great deal easier for villagers, but the other side of the coin is that the same increase in motor car population has happened everywhere and the traffic explosion all over the country has turned the London Road into a mini-motorway. It's a safe guess that today more cars pass through the village in an hour than passed through in a day in pre-War Poulton – and at speeds that make crossing the London Road as dangerous as scaling the north face of the Eiger, particularly for the slow-moving elderly. The major grumble from Poulton residents seems to be the speed of drivers coming through the village, and all the warning signs and speed bumps installed haven't really made much difference. That the London Road, officially the A417, is a dangerous road is without question; hardly a year passes without at least one fatality on the stretch between Cirencester and Lechlade.

Anatomy of Poulton in 2009

In 1993 the author sent questionnaires to every Poulton household asking for anomymous information to give a picture of life in the village then, which appeared in the first edition. In 2009 a new questionnaire was sent out to the 174 households to bring the statistics up to date. As in 1993, only a little over a third of the residents returned the questionnaires, so the statistics may or may not accurately represent the village as a whole, but 34% is pehaps a better sample than many national polls achieve. The reader is left to judge the validity of the these statistics as there is no way of knowing which residents completed the forms and which two-thirds did not bother.

The Households

Whereas so many of the cottages used to belong to big estates like the Priory or Poulton Fields or Home Farm, and were inhabited by rent-paying tenants, our sample in 2009 showed 92% of the householders owned their own houses, and unlike other villages which have many cottages used as weekend 'holiday homes', Poulton has only one or two (though several residents offer 'holiday lets' cottages on their property). Otherwise the houses are principal homes, with the current population (2012) standing at 410, of which roughly 100 are children and 100 are pensioners.

In 1993 Mrs Baylis recalled the days when there was one electric cooker in the entire village and only three light bulbs allowed in any one house. The 2009 poll showed 93% of all houses had central heating and every household but one had a washing machine and a television – in fact there were nearly 3 TV sets per household – and 86% also had at least one

DVD recorder, 80% of the households had a dishwasher, 90% had a microwave oven, and households averaged 1.7 personal computers each, nearly all on internet broadband. Of pets, 38% of householders owned dogs (some more than one) and 21% kept cats; other pets listed ranged from the predictable, commonplace guinea pigs, hamsters, rabbits and fish to the more bizarre; one household reported lizards and snakes as their family pets.

Transport and Travel

Before World War II, private cars were few and most of the population relied on Tommy and Des Little's Poulton Bus to get into Cirencester. In 2012, there are five regular buses a day into Cirencester for those who rely on public transport, but they are few and their numbers are dwindling. All but one household in our sample had at least one private car and enough families had two or more to bring the average to 1.8 cars per household (and that's not counting one Poulton obsessive collector who owns over 20 cars of various marques and vintages).

One legendary former resident, a student at the Royal Agricultural College, actually commuted from Poulton to his classes in Cirencester in his private helicopter, kept in a field in Bell Lane. The story goes that after his driving licence was suspended for a year, his rich daddy provided the helicopter to overcome his son's imposed immobility [if you can't drive – fly!]. The young man's neighbours, who had their serenity shattered every time he took off or landed, were greatly relieved when he finally flew out of Poulton for the last time.

Whereas a trip up to London was, in times past, a fairly major journey for the village folk, even in 1993, 70% of the population travelled abroad at a rate of 2.3 times during the year. 50% of those took their holidays in countries on the Continent of Europe, and the other 50% went on long haul journeys to Africa, Asia, Australia, the West Indies and, most commonly and frequently, to the United States.

Employment and Business

Aside from the villagers who are retired, only three in our

sample were temporarily unemployed. Of those still working (in jobs other than 'housewife'), 33% travelled elsewhere to work, primarily to London, Cirencester, Swindon, Oxford, and Cheltenham and one commuted to Sheffield.

Education and medicine were the most common occupations, while other residents listed employment in the broad fields of sales, business, architecture, catering, accountancy, admin, law, engineering, journalism and defence. Very few are now engaged in any form of agriculture in this formerly farming community.

Businesses

There are a number of commercial enterprises located in the village at the time of writing: the commercial glasshouses at the Butts, which cultivate alstroemeria for florists (but locals can pop in to pick up a bunch or two at favourable retail prices) and F. Pitt and Sons, builders and Main-Care building services at Betty's Grave; there are several Bed and Breakfast houses, and in Bell Lane Yard there is Bell SAS, a secretarial agency, Hoh Ltd. internet services, George Newman's Timber Preservation company and mechanic Trevor Carr's Poulton Workshops, a car repair and servicing garage popular for local MOTs. In recent years new office and workshop units have been created for small businesses. The Priory estate has developed *Priory Court* as a business park that houses

commercial greenhouses for alstroemeria at the Butts

Priory Court business park, home of various new offices from computer software developers to language translation services.

14 offices of various kinds including computer systems and software companies, a commercial property agency, a language translation service, a surveyor and a sales and marketing company, and in *Butts Courtyard*, where Performance Cycles offers a comprehensive service for bikes and cyclists from sales and repair to sports massage and coaching.

Performance Cycles, a cycling centre in the Butts Courtyard

Education

Our 2009 sample showed that 42% had their secondary education at a comprehensive (or its equivalent) state school and 31% at state grammar schools. 27% were educated privately at independent schools. 66% of this sample reported they had gone on to institutions of higher education – universities, colleges or polytechnics – where they achieved a degree, diploma, or professional qualifications of one kind or another.

Religion

63% of Poulton adults from our sample listed the Church of England as their religious preference. Of the others, 8% were Roman Catholic, and 4% belonged to other Christian sects, primarily Baptist and Methodist. No other religions were cited, but 13% claimed they were atheists and 12% ticked agnostic (a considerable increase since the 1993 poll) and the remaining entered 'none'. Church attendance was another matter; 20% of those who claimed C of E affiliation said they didn't attend even one church service during a year, and of the 80% who did, the average was 15.5 services each. Only two-thirds of the Roman Catholics attended masses, but those who did averaged 23.6 annual attendances each. The assorted Protestants averaged 7.4 church services over the year.

Poulton Parish Church

Attendance at St. Michael and All Angels' church, like Anglican churches all over the land, has been steadily declining, and today a church that was built to accommodate a congregation of 290, only fills about 5% to 10% of those pews at ordinary Sunday services. In 1994 the Poulton vicar was also in charge of four other parish churches. Since then the benefice has increased to six other churches, as well as attending to the pastoral needs of the Royal Agricultural College in Cirencester, as the thin red line becomes more and more stretched.

It is nothing new that Poulton's vicars have caused controversy and have divided the congregation, none more than the pacifist anti-hunting vicar 'Father' Gott. The appointment of Annette Woolcock as vicar in 2000 indeed caused some dissention amongst some Poulton parishioners, not perhaps only because she was the first woman priest, but many traditional worshippers were unhappy about her style of liturgy, which incorporated new hymns and modern litany with the inclusion of often noisy children at normally adult communion services. This suited a number of younger church-going families, but disturbed many older members who preferred traditional hymns and the more elegant prose of the *Book of Common Prayer,* some of whom quit Poulton to find services more to their liking elsewhere in the area. Our research shows that 66% of churchgoers exclusively worship in the Poulton benefice but 23% go elsewhere to attend Anglican services with other vicars. 11% seem to go back and forth. In any case, for whatever reasons, Annette Woolcock resigned the benefice and in 2011 was replaced by the Rev. John Swanton, who seems, as of now, well-received by all factions.

The financial demands of the Poulton church is a perennial concern – not just the upkeep of the physical structure of St Michael's, but the very appreciable sums of money the church is required to send as dues to the Diocese of Gloucester. For its continued existence, the church stalwarts are forced to stage a number of fund raising events every year to try to keep St Michael's functioning for what amounts to be only one or two services in Poulton per month. It would doubtless be far more practical to amalgamate a number of the local parishes and make the smaller seldom-used or sparsely-attended churches redundant, but, understandably, no village wants to close down its own historic church, so the desperation for funding will no doubt continue well into the foreseeable future.

Poulton Rates Poulton

The questionnaire asked the residents to rate the village on a scale of 0 to 10 for Friendliness, Community Spirit, Amenities and Activities. The results of our sample are expressed in averages:

Friendliness: 7.5
Community Spirit 8.6
Amenities: 7.0
Activities: 6.7

Two householders entered zero for both amenities and activities. This may be somewhat surprising to a number of residents who gave a rating of 10 for both categories and might with some justification believe that Poulton offers rather more amenities and activities than other villages in the area.

The questionnaire allowed space for people to write comments about the village if they so desired. Not many did, but the most common complaint was the amount of traffic through the village, particularly buses, and called for more controls to curb speeding. There were also grievances that not enough of the residents participate in village affairs and that too many villagers drop litter and one complained of teenage behaviour. There were also individual requests for the village to provide free Wi-Fi, street lamps, table tennis in the evenings, a garden club and social networking.

POULTON PROVISIONS

A valuable amenity; a well-stocked local shop and post office is a rarity in villages today. Since David and Deborah Fowles took over the shop, the premises and the stock have been greatly expanded. The village wishes them success.

An important element of English village life - a friendly pub that serves food and drink to travellers and locals alike.

The Falcon Inn

Poulton's only village pub since the the *New Inn* ale house closed down in 1958 has had a volatile history in the past twenty or so years; the publicans have come and gone at a great rate, many of them extremely unsuitable as 'mine host' of a village pub. In the 1990s the freehold was bought by Tatyan, a Chinese restaurateur from Cirencester, and for some time he and his relations were in the kitchen offering excellent Chinese cuisine, unique to country pubs, but when he went back to his Cirencester restaurant leaving a series of less than proficient local English cooks in charge, the food went rapidly downhill. When the pub was near its nadir, a pair of young men, one of whom was an established chef, bought it from Tatyan and turned it into a gastro-pub, serving *haute cuisine* at predictably *haute* prices. Out went the darts board and the skittles alley; the drinking areas, formerly popular with laddish locals, the ladies' darts team and thirsty ramblers, became candle-lit dining-only areas that left little space or welcome for the beer and crisps crowd. The Falcon Inn virtually became an up-market restaurant.

As long as these proprietors were there, the standard of the food was high and the pub flourished in its new role as a posh eatery. In time however the young publicans wanted to move on and sold it to a giant chain of pub owners, *Enterprise Inns*, who leased it to a feckless manager, and down it sank again, hitting rock bottom in 2007 when the company was forced to close the Falcon completely, leaving it dark and deserted for the best part of eight months, to the great consternation of most Poulton residents who, even those who had never been frequent customers, felt a functioning pub essential to the soul of an English village.

In July 2008 the Falcon Inn re-opened, leased by a married couple, but within six months they had squandered a lot of local goodwill. A successful pub needs a full-time hands-on landlord and/or landlady who knows and welcomes their customers personally and is open daily and remains open until the expected closing time, customers or no. This, alas, was not so when it was managed by this pair of publicans. When the disgruntled locals thinned out, and the turn-over plumetted accordingly, they put the lease back on the market, but failing to find a new leaseholder for a business in the red, they scarpered, and the Falcon closed down yet again.

By January 2009, the freehold owners, Enterprise Inns, were reported to be massively in debt and the future of the Falcon Inn was looking very bleak indeed. However disappointing the last publicans had been, few Poulton residents would wish the pub to close forever and be converted into a private residence, as has happened to so many other village pubs in the last few years. Fortunately Natalie and Gianni Gray came along and bought the pub freehold, so it is again open, described by them as *"A traditional British country dining pub with a focus on locally brewed cask ales, an interesting wine list and classic English dishes"*. We all hope the Falcon Inn will continue to flourish as a convenient family restaurant as well as a watering hole, as it has been since the stagecoaches to London stopped by for a pint of ale, a hot meal and a fresh team of horses.

The Village Hall

Ever since 1932, when Major Mitchell presented Poulton with a barn to be converted into the village hall, the building has served a wide variety of uses – a hub of village life instrumental in bringing the community together. Not only did dances in the hall keep spirits up during World War II, but it even served then as a dormitory for evacuees when Poulton's child population trebled as a result of the bombing of London. It has been the site, too, of many a national celebration, from VE Day festivities in 1945 and celebrations to mark the Coronation of Queen Elizabeth II in 1953, to a dinner dance for the Queen's Golden Jubilee in 2002 and a barbecue lunch and festive dinner with cabaret to celebrate the Queen's Diamond Jubilee in 2012.

Today the hall provides the venue for many meetings and community projects: the occasional harvest suppers, quiz nights, horse race evenings, Christmas fêtes and gala evenings with seasonal musical entertainment, Burns Night suppers with Scottish reeling and other themed dinners with cabaret and dancing.

The hall is the venue for the monthly meetings of the Women's Institute and the Poulton Parish Council, the rural cinema film nights, two weekly

Poulton children celebrate the Coronation of Elizabeth II in 1953 at a tea party in the hall. In 2002 the Queen's Golden Jubilee was celebrated with a dinner dance.

60 years on, Poulton residents celebrate the Queen's Diamond Jubilee by coming together in the hall for the Big Lunch barbecue on 3 June, 2012.

playgroups for toddlers, weekly 'keep fit' classes, practice sessions of the Poulton table tennis team, and a meeting place for a Youth Club. In addition, it is regularly hired out for private birthday parties, post-funeral receptions, as a rehearsal hall for drama groups and stage productions, and used as the polling station for local and general elections.

Ukrainian bass Vasily Sevenko sings at 'An Evening in Kiev', 1993 – dinner with cabaret raised thousands of pounds for medicine for child victims of Chernobyl.

Burns Night Gala suppers held in the village hall in '95, '96. '98 '02 '04 & '06 (left) *Tom and Sally Boyd present the steaming haggis for William Bell to deliver the traditional Burns address to the 'Great chieftain o the puddin'-race'.* (right) *After-dinner reeling to a live Scottish band.*

In 1995, the author and his wife Sally founded Poulton Productions, a not-for-profit organisation designed to create, sponsor and promote live entertainment and to raise funds for charities and worthy projects. The first few of these events provided the money to buy an electric piano and stage lighting for the hall, which enabled a large number of musical entertainments to take place, from jazz bands to opera, including two village productions, *Party Pieces* in 1995 and the Victorian *Poulton Music Hall* in 1996.

'An Evening in New Orleans' – dinner and dixieland jazz to fund stage lights and a new electric piano

POULTON VILLAGE LOCAL TALENT SHOWS

(above) *PARTY PIECES* **1995** - l to r, *three young Poulton housewives as The Supremes; the Diddymen; The Women's Institute Can-Can, and the Oldies chorus.* Below: *THE POULTON MUSIC HALL 1996. The shows played to packed houses for three performances each.*

THE POULTON MUSIC HALL (clockwise) The Chairman, Stephen Langton, introduces the famous and traditional Victorian music hall numbers performed by local talent: *Daddy Wouldn't Buy Me a Bow Wow; You Are My Honeysuckle, I Am the Bee; Any Old Iron; There Was I, Waiting at the Church; The Man who Broke the Bank at Monte Carlo; Daisy Bell (A Bicycle Made for Two)*

Poulton in the Twenty-first Century

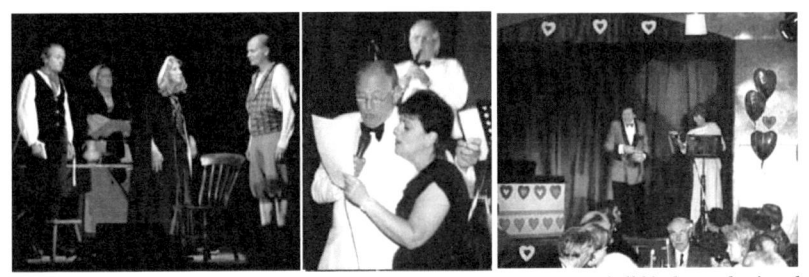

Since 1995 Poulton Productions has to date produced over 60 events of all kinds, professional and amateur. (l to r) *The Festival Players' production of* Cathleen ni Houlihan *by W. B. Yeats; Kathy Folkestad and Stephen Langton sing hits from 1952 at the Queen's Jubilee dinner; the author and his wife host a candle-lit Valentine's Day dinner with cabaret for charity.*

Bel Canto Opera performed several operas with orchestra in the hall: (l to r) **Doctor Miracle** *by Bizet,* **The Impresario** *by Mozart, and* **Trouble in Tahiti** *by Leonard Bernstein*

Anup Kumar Biswas, the distinguished Indian cellist, with children from the Mathieson Music School, Calcutta, performed at several Indian buffet dinners to raise funds for the school.

(l to r) *Royal harpist to the Prince of Wales, Jemima Phillips, played at several Christmas Festive Evenings; in 2008, a production of the West End musical* Chess, *and, in 2009,* the Best of Broadway, *a musical revue staged in the hall by the Rolling Stock Theatre Company*

In 2006, the hall received a generous grant that enabled the committee to put in central heating, buy more comfortable upholstered chairs to replace the hard wooden ones that were handed down when the village school closed, and to instal a large cinema screen, electrically lowered to fill the stage area, plus DVD projection equipment and broadband installation. Stuart Russell and his late wife Liz formed the Poulton *One 'n' Nine Club* to show one or two movies every month, from Hollywood blockbusters to art house films. Though opinions quite naturally differ about the choice of films, attendance has been steady enough for the *One 'n' Nine Club* to be considered a successful and welcome addition to village social life.

The Children's Playground

Those finicky fellows from the Health and Safety Executive, whose goal is to remove the slightest hint of risk from every detail of our lives, decided, in the 1990s, that the swings, slides, carousel etc. in the Poulton children's playground, which had been used without known accident for several past generations of Poulton children, were too dangerous for today's more fragile kiddies. Thus was the Parish Council compelled to replace all the apparati with new, and of course very expensive, equipment. As a result of the renovation, the Poulton playground now boasts a far wider variety of facilities for tots, toddlers and teens – including a picnic table and benches for exhausted grannies.

Poulton's Mediaeval Michaelmas Festival
27th and 28th September, 1997

In the *Mediaeval Poulton* chapter of this book, there is reference to the Diocese of Salisbury appointing Thomas de Lecchelade first rector of Poulton in 1297, the same year King Henry III confirmed Nicholas de St Maur as hereditary Lord of Poulton Manor, granting Poulton the right to stage a yearly fair at Michaelmas, from 28th to 30th September. It was Geoff Chapman, a mover and shaker in most Poulton institutions, who came to the author with the idea of marking the 700th anniversary of these events by staging a mediaeval celebration for all the village. Most of the residents took to the idea and entered into the spirit by flying colourful heraldic flags from their houses and many dressed themselves and their children in mediaeval costume for the weekend.

Costumed residents assemble for the grand opening parade

The ceremonies began at noon on the Saturday with a parade down the London Road from Bell Lane junction to the cricket grounds, pausing at the fair's centrepiece – a large marquee erected on the children's playgound in Cricklade Street, to raise the flag of St George and officially proclaim the start of the two-day Michaelmas festivities.

The procession passes the Falcon Inn and halts in Cricklade Street to hoist St George's flag to mark the beginning of the Poulton Michaelmas Fair.

There were stalls and entertainments of all kinds at Englands, the cricket grounds, and a variety of games for all ages: archery, walking the greasy pole and, for the heartier men (and surprisingly for a few intrepid ladies) a rough-and-tumble football match using mediaeval rules and a ball made of a pig's bladder, a sport which caused the odd minor casualty amongst players and spectators who were too close to the playing area.

A few plucky lasses joined the lads for a rough-and-tumble game of mediaeval football with a pig's bladder.

At night guests attended a mediaeval banquet in a marquee lined with heraldic coats of arms; a whole sheep was roasted on a spit, the meat washed down with mead, and diners were presented with a wooden spoon, rustic pottery mugs and earthenware plates specially potted for the event. Entertainment was provided by a troupe of professional jugglers, jousters, broad-sword fighters and strolling troubadours. After dinner, local thespians presented the famous mediaeval morality play *Everyman*, with a finale of human skeletons performing the *Dance of Death*.

A troupe of professional minstrels, jugglers, jousters and knights errant entertained nobly at the banquet.

Michaelmas Fair organisers Tom and Sally Boyd and Geoff and Rosemarie Chapman watch the Dance of Death (right) *that concluded the mediaeval morality play* **Everyman**

Michaelmas Festival
Sunday, 28th September, 1997

The Sunday festivities began with an *al fresco* church service at the ancient cemetery at Poulton Priory where the original 13th century parish church stood, and the earliest Poultonians were hatched, matched and dispatched.

The vicar Peter Naylor holds a service on the spot where Poulton's first appointed rector said mass at St. Michael's 700 years before.

In the afternoon the children's playground became the centre of re-enactment jollity, with a falconer giving flying displays with his birds of prey, and all sorts of games for the kiddies. Stalls and period tents sold reproduction trinkets and served refreshments, and the

*The Sunday fair catered for all ages, with games, competitions, refreshments and entertainments typical of the middle-ages. (*far right) *the professional falconer explained the training of birds of prey and demonstrated with flying displays of owls and falcons.*

locals were greeted by a dancing bear, which proved contentious to say the least. That it was actually – and fairly obviously – an actor in a bear suit did not mitigate the disapproval of some local vigilantes from the RSPCA who made angry protests in telephone calls and letters to the *Wilts & Glos Standard* claiming that even the representation of a dancing bear, albeit a human in a bear costume, was

The offending dancing bear and his keeper

231

offensive to their principles and demeaning to the dignity of all living members of the bear species throughout the world. The letters provoked humorous replies to the *Standard* from some supportive Poulton residents, followed by more rant from the animal welfare ladies which went on for some weeks, getting nuttier and funnier and providing more entertainment than the offending dancing bear itself. Surprisingly in this day and age no member of the bear community has filed a complaint about the indignity and claimed compensation from a tribunal for the specist insult. Those who missed the fabulous Michaelmas centenary celebrations will have to hang around till 2097 for the next one.

The children's playground decked out in mediaeval splendour for the Michaelmas fair

Poulton Gold

In September 2004 a spectacular discovery of 3000-year-old Bronze Age articles was found by a metal detectorist in an isolated field in Poulton. A survey and excavation was carried out by the Gloucestershire County Council Archaeology Service to retrieve the remainder of the hoard (which dates back to 1300 BC and included 67 fragments of gold jewellery), and to investigate the location to try to find out how and why the very rich assemblage of gold had been buried in that place. Most of the gold objects are fragmentary which makes it difficult to determine the number and type of objects represented. Analysis by experts surmised that (above) *A Bronze Age knife, part of the hoard found in an isolated field.*

(left), *the 3000-year-old Poulton Gold, now on display at the Corinium Museum in Cirencester.*

the objects include torc fragments, finger-ring fragments, bracelet fragments, penannular rings, sheet gold-work and the tip of a bronze spearhead. In addition, three of the bronze objects can be described as tools, possibly used for applying decoration to gold objects. The stash also includes an unusually large bronze tanged knife which could have been used for cutting up artefacts. No one knows whether it was an offering to the gods, buried for safe keeping but never reclaimed, or just a load of old scrap waiting to be melted down for other purposes. The gold was assessed and recorded as Treasure at the British Museum and the proceeds of the sale were split between the landowner and the finder.

The Cotswold District Council-owned Corinium Museum in Cirencester launched a £20,000 appeal [The *Going for Gold* appeal] to buy the hoard in October 2006, and museum staff were impressed by the response. The *Wilts. & Glos Standard* reported in March, 2007: 'The 3,000-year-old gold arrived at the [Corinium] museum last week after a successful fundraising campaign to buy the gold and keep it in the Cotswolds. Public donations of over £3,000 rolled in during the first three months enabling the museum to secure £17,000 worth of grant money from the MLA/V&A Purchase Fund, The Headley Trust and The National Art Fund'. John Paddock, Cotswold District Council's Curator of Museums, was quoted as saying: 'We are thrilled that public support

Dr John Paddock, then curator of the Corinium Museum, displays the stash of Poulton Gold

for the appeal has enabled us to buy the only known collection of Bronze Age gold-work from the Cotswolds. Local donations were the key to securing the grant funding. We couldn't have done it without the support of residents and visitors to the museum'.

But not all had been smooth sailing in those Poulton fields; a degree of in-fighting appears to have gone on between the Gloucestershire archaeologists and the finder of this unique Treasure Trove. The detectorist Steve Taylor, a gardener from Cheltenham, complained *'After the discovery of the Poulton hoard, which should have been the find of a lifetime, I felt I had been treated unfairly by the archaeologist involved in the excavation'*, who, he claimed had made various unsubstantiated accusations against him. *'After this incident'*, he wrote, *'I will never work with the archaeologists again, and has certainly tainted my view of them'*.

One such accusation by a Gloucestershire Council Sites and Monuments Records Officer, Tim Grubb, is posted on the Hidden Treasure website: *'I will be frank, I have enough evidence to consider him [Taylor] a nighthawk'* (a metal detectorist who illegally steals antiquities without the landowner's permission). About the accusations, Taylor replied *'If it hadn't been for the high cost of litigation and the time involved in a long protracted court case, these people would have been sued through the courts for libel'*.

A team of Gloucestershire archaeologists on the site of the Poulton dig in 2005

Whatever the case, Dr Alison Brookes, the Corinium Museum's Collections Management Officer, said: 'It is a very positive addition to our collection.' The hoard is now on permanent display in the Prehistory Gallery of the Museum, which is open Monday to Saturday from 10am to 5pm and from 2pm-5pm on Sundays.

Open-Air Theatre in Poulton

Since the summer of 1995, troupes of touring professional actors with the Festival Players and the Rain or Shine Theatre Company have presented seventeen different plays by William Shakespeare, from the favourite lighter comedies to *Hamlet, Henry V and Richard III*, interspersed with a few of the Restoration romps by Goldsmith, Sheridan and Vanbrugh in the gardens of Poulton House in summer.

The Rain or Shine Company's production of Sir John Vanbrugh's 17th century comedy of manners, The Provok'd Wife, *still drawing belly-laughs after 300 years*

The companies bring their own scenery, lighting and stages, and put on thoroughly polished performances for an audience of up to 200, who bring their own picnics, seating, blankets, umbrellas, and often their attentive and well-behaved children. Open-air *anything* in England is a risky enough proposition, but at the time of writing, of the 33 plays performed over 17 years, inclement weather only thrice forced the performers and audience to cross the road to the dry shelter of the village hall. Otherwise actors and audience played on and stayed on through what was often an unseasonal cold snap and/or an unforeseen drizzle. The show must go on!

Thane Bettany, father of the film star Paul Bettany, as Shylock in Act I of the Festival Players' production of The Merchant of Venice *(Act II was in the village hall)*

The plucky Poulton audience come prepared to brave the foul weather for the plays in Poulton House gardens.

235

The Cricket Club at Englands

The Poulton Cricket Club was given the field known as 'Englands' for a pitch in 1979, and the villagers raised £3,500 to buy a redundant telephone exchange at Tetbury which they re-erected in Poulton to serve as a pavilion for both the football and cricket clubs. In 2005 the club, which is ECB ClubMark accredited, was given a considerable lottery grant from Rural Renaissance, largely due to the tireless efforts of

(l) The foundations for the new pavilion in 2005. (r) The new pavilion was completed in 2008.

the PCC President Geoff Chapman, which, together with local fund raising that includes an annual village fête, enabled the club to begin the construction of a new pavilion, incorporating showers, changing rooms and hospitality area. The work was completed in 2008 at a cost of around £500,000 and was officially opened by the committee in July of that year.

There are today about 40 members of the PCC between the ages of 18 and 56 – the average age being 23. Poulton Cricket runs a First XI, a Second XI and a Sunday Cricket Team, playing every Saturday, Sunday and Wednesday during the season, which is roughly from May to September.

The members of the Poulton Cricket Club Committee jointly cut the ribbon across the verandah at the official opening of the new pavilion at Englands in July 2008.

The club also has a junior members section which caters for over 130 youngsters between the ages of 6 and 18, and with many of the older youngsters playing in the successful 1st and 2nd teams during the summer months. It has a Junior Team for those aged between 6 and 17, running sides at Under 9, Under 11, Under 13 and Under 15 teams, with each squad of players excelling in District and County leagues and cup matches. Poulton Cricket Club prides itself on the opportunities it provides for children of whatever age and level of ability. As of writing in 2012 it has 154 children registered and over 80 regularly turning out on Saturday mornings for coaching at the different age groups each week.

Poulton Cricket Club's 2012 Under-15 cup-winning team, coached at Englands on Saturday mornings

The First XI play in the top division of the Gloucestershire County Cricket League and the Second XI play in the Cotswold District League. The Sunday Team plays friendly cricket with sides in the CDC area, providing an additional opportunity to enjoy cricket outside the competitive leagues and to provide additional experience of adult cricket for the better and older juniors at the club.

One of the club's former stalwarts, Gordon Paine, who joined the Poulton XI in 1955 and was the Club's Chairman from 1984 until his death in 1990, penned the following, which the club reckons sums up 'the Poulton way of cricket':

'Cricket – now what's in a name?
To some it's just a silly game,
But not to those who like to watch and play,
Nothing could be nicer on a summer's day
Than to hear the crack of ball on bat,
Now what could be a nicer sound than that ...
Cricket – now what's in a name?
I hope you'll agree, a very nice game,
And how lucky we are to play for a club
That always ends up in the local pub.'

Post-Agricultural Poulton

The transition of Poulton from a rural farming village into a cosmopolitan post-agricultural community left it with a number of barns, stables, granaries and other farm buildings of one kind or another which were no longer useful. In recent years many of these have been re-developed into *des-res* family homes which were then sold off for whacking great sums. This has given Poulton a fair amount of new housing and has added to the overall value of property in the village.

Hester's Barn on Poulton Fields Farm being landscaped after conversion of a redundant 18th century barn into an elegant family house. Many such conversions have added to Poulton's residential housing pool.

From Footpaths to Pavements

The shabby condition of the footpaths along the streets had been a cause for constant complaint by the villagers for many years. In fact, between the post office and the children's playground there were no footpaths at all, which meant children had to walk in the busy and dangerous London Road to catch the school bus every morning – a nightmare for parents. In stages between 2003 and 2008 the Poulton Parish Council, financially aided by the Cotswold District Council and the WI, re-surfaced the dodgy pavements and cut back bits of walls to put in smooth and safe walkways where previously none existed.

For years pedestrians had to walk this stretch in the busy road itself. This new pavement was installed in 2006.

The Old Priory Graveyard

In the first edition of this book, I made a plea for the restoration of the old Priory graveyard, which had become derelict. I had spent a certain amount of time there researching the book, and when stumbling upon the grave markers of those late residents of Poulton whom I had written about, I felt as if they were old friends in an unworthy setting.

In his book *The Buildings of England* David Verey wrote of Poulton: "The tombs are of high quality design and execution, showing good use of architectural forms, carved decoration and inscription". Some of the tombs are indeed fine examples of local masonry and others are interesting for their inscriptions and epitaphs, such as that of Thomas Rudge, who died in Poulton in 1864, at the untimely age of 49:

Gravestone of tailor Samuel Sambleson's wife Elizabeth who died in 1865, aged 60.

ALL YOU THAT BY ME PASS ALONG
O THINK HOW SUDDEN I WAS GONE
DEATH DO NOT ALWAYS WARNING GIVE
THEREFORE BE CAREFUL HOW YOU LIVE.

The pity was that it was unlikely anyone then could ever 'pass along' by Thomas Rudge's grave, or take heed of his contemplative inscription, as the old churchyard was so decrepit and the table-top tombs so grimy and the headstones stacked up so that the messages and the carving on these once-handsome tombs and stones could hardly be seen. Considering the love and

Ornately carved tombstone at the Priory, displaying a memento mori skull

239

sentiment, not to mention the expense, lavished on the grave markers by so many Poulton families in order to provide a lasting memorial to their beloved parents, wives, husbands and children, it was shameful that the old churchyard had fallen into such disrepair. Many of their descendants still live in the area, and many come to Poulton from America, Canada, Australia etc. specially to visit the graves of their ancestors

After the Restoration in 1660 the surfaces of the tombs were highly decorated, often including cherubs, drapery, fruit and floral motifs. This can be seen above on the ornamented tomb of William Tipper, a Poulton farmer buried here in 1684, which is the oldest of the 17 restored box tombs.

Restoration of the table-top tombs 2012

The churchyard is "owned" by the vicar and governing body of St Michael's Church, but the Poulton Parish Council has long been responsible for the care and maintenance of the graves. When Geoff Chapman was chairman of the Council, he campaigned tirelessly for funding to have the table-top or chest tombs renovated. In 2012 he eventually received a grant of over £30,000 from the Heritage Lottery Fund that allowed 17 of the tombs, dating from 1684 to 1870, to be repaired.

A table-top tomb is a memorial shaped like a stone box, the whole of which is above ground. The body was usually buried beneath the memorial, not in the chest itself. The chests are usually decorated only on their sides, however there are some spectacular exceptions, such as the 'bale' tombs of the Cotswolds (so called because the top was thought to represent bales of wool). The Poulton tomb of Arthur Hood, a local gentleman who was buried in 1734, is an excellent example of a bale tomb.

'Bale' tombs, peculiar to this area, were decorated on top to represent bales of wool. Arthur Hood, who was buried beneath in 1734, is likely to have had connections with the prosperous Cotswold woollen trade.

Although the old churchyard was technically closed in 1884, the closure order still allows burials, but the graves must be lined with brick to avoid contamination of the soil. By the mid-nineteenth century the Victorians discovered that the decaying bodies beneath tombs were polluting the water table. When the lid of the 1851 table tomb of Henry Lane was pried off, his bones were, surprisingly, discovered inside the chest, which was in fact a brick-lined vault covered with slabs of stones. The Diocese recommended that his remains be buried in the earth beneath the monument, as the other bodies are, and the chest tomb be reassembled on top.

The tomb of Henry Lane 1780-1851 the younger brother of William Jenner Lane 1776-1862, one of the Poulton dynasty of Jenners, Lanes and Hills much written about in the Georgian Poulton chapter. This was the last of the table-top tombs and the only one that contained the mortal remains within a brick-lined vault inside the chest. (pictured right)

Fourteen of the seventeen restored chest tombs are grade II listed by English Heritage. John Swanton, the current Vicar of Poulton writes: "It is great that we are able to care for our heritage in this way by repairing these historic table top tombs. Their future is now secure for another few hundred years." Richard Bellamy, chief spokesman for the Heritage Lottery Fund said: "We are delighted to support this project which will ensure that an important part of Poulton's past is protected for the future." The generous Heritage Lottery Fund grant of £36,000 also covered a seat in the churchyard, funds for young people to research the history of the tombs and the costs of printing this book.

Poulton in the Future

The considerable changes in Poulton's village life are clear to see; the residents today are far more affluent, more mobile and more cosmopolitan. The rôles of the church, the pub and the village shop have diminished over the years, and local post offices are under constant threat of being shut down by Royal Mail. It is a struggle, in this rapidly changing world, to keep these village amenities in operation.

On the other hand, there is certainly more social mobility and integration now than in times past, and even amongst the recently arrived residents, whether young families, singletons or retired Darbys and Joans, there is still, in Poulton, a sense of belonging to a community. In any society there are bound to be people who are more civic minded than others, and indeed those who devote the time and energy to take on the burden of administering village structures and organisations such as the Parish Council, the Village Hall, the Parochial Church Council, the Allotments Commission, the Neighbourhood Watch etc. are relatively few, and seem to get ever fewer, and the volunteers tend to be the same committed people again and again, but the majority of residents seem supportive of village institutions, even if they are too busy or disinclined to play an active rôle, and most, even today I would think, have a genuine concern for others in the community.

This has an impressive way of revealing itself when there are instances of illness, bereavement, or other misfortunes of one kind or another. The floods of 2007 can serve as an example of community support; the intense and continuous rain caused the Poulton brook to overflow to such an extent that the A417 was quite submerged and became impassable. Cars trying to get through found the water rising above the wheels and several stalled in a torrent. Villagers appeared with waterproof thigh boots and carried the drivers and passengers on their backs to dry ground. They did the same for elderly householders in Stoney Pool who became trapped by the deluge invading their homes. A number of the houses near Poulton Bridge had two and a half feet of flood water gushing into their ground floors and had to be evacuated. The evacuees were offered food and lodging by other Poulton residents until the water subsided. Then, when the monumental job of cleaning and sorting out the damage from the water began, village volunteers from houses on higher ground went in to the flood-damaged houses for days to help the occupants in their attempt to get back to normal. So great was the destruction in some of the worst-hit houses that the householders weren't able to return and live there for weeks or even months. Since then the county and district councils have widened the brook and installed a new drainage system, so with luck such flooding is a thing of the past.

It is hoped that this book will, by its documentation, draw attention to the richness that has been the long history of this small Cotswold village, and thereby encourage a respect and an appreciation for the continuity and heritage that is passed on to each generation who make their home in Poulton. When we, the present lot, are dead and gone, it will be the residents of tomorrow, now unknown and perhaps unborn, who will determine the future of this world in a grain of sand. Let us hope they look after it judiciously so that new chapters can be added by someone in the centuries to come.

And so life goes on. As of now, St Michael and All Angels Church continues to perform the ancient rituals and ceremonies that have served generations in the Parish of Poulton for centuries.

SELECT BIBLIOGRAPHY
Principal published sources cited or quoted

Barker, E. The Character of England, Oxford University Press, 1947

Bassett, S. The Origins of Anglo-Saxon Kingdoms, Leicester University Press

Binney, M. Poulton Manor, Gloucestershire, article in Country Life May 27, 1976

Branigan, K. & Fowler, P.J. The Roman West Country, David & Charles Inc., North Pomfret, Vermont, 1976

Burke, J. Life in the Villa in Roman Britain, BT Batsford Ltd., London

Campbell, J. The Anglo-Saxons, Phaidon, London

Church history booklet St. Mary the Virgin, Kempsford

Committee for Archeology in Gloucestershire Handbook of Gloucestershire Archeology, The Bristol & Gloucestershire Archeological Society, 1985

Domesday Book of 1086

Hackett, Gen. Sir J. The Profession of Arms, Sidgwick & Jackson, London, 1983

Heighway, C. Anglo-Saxon Gloucestershire, Alan Sutton & Gloucester County Library

Hill, B. St. Michael's and All Angels, Poulton, 1874–1974 Church history

Hilton, R.H. Peasants Knights and Heretics – Studies in Medieval English Social History, Cambridge University Press, 1981

Hindley, G. England in the Age of Caxton, Granada, 1979

Jackson, R. Dark Age Britain, Patrick Stephens, Cambridge

Kelly's Directory. Poulton, Gloucestershire

Kruta, V. & Forman, W. The Celts of the West, Orbis, London, 1985

Lewis, J. A History of Fairford, Hendon Publishing Co., Lancashire, 1982

Lewis, J. A History of Fairford, Hendon Publishing Co., Lancashire, 1982

Lewis, J. Poulton, article in Cotswold Life, June 1974

Lewis, J. Cotswold Characteristics, Countryside Publications Ltd., Lancashire, 1983

Lewis, J. Cotswold Villages, Robert Hale & Co., London, 1974

McWhirr, A. Houses in Roman Cirencester, Alan Sutton Publishing Ltd., Gloucester, 1986

Myres, J.N.L .The English Settlements, Clarendon Press, Oxford

Nohl, J. The Black Death, A Chronicle of the Plague, Unwin Books, London, 1926

Rickert, E. Chaucer's World, Columbia University Press, New York,1948

Ross, A . The Pagan Celts, BT Batsford Ltd, London

Royal Commission on Historical Monuments Iron Age and Romano British Monuments in the Gloucestershire Cotswolds, HMSO London, 1976

Thompson, R. 'When they say no at Poulton, they really mean it. . . .' Evening Post, March 29, 1967

Tomlin, A. Castle Eaton's St Mary the Virgin Church, Church history booklet, 1992

Trevelyan, G.M. English Social History, Longmans, Green & Co., 1952

The Victoria History of Wiltshire

Wacher, J. & McWhirr, A. Early Roman Occupation at Cirencester, Corinium Museum, Cirencester, 1982

Wacher, J. The Coming of Rome, Britain before the Conquest, Routledge & Kegan Paul, London & Henley

Welsford, J. Cirencester - A History and Guide, Alan Sutton Publishing Ltd., Gloucester, 1987

Websites: www Anglo-Saxon Charters; www The National Archives; www.hidden-treasure.co.uk

Wilkinson, B. The Later Middle Ages in England 1216—1485, Longmans, 1969

Wilts & Gloucestershire Standard   Many assorted articles

Ziegler, P. The Black Death, Alan Sutton,1969

INDEX

Adams family 85,87-89,114-115,142,151,16
1,195,201,202
Adams, Reg 89,132,141,150,152,164,207
Adams, Sally 79
Alma's Cottage 80-1,201
Arkwright, General & Kitty 125,206
Ash family 109-110,
141-143,149,151,152,156,162,164,166,207-208
Axe & Compass inn (see Figaro, Strafford, Freeth) 70,75,115,129
Ball, Queenie (née Little) 125,141,149-150,153,160,179-180,197,207,211,212,213
Banbury, Lord(s) 196,204
Barnard, John, publican of Red Lion 73
Bastoe, Betty (Betty's Grave) 95-97
Baylis, Freda 141,148,151,159-60,165-166,171-180,214,216
Bedwell family 82-5,129
Betty's Grave (see Bastoe)
Bishop family 87
Boyd, Tom and Sally 225, 230
Brookes, Alison 234
Burnett, Peggy 174
Butterfield, Wm. architect 123-4,126-9
Butts development 216
Campbell, Evelyn, Ian 203-205,206-211
Carpenter, Richard & Ben 133-139
Carr, Trevor 218
Cartwright, Nancy & Diana 154,167,176,178
Chapman Geoff 229, 230, 236, 240
Cilcennin, Lord (see Thomas)
Clarke, Lady Elizabeth aka Langton,
181,182-191,185,188
Clarke, Humphrey 187,190
Cole (see Esmond Matthews)
Corinium Museum (John Paddock, Alison Brookes) 233-234
Cricklade St. no. 10 (Betty Bastoe's house) 95 (see Betty's Grave & Shrive)
Cripps family 84-85,110
Crouch, Janet (née Hill) 139 (see Jenners, Lanes & Hills 100-8 ff.)
Edwards family 87,109,140,147,149, 156, 157-160,164-165,167,210
Esmond-Matthews, Joan 167-170,171
Falcon Inn (pub) 70,74,115,132, 141,142.222-223
Festival Players Company - 235

Figaro (house, see Axe & Compass, Strafford, Freeth)
Firs, the (House) 103 (see W.J. Lane & Poulton Fields)
Fowles, David and Deborah 161,221
Franklyn, P. (schoolmaster) 123,147,150
Freeth, Wilf 75, 87, 208
Gamble, Sir David 89,170,209
Gardner family (see Lavin)87,142,149
Gassor 200-202
Gott, the Revd Desmond
117,171,205,206,207-209,220
Gray, Gianni and Natalie (see Falcon Inn) 223
Green Close aka Gable Cottage 201 (see Gassor)
Greenwood,Eric 196
Griffin (see Ockwell)
Hammond, Walter 153
Harrison family 8
Hester's Barn 238
Higgins, Peter 199
Hill family 34, 89, 99-104, 105, 106, 107, 108-9,123,126,130-131,141-143,149,151, 161,173
Hillside (house) 89
Home Farm (house)107 (see Hill)
Hope-Simpson, Edgar 199-200
House on the Corner 85,89,114,201
Hutchinson, the Revd H.S, 34, 117,206
Jenners, (house) aka The Gables 83-84
Jenner family 100-103
Jobbins family 89,141-143,156,162-163,165,171,176,201
Joicey, Maj. James 95,117, 120-122,146,149,155-156
Keble, the Revd John & son 98-99,110,116
Lafford, Wilf 191-193
Lane family 85,89,100-105
Langton, John & Stephen 182,186-187,190,204,226
Lavin, Joan (nee Gardner),141,160
Little, Tommy & Des 142,146-147, 149,153,197,211,217
London Road nos. 12 & 14 85
Luckett family 157,165
Mackay, Commander & Mrs John 200
Malden, George (see Tanner)
Manor House 82, 83-85

246

INDEX

Marshall,H. J. 115,117,126 (see Priory)
Mayne, the Revd W.J. 113,115,117,131
McMaster-Yair, the Revd A.J. 152
Mediaeval Festival 227-230
Miles, Mrs (churchwarden) 206-207
Mission Room/ Methodist chapel 111, 112
Mitchell, Clarissa 185-186,188-189
Mitchell, Major A.B. & family 68,122, 155-156,160,172,177-178,196,197-198,206,224
Montgomery, Earl Roger, 26,29
Moss, Dennis 229
Nesham 117,188,190,204-205,209,211
New Inn, 81,156
Newman, George 216
Nunn, Jim 193
Ockwell (see Griffin) 109,125,142,148,149
Old Farmhouse 85
Old Forge 85, 133-139 (see Carpenter, and Clarke)
Packhorse Inn (House) 70,74, 199(see Hope-Simpson)
Paddock, John 231-232
Paine, Gordon 237
Parish Church (see St Michael & All Angels)
Parish Council 228, 238,240
Parker-Jervis, Capt. Robt. St Vincent 194-6
Peach & Pear Tree Cottage 85
Peters, Diana 181,188,189
Pitt, Frank 141 & sons, 218
Player, Capt. Stephen 68
Poulton Cricket Club 120-2, 153-156,236
Poulton Fields 68,81,103,(see The Firs, W.J. Lane, S. Player & Lord Wigram)
Poulton House 196, 202,203-209,235
Poulton Manor 81,82, 83-5 (see Bedwell, Cartwright, Gamble)
Poulton Parish Church (see St Michael & All Angels)
Poulton Priory 34-43, 49,62-3,95. 117-9, 155-156, 196, 214 Mansion 121,122 (see Marshall, Joicey, Mitchell)
Poulton School (Old School House) 81,123, 124,125,146
Price, 87, Aubrey 157-158 and John 156
Priory Court 218 (Poulton Priory Estate)
Rain or Shine Theatre Company - 233
Ranbury Farm & Cottages 191-193 (see Wood,Lafford,Greenwood, Mackay)

Ready Token House (Inn) 70, 75, 76,77, 78,79
Red Lion pub (see Barnard) 70,73, 94
Rickards, Sq. Leader Aubrey 203
Rootes, Rob and Sue 161,221
Rudge, Thomas 237
Russell, Stuart & Liz 161
Sambleson (or Samblesohn) family 111-114,162
Sanford, Anthony & Erica Mary 125,206,208,210
Siward, Lord of the Manor 26
Seymour, aka St Maur aka Sancto Mauro 29-32,35-36, 61
Shrive, Mrs Jack 210
Southcott 107 (see Hill, Thomas)
Southcott Cottage 85
St Michael & All Angels Church (aka Poulton Parish Church) 37, 39, 64-5,82,98,10 6,116,126,127,128,129,142-144,178,207-208, 219,220, 240
Stevens, Richard 117-119
Strafford family 75,129,142,144,145,148, 152,163-165,167,180
Strange, Hilda (née Strafford) 122,129,141-148,152
Swanton, Revd John 220, 241
Tanner family 74-75, 149,151,161,164,191
Tatyan 222
Taylor, Steve 232
Thomas, Annie, Joan & James (Lord Cilcennin) 157-159,165,181
Thomas de Lecchelade 227
Thorne, Margaret (see Tanner) 141,163
Tidmarsh, Revd F.H.E, Vicar 12,117, 206
Tilling, Joseph & Ernest 111,112,131-132,161-162
Titley family 108, 110 (see Hill)
Verey, Rosemary 80, David 129,239
Vicarage Cottage 62
Vicarage aka Old Vicarage, 115,116,117
Village Hall 224 - 227,228
Weeks, Billy 165-166
Wheeler family, 87
Wigram, Lt Col the Lord 206, 208
Women's Institute (WI) 214, 224, 226
Wood, Dick 191-193
Woolcock, Annette 220
Worsley, Violette (see Mitchell) 196-8

247

About the Author

TOM BOYD was born in the USA but has spent the majority of his adult life in England. He originally came to London as a student at the Guildhall School of Music and Drama, and while there wrote book, music and lyrics for a musical *Tom Sawyer,* performed by the college in 1956. It was given a professional production in London at Theatre Royal, Stratford East in 1960/61, and revived 50 years later, in the Poulton Village Hall, for Mark Twain's centenary in 2010.

Over the years Tom Boyd has written scripts and music for ITV, BBC World Service and BBC TV and a slew of TV and cinema commercials and jingles for various advertising agencies in London; he was also a journalist and international correspondent for *Speak Up* magazine, published in Italy, Spain, France, former Jugoslavia and Brazil.

Together with his wife Sally, he ran an English restaurant, *the Chelsea House*, in Los Angeles, and a language school in Hampstead where he wrote and produced recorded English language teaching materials.

Since moving to Poulton in 1986 he has written English translations of librettos for 12 different operas performed by Bel Canto Opera, of which he was a director. He is also the author of several other books: *In Their Own Words, Britain and America in Contrast, A Bowl of Cherries* and *All in the Family.*

He feels fortunate to have ended up, as it were, in Poulton and is delighted that his children and grandchildren are all living nearby in the Cotswolds.